•Bartholomew•

# EDIN
# Stree nder
# STREET ATLAS

## CONTENTS

| | |
|---|---|
| Legend | 3 |
| Key to Map Pages | 4 |
| City Centre Map | 6 |
| Map Pages | 8 |
| Index | 52 |

Bartholomew
*A Division of* HarperCollins*Publishers*

Bartholomew is a Division of HarperCollins Publishers

ISBN 0 7028 1858 5

Printed in Hong Kong



F/B 6663 UNU

# Legend

main through road

dual carriageway

main link road

other roads

lane, drive

tourist information centre

car park

post office

public building

church

tower block

King's theatre

Cannon cinema

Usher Hall public hall

Huntly Ho. Mus. museum or gallery

library

primary school

secondary school

hospital

police station

fire station

railways/main station

airport coach terminal

woodland

built-up area

viewpoint

golf course

swimming pool

sailing centre

caravan / camping site

**Scale of main map pages - 1:15 000 (4.2 inches to 1 mile)**

0 0.5 1 1.5 km

0 ¼ ½ ¾ mile

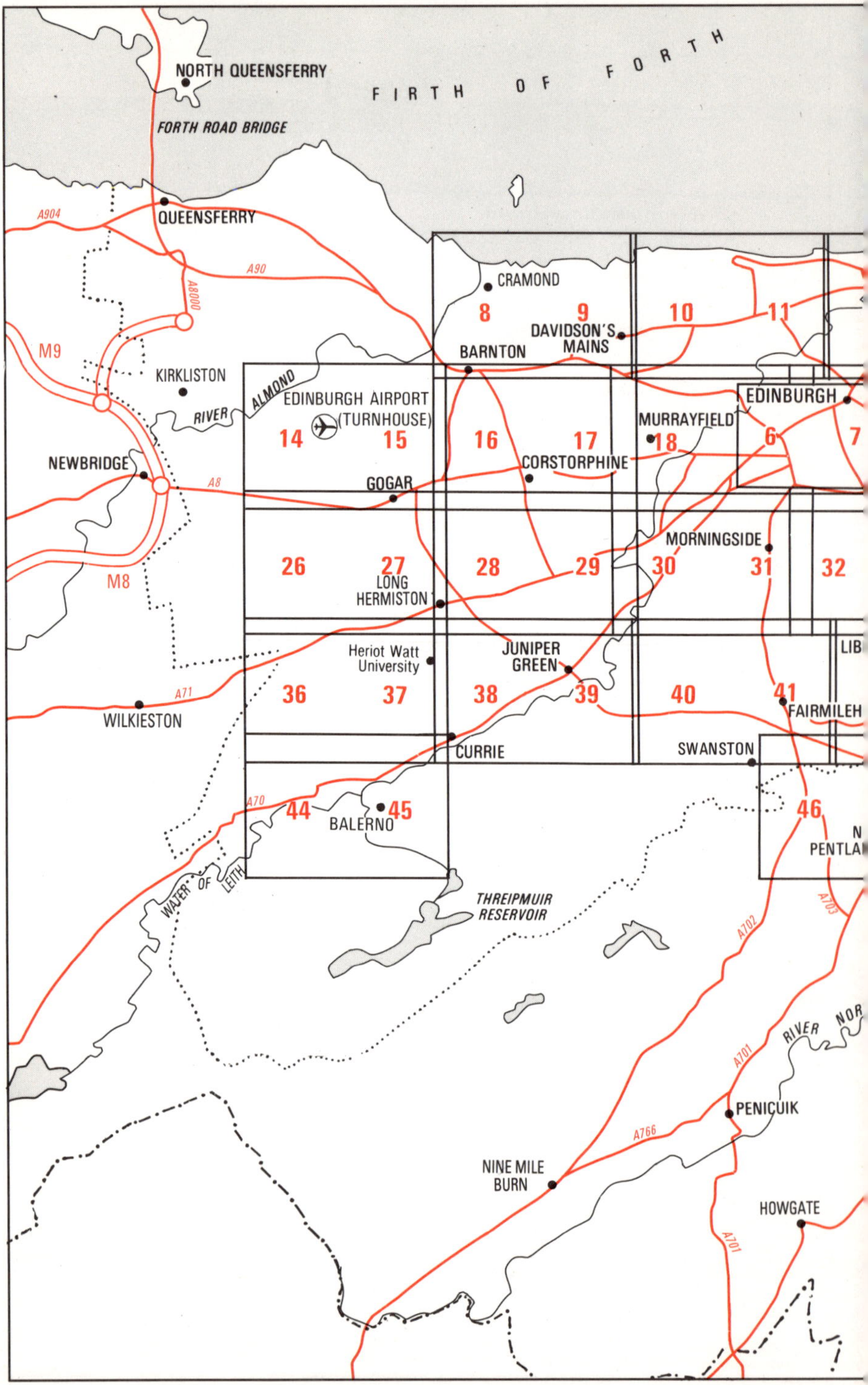
FIRTH OF FORTH
NORTH QUEENSFERRY
FORTH ROAD BRIDGE
QUEENSFERRY
A904
A90
A8000
M9
KIRKLISTON
RIVER ALMOND
NEWBRIDGE
A8
M8
CRAMOND
8
9
DAVIDSON'S MAINS
10
11
BARNTON
EDINBURGH AIRPORT (TURNHOUSE)
14
15
16
17
MURRAYFIELD
18
EDINBURGH
6
7
CORSTORPHINE
GOGAR
26
27
LONG HERMISTON
28
29
30
MORNINGSIDE
31
32
Heriot Watt University
JUNIPER GREEN
36
37
38
39
40
41
FAIRMILEH
LIB
A71
WILKIESTON
CURRIE
SWANSTON
A70
44
45
BALERNO
46
N PENTLA
WATER OF LEITH
THREIPMUIR RESERVOIR
A702
A703
RIVER NOR
A701
PENICUIK
A766
NINE MILE BURN
HOWGATE

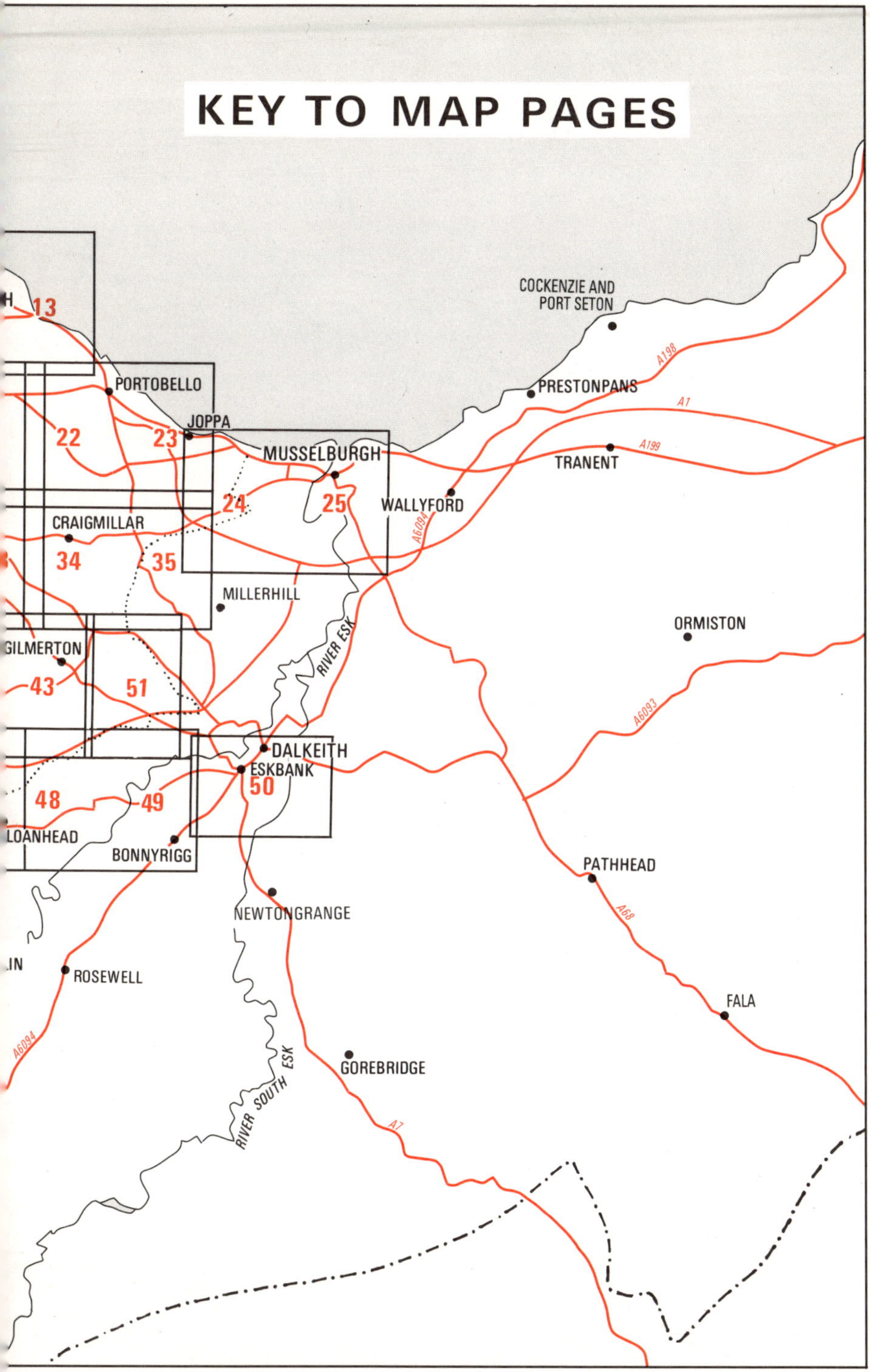
KEY TO MAP PAGES
13
PORTOBELLO
JOPPA
22
23
MUSSELBURGH
24
25
CRAIGMILLAR
34
35
MILLERHILL
GILMERTON
43
51
DALKEITH
ESKBANK
50
48
49
LOANHEAD
BONNYRIGG
COCKENZIE AND
PORT SETON
PRESTONPANS
A198
A1
TRANENT
A199
WALLYFORD
A6094
ORMISTON
RIVER ESK
A6093
PATHHEAD
A68
NEWTONGRANGE
ROSEWELL
FALA
GOREBRIDGE
RIVER SOUTH ESK
A7

L Scale 1:10 000 25 M

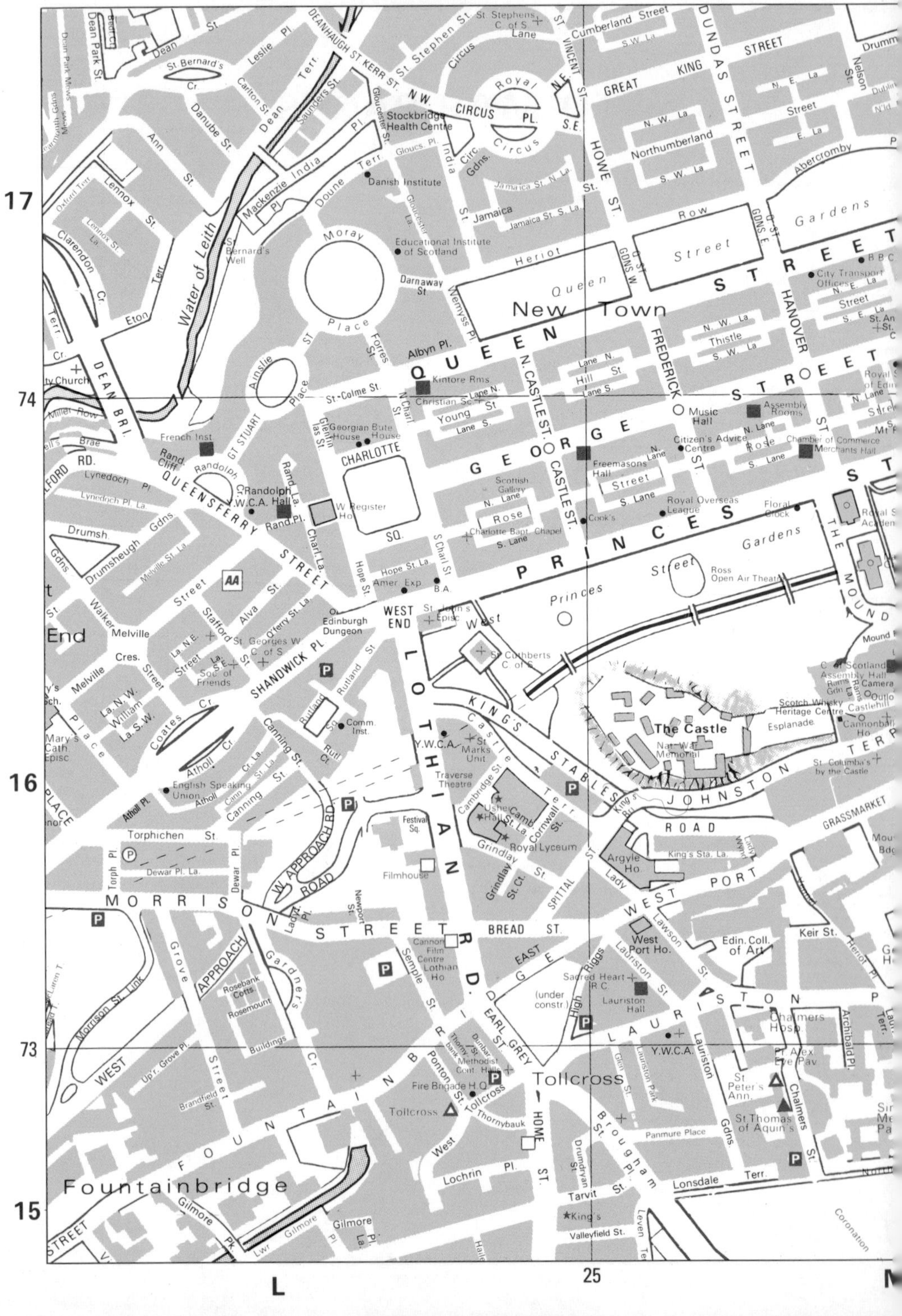

26
N
17
74
16
73
15
LONDON ROAD
Royal Terrace Gardens
Royal Terrace
CALTON
Regent Gardens
Calton
HILL
City Observatory
Edinburgh Experience
National Mon.
Nelson Mon
St. Andrew's Ho
Crown Office Bldgs.
REGENT ROAD
Regent Terr.
Regent Road Park
Calton New Burial Ground
Burns Mon
Nether Craigwell
Calton Road
ABBEYHILL
Palace of Holyroodhouse
Queen Mary's Bath Ho.
Abbey Strand
White Horse Close
Horse Wynd
Queensberry House Hosp.
Royal Mile
CANONGATE
Canongate
Canongate Church C. of S.
Canongate Tolbooth and People's Story
Huntly Ho. Mus.
Acheson House (Scot. Craft Centre)
Moray Ho Coll. of Ed.
HOLYROOD ROAD
Lochview Ct.
Holyrood Ct.
QUEEN'S DRIVE
Salisbury
Radical
Dumbiedykes
Dumbiedykes Rd.
Viewcraig Gdns.
Pleasance Sports Ctre. (Edin. Univ.)
Pleasance Thea.
PLEASANCE
New Arthur Pl.
Brown St.
Lothian Region Health Board
Carnegie Ct.
St Leonards
ST LEONARD'S
Rankeillor St.
Montague St.
Parkside St.
Bowmont Pl.
Forbes St.
St Leonard's Hill
St Leonard's Crag
St Leonard's Bank
YORK PL.
Albany St.
Barony St.
BROUGHTON ST.
Forth St.
St Mary's
St. Paul's and St. George's Episc.
PICARDY PL.
St. Mary's Cath. R.C.
LEITH ST.
LEITH WLK.
Playhouse
Greenside
St. James Centre
Bus Sta.
New St. Andrews Ho
Royal Bank of Scotl
Register Ho.
Melville Mon.
Wellington Mon.
WATERLOO PL.
G.P.O.
NORTH BRIDGE
Waverley Market
Waverley Steps
WAVERLEY BRIDGE
Waverley Sta.
Ticket Centre & Tattoo Office
Fruit Market Gallery
City Art Centre
Market St.
Jeffrey St.
Scottish Poetry Lib.
Brass Rubbing Cen.
John Knox's Ho
Netherbow Centre C. of S
Old St Pauls Episc.
Cockburn St.
Festival Offices
City Chambers
Bank of Scotl.
HIGH ST.
St. Giles Cath. C. of S.
Parl't Sq.
Parliament Ho.
County Hall
National Lib.
The Tron
Festival Fringe Office
Mus. of Childhood
Scottish Mus. of Experience
Chessels Court
St. Cecilia's Hall
SOUTH BRIDGE
COWGATE
GEORGE IV BRI.
Wilkie Ho.
Adam Ho
Edinburgh Dental Hosp. & Sch.
CHAMBERS ST.
Edin. Univ. Old Coll.
Talbot Rice Art Gall.
Royal Mus. of Scot.
Lecture Thea.
Infirmary St.
St. Patrick's
Drummond St.
Surgeons' Hall
NICOLSON ST.
Nicolson Sq.
Reekie's Ct.
Methodist Chapel
Richmond Place
CANDLEMAKER ROW
Greyfriars Kirk C. of S.
Bristo Port
Bristo Pl.
Forrest Rd
Forrest Hill
Student Centre
Potterrow
Bristo Sq.
TEVIOT PL.
McEwan Hall
Medical Sch.
Crichton St.
Appleton Tower
George Sq.
David Hume Tower
School of Scottish Studies
Univ. Library
Univ. Thea.
Buccleuch Pl.
Edin. Univ. Extra Mural Studies
Buccleuch and Greyfriars Free C. of S.
W. Crosscauseway
BUCCLEUCH ST.
Odeon
CLERK ST.
Archers Hall
Meadow Lane
Boys Brigade Walk
Middle Meadow Walk

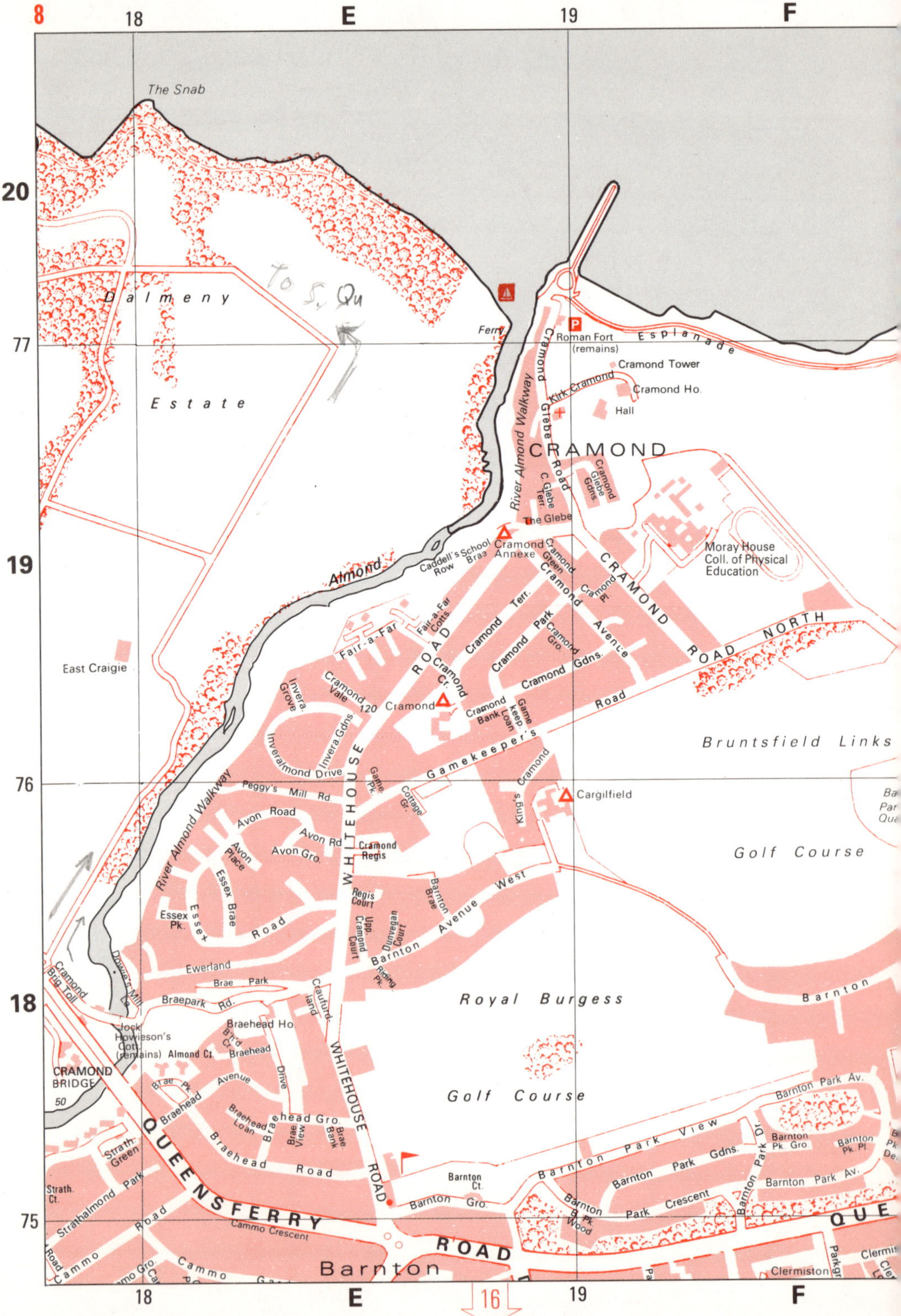
18
E
19
F
20
77
19
76
18
75
The Snab
Dalmeny
Estate
Ferry
Roman Fort
(remains)
Esplanade
Cramond Tower
Kirk Cramond
Cramond Ho.
Hall
CRAMOND
Cramond Glebe Road
C. Glebe Terr.
Cramond Glebe Gdns.
The Glebe
River Almond Walkway
Cramond Annexe
Caddell's Row
School Brae
Cramond Green
Cramond Terr.
Cramond Cr.
CRAMOND
Cramond Avenue
Moray House
Coll. of Physical
Education
Almond
East Craigie
Fair-a-Far
Fair-a-Far Cotts.
ROAD
Cramond Park
Cramond Gro.
Cramond Gdns.
ROAD NORTH
Cramond Cr.
Cramond Vale
Invera. Grove
120
Cramond
Cramond Bank
Game keeper's Loan
Road
Gamekeeper's
Bruntsfield Links
Inveralmond Drive
Invera.Gdns
WHITEHOUSE
Game Pk.
King's Cramond
Cargilfield
Peggy's Mill Rd.
Cottage Gr.
Avon Road
Avon Rd
Avon Place
Avon Gro.
Cramond Regis
Golf Course
River Almond Walkway
Essex Brae
Essex Pk.
Essex Road
Regis Court
Upp. Cramond Court
Dunvegan Court
Barnton Brae
Barnton Avenue West
Ewerland
Dowie's Mill La.
Riding Pk.
Cramond Brig Toll
Brae Park
Braepark Rd.
Cauford-land
Royal Burgess
Barnton
Jock Howieson's Cott. (remains)
Almond Ct.
Braehead Ho.
B'h'd Ct.
Braehead
CRAMOND BRIDGE
50
Brae Pk.
Braehead Avenue
Drive
WHITEHOUSE ROAD
Golf Course
Barnton Park Av.
Braehead Loan
Braehead Gro.
Brae View
Brae Bank
QUEENSFERRY
Strath. Green
Braehead Road
Barnton Park View
Barnton Pk. Gro
Barnton Pk. Pl
Barnton Park Gdns.
Barnton Park Dr.
Strath. Ct.
Strathalmond Park
Barnton Ct.
Barnton Park Avenue
Barnton Park Av.
Barnton Gro.
Barnton Pk. Wood
Park Crescent
Road
Cammo Crescent
ROAD
QUE
Cammo Road
Cammo Gro.
Cammo
Barnton
Clermiston
18
E
19
F

16

20
G
21
H
Gran
20
19
18
77
76
75
10
17
Esplanade
Marine Drive
MARINE DRIVE
Craigroyston Ho.
Muirhouse
84
Civil Service
Sports Ground
Silverknowes
Golf Course
(Public)
SILVERKNOWES ROAD
Salvesen
Salv. Terr.
Salvesen Gdns.
Salv. Gro.
Salvesen Cr.
Muirhouse Mains
PARKWAY
MUIRHOUSE
Silverknowes Park
May Ct.
Fidra Ct.
Pennywell Pl.
Pennywell Gro.
Pennywell Gardens
Penn. Medway
Gunnet Ct.
Birnie's Ct.
Muirho. View
Oxcars Ct.
Inchmickery Ct.
Martello Ct.
Muirho. Gro.
Muirhouse Gdns.
SILVERKNOWES PARKWAY
Muirhouse
Muirhouse Drive
Muirho. Loan
Muirhouse Medway
Muirho. Way
Muirhouse Park
Muirhouse Pl. W
Muirho. Pk.
Muirhouse Terr.
Muirhouse Green
Muirho. Bank
Muirhouse Park
Muirhouse
Silverknowes
Lauriston Castle
Lauriston Farm
LAURISTON FARM RD.
SILVERKNOWES RD.
Silverknowes Pl.
Silverknowes
Silverknowes Gardens
Silv. Eastway
Silverknowes Grove
Silverknowes Court
Silverknowes Hill
Silverknowes Bank
Silverknowes Crescent
Silverknowes Av.
Silverknowes Loan
Silverknowes Brae
Silv. Green
Silv. Midway
Silverknowes View
Silv. Southway
Silverknowes Drive
Silverknowes Terrace
Silv. Loan
SILVERKNOWES RD. EAST
Silv. Dell
Silv. Neuk
Silv. Rd. S.
MOND
ROAD
Barnton
Northlawn Terr.
Easter Park Drive
Garden Terr.
Barnton Pk.
Barnton Gardens
SOUTH
Barnton Loan
Barnton Av.
S. Barnton Av.
E. Barnton Avenue
E.B. Gdns.
Safeway Shopping Centre
The Green
DAVIDSONS MAINS
MAIN STREET
Quality St. La.
QUALITY ST.
Corb. Pl.
Corbiehill Cr.
Corb. Terr.
Marchfield Park La.
Davidson's Mains
Vivian Terr.
David Gdns.
CORBIEHILL ROAD
Corbiehill Gro.
Corbiehill Gdns.
Corbiehill Av.
Corbiehill Pk.
Marchfield Pk.
Marchf. Gro.
Marchf. Terr.
Ho'Hill Brae
H o'H Pl.
H. o'Hill Gro.
Ho'Hill Green
House o'Hill Cr.
House o'Hill Av.
House o'Hill Road
H o'Hill Row
House o'Hill Gdns.
Wester Drylaw
Drylaw Ho. P.
Dry
Drylaw Gdns.
Drylaw Cr.
Drylaw Green
Whitehall
The Royal High School
204
Davidson's Mains Park
FERRY ROAD
HILLHOUSE ROAD
Hillpark Ct.
H'pk Dr.
Hillpark Avenue
Hillp'k Gdns.
Hillpark Cr.
Hillpark Way
Hillpark Loan
H.Wd.
Barnton Quarry
CLERMISTON
CRAI

H
22
J
23
K
20
77
19
76
18
75
9
18
Granton Point
West Shore Road
West Harbour Road
West Pier
Sealcarr
Chestnut St.
Royston Ho.
Caroline Pk.
West Broompark
Granton Pk. Av.
GRANT
Granton Medway
Granton
Gas Works
Caroline Park Avenue
Govt. Training Centre
Granton Ho.
Gypsy Brae
West Shore Road
groyston Ho.
WEST GRANTON ROAD
Caroline Pk. Gro.
Royston Mains Crescent
Royston Mains Av.
Royston Mains Gdns.
Royston Mains Rd.
Royston Mains St.
Royston Mains Pl.
Royston
BOSWALL PA
PILTON DR. N.
Wardieburn Pl. N.
Wardieburn Pl. W.
Wardieburn Pl. S.
Wardieburn Rd.
Wardieburn St. West
Wardiebu
Salvesen Gro.
Salv. Gdns.
Salv. Terr.
Pennywell Villas
Pennywell Cotts.
W. Granton Terr.
W. Granton Cres
W. Gr. Row
W. Gr. Gdns.
W. Gr. View
W. Gr. Drive
W. Gr. Green
W. Gr. Pl.
Granton Loan
W. Gr. Grove
W. Pilton Dr.
W. Pilton Ln.
W. Pilton St.
W. Pilton Gr.
West Pilton Terr.
W. P. Rd
W. P. St.
West Pilton Crescent
West Pilton Bank
W. Pilton Lea
Craigmuir
Pirniehall
Pennywell Pl.
Pennywell Gro.
Pennywell Gardens
Northview Ct.
PENNYWELL RD.
W. P. Crossway
West Pilton Rise
West Pilton Gdns.
West Pilton
West Pilton Park
Inchcolm Ct.
Inchgarvie Ct.
West Pilton Place
West Ferry Road
West Park
W. P. View
Muirhouse
Muirhouse Cr.
Penn. Ct.
Muirhouse Loan
Muirho. Way
Muirhouse Av.
Muirho. Pl. W.
Muirho. Pl. E.
Craigroyston
Muirhouse
W. Pilton Gro.
W. Pilton Av.
Pilton Drive
St. David's
Inchview
Ferry Road
Ferry Rd Gdns
Ferry Rd Pl
Ferry Rd Gro
Ferry Rd Av.
Crewe Road West
CREWE ROAD NORTH
Crewe Path
Crewe Loan
Crewe Place
Crewe Bank
Crewe Crescent
Crewe Gro.
Crewe Terr.
Crewe Rd. Gdns.
Pilton
Pilton Place
Pilton Loan
PILTON DRIVE
Pilton Park
Pilton Gdns
East Pilton Park
Pilton Ave
Ainslie Park Recreation Centre
Ainslie Park
Northern General Hospital
CREWE TOLL
FERRY ROAD
Green Bank
Drylaw Place
Wester Drylaw
Easter Drylaw Place
E. Dry. Loan
E. Drylaw Way
E. Drylaw View
E. Drylaw Bank
Drylaw View
Drylaw Drive
E. Drylaw Gardens
E. Drylaw Gro.
E. Dry Av.
E. Drylaw Avenue
Easter Drylaw Drive
Drylaw Ho.
Drylaw Ho. Gdns.
Drylaw
Drylaw Ho. Padd.
W. D. Park
W. Drylaw Av.
Wester Drylaw Drive
Ferryhill
GROATHILL ROAD NORTH
Drylaw
H. o'Hill Row
House o'Hill Gdns
Drylaw Gdns
Drylaw Crescent
Drylaw Green
W. Drylaw Row
Whitehall Ct.
TELFORD ROAD
Telford College
West Werberside
East Werberside
North Werberside Rd.
North Werber Park
North Werber Place
North Werber Park
Telf. Pl.
Telford Drive
Telf. Gdns.
Grigor Dr.
Grigor Terr.
Grigor Avenue
Grigor Gdns
Davidson Park
Davidson Rd.
CREWE ROAD SOUTH
W. Woods
Porterfield Rd.
Western General Hospital
Craigleith Hill Green
Craigleith
Carrin
Police H.

24 L 25 M

20
77
19
76
18
75

24 19 L 25 20 M

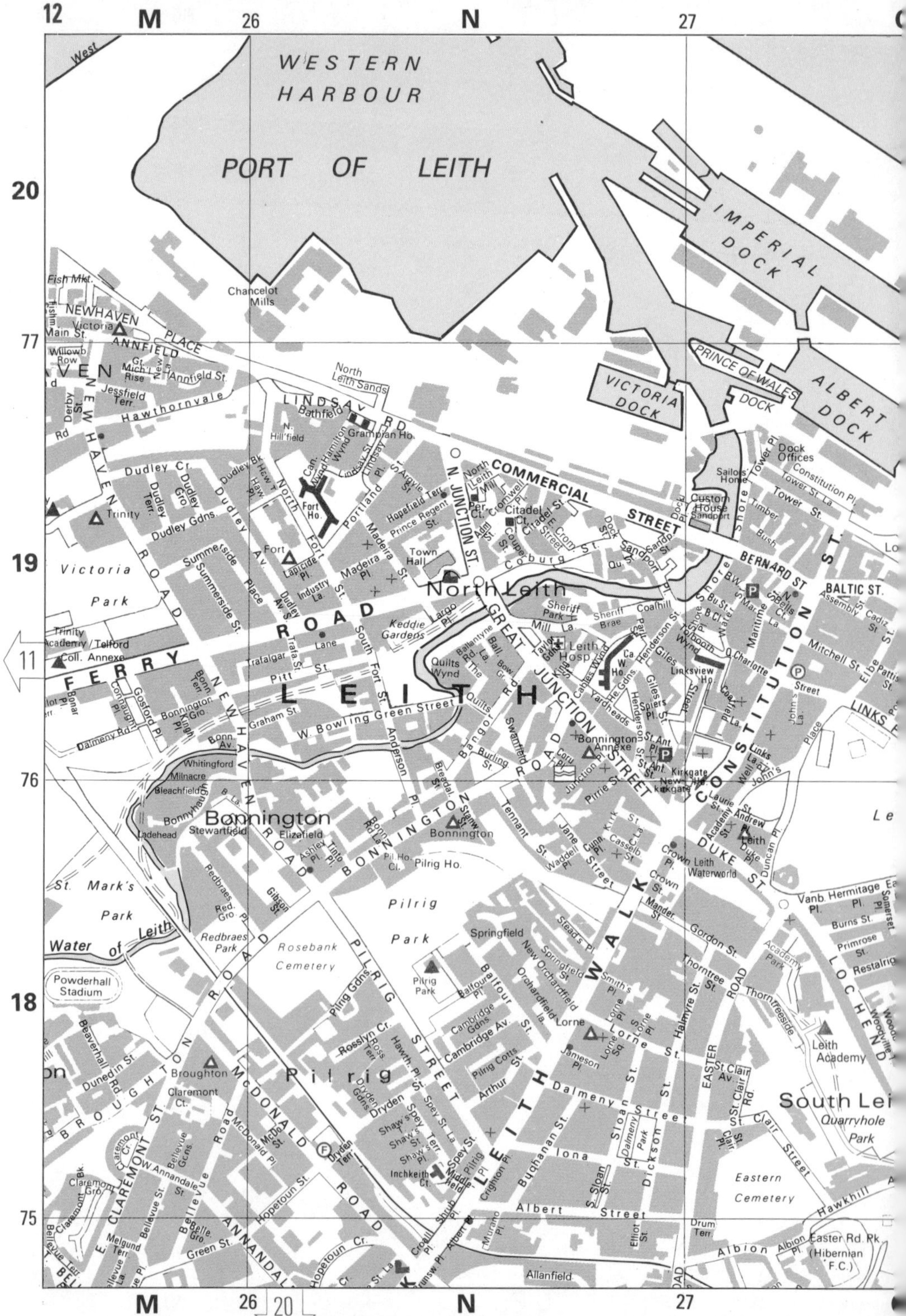
M
26
N
27
20
19
18
77
76
75
11
20
WESTERN HARBOUR
PORT OF LEITH
IMPERIAL DOCK
VICTORIA DOCK
PRINCE OF WALES DOCK
ALBERT DOCK
West
Fish Mkt.
NEWHAVEN
Main St.
Victoria
ANNFIELD
PLACE
Willowb. Row
Gt. Mich'l Rise
Annfield St.
Jessfield Terr.
Hawthornvale
Chancelot Mills
North Leith Sands
LINDSAY RD
Bathfield
N. Hill'field
Grampian Ho.
Fort Ho.
Dock Offices
Constitution Pl.
Tower St. La.
Tower St.
Sailors' Home
Custom House
Sandport
COMMERCIAL STREET
N. JUNCTION ST.
Citadel Ct.
Citadel St.
Coburg St.
Dudley Cr.
Dudley Gro.
Dudley Terr.
Dudley Gdns.
Dudley Av.
Trinity
Victoria Park
Summerside Place
Summerside St.
Fort
Lapicide Pl.
Industry La.
Madeira Pl.
Madeira St.
Portland St.
Hopefield Terr.
Prince Regent St.
Town Hall
North Leith
BERNARD ST
BALTIC ST.
Trinity Academy / Telford Coll. Annexe
FERRY ROAD
Keddie Gardens
Largo Pl.
Sheriff Park
Sheriff Brae
Coalhill
Mill La.
Leith Hosp.
Henderson St.
Giles St.
Linksview Ho.
Charlotte
Mitchell St.
Cadiz St.
Elbe St.
Trafalgar Lane
Pitt St.
Quilts Wynd
Ballantyne Rd.
LEITH
GREAT JUNCTION ST.
CONSTITUTION ST.
LINKS PL.
Bonnington Gro.
Gosford Pl.
Connaught Pl.
Bonar Pl.
Dalmeny Rd
Graham St.
W. Bowling Green Street
South Fort St.
Anderson Pl.
Bangor Rd.
Swanfield
Burling St.
Bonnington Annexe
Kirkgate
New Kirkgate
Links
John's Place
NEWHAVEN ROAD
Whitingford
Milnacre
Bleachfield
Bonnyhaugh
Ladehead
Bonnington
Stewartfield
Elizafield
BONNINGTON ROAD
Tennant St.
Pirrie St.
Jane Street
Laurie St.
Andrew St.
Leith
Duncan Pl.
DUKE ST.
Crown Pl.
Leith Waterworld
Pilrig Ho.
Pilrig Park
St. Mark's Park
Redbraes Pl.
Redbraes Park
Gibson St.
Water of Leith
Powderhall Stadium
Rosebank Cemetery
PILRIG STREET
Pilrig Gdns.
Springfield
Balfour St.
Orchardfield La.
Smith's Pl.
Lorne
Lorne St.
Gordon St.
Thorntree St.
EASTER ROAD
Halmyre St.
Vanb. Pl.
Hermitage Pl.
Somerset Pl.
Burns St.
Primrose St.
Restalrig
Academy Park
LOCHEND
Leith Academy
Thorntreeside
Beaverhall Rd.
Dunedin St.
Broughton
BROUGHTON ST.
Claremont Ct.
McDONALD ROAD
Pilrig
Rosslyn Cr.
Cambridge Gdns.
Cambridge Av.
Pilrig Cotts.
Arthur St.
Jameson Pl.
Dalmeny Street
LEITH WALK
St. Clair Av.
St. Clair Rd.
St. Clair Street
South Leith
Quarryhole Park
Dryden Gdns.
Dryden St.
Shaw's Pl.
Spey Terr.
Spey St.
Inchkeith Ct.
Crighton Pl.
Buchanan St.
Iona St.
Sloan St.
Dickson St.
Dalmeny Park
E. CLAREMONT ST.
W. Annandale St.
Bellevue Gdns.
Bellevue St.
Bellevue Gro.
Melgund Terr.
Green St.
Hopetoun St.
Hopetoun Cr.
ANNANDALE ST.
Albert Street
Albert Pl.
Murano Pl.
Elliot St.
Drum Terr.
Eastern Cemetery
Hawkhill
Albion Pl.
Albion
Easter Rd. Pk. (Hibernian F.C.)
Allanfield

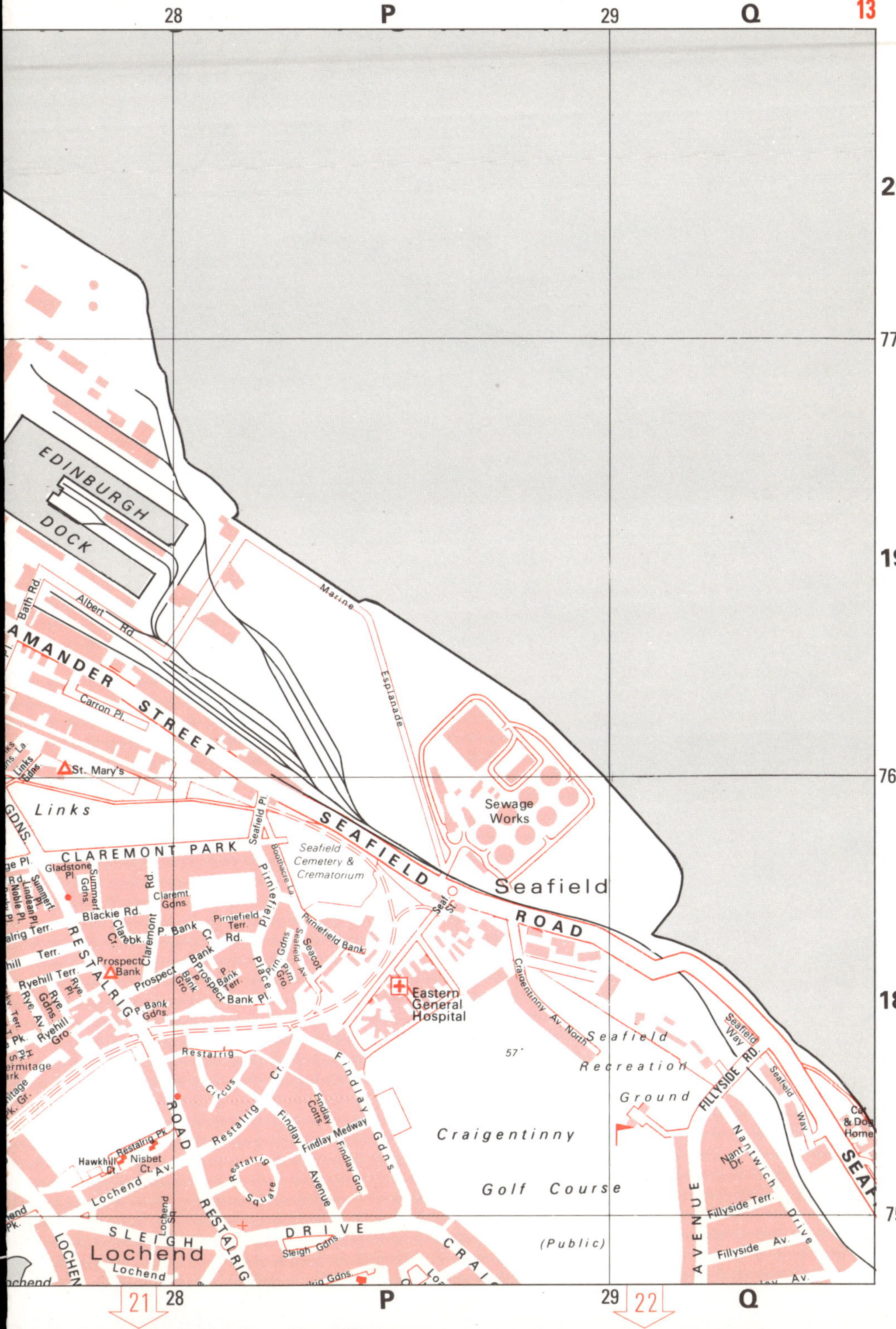
28
P
29
Q
20
77
19
76
18
75
EDINBURGH DOCK
Bath Rd.
Albert Rd.
SALAMANDER STREET
Carron Pl.
St. Mary's
Links
Marine Esplanade
Sewage Works
Seafield
SEAFIELD ROAD
Seafield Pl.
CLAREMONT PARK
Seafield Cemetery & Crematorium
Boothacre La.
Gladstone Pl.
Summerf. Gdns.
Claremont Rd.
Claremt. Gdns.
Blackie Rd.
Pirniefield Place
Pirniefield Terr.
Pirniefield Bank
Seafield Av.
Seacot
Seaf. St.
Prospect Bank
P. Bank Cr.
P. Bank Rd.
Prospect Bank Pl.
Prospect Bank Gro.
P. Bank Gdns.
Ryehill Terr.
Ryehill Gro.
RESTALRIG
Restalrig
Restalrig Circus
Restalrig Cr.
Restalrig Square
Findlay Gdns.
Findlay Cotts.
Findlay Medway
Findlay Avenue
Findlay Gro.
Eastern General Hospital
Craigentinny Av. North
Seafield Recreation Ground
57
Craigentinny Golf Course (Public)
Seafield Way
FILLYSIDE RD.
Cat & Dog Home
Nantwich Dr.
Nantwich Drive
Fillyside Terr.
Fillyside Av.
AVENUE
Restalrig Pk.
Nisbet Ct.
Hawkhill Ct.
Lochend Av.
Lochend Sq.
ROAD
SLEIGH DRIVE
Sleigh Gdns.
Lochend
CRAIG
21
22

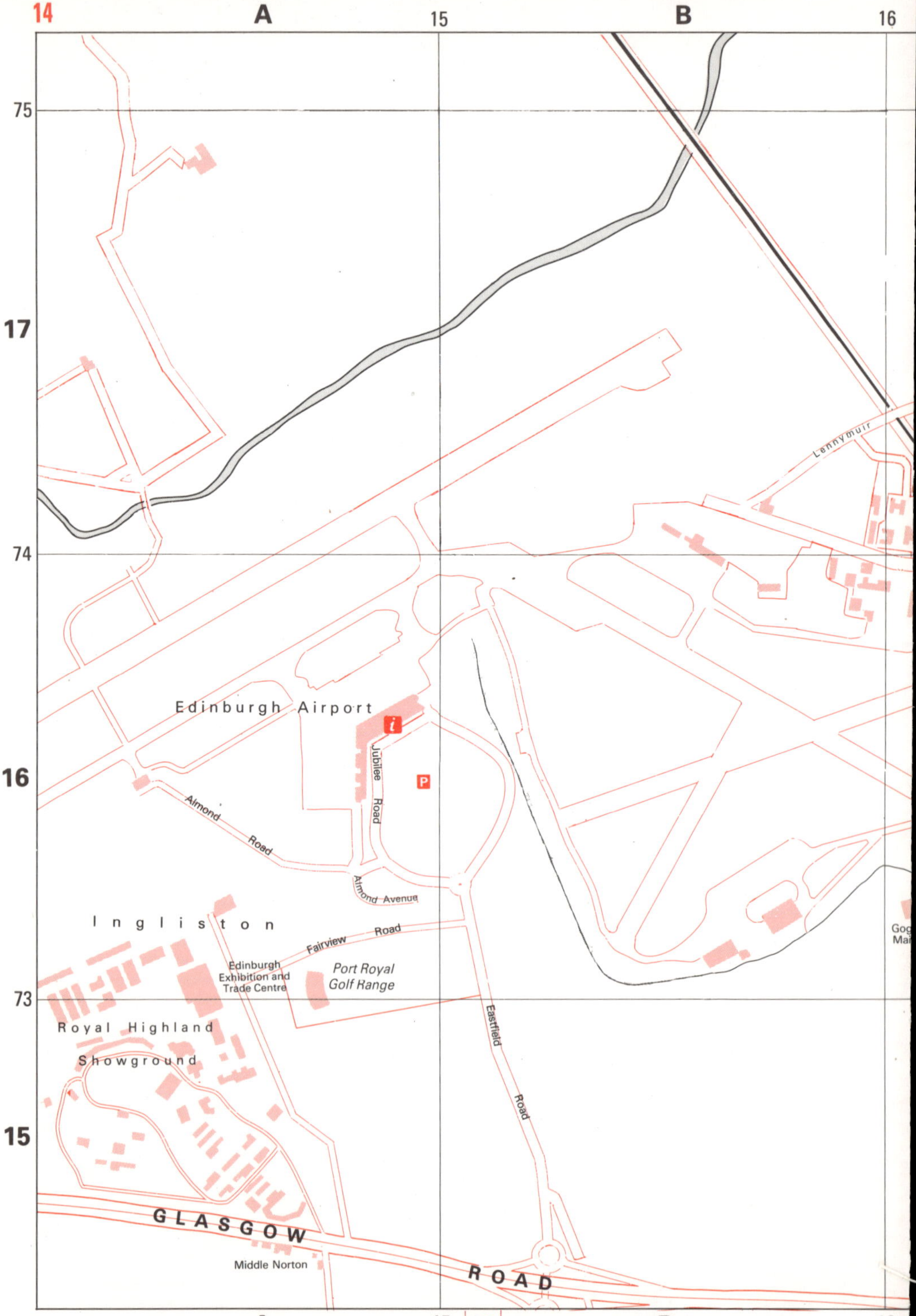
A
15
B
16
75
17
74
16
73
15
Lennymuir
Edinburgh Airport
Jubilee Road
Almond Road
Almond Avenue
Ingliston
Fairview Road
Edinburgh Exhibition and Trade Centre
Port Royal Golf Range
Royal Highland Showground
Eastfield Road
GLASGOW ROAD
Middle Norton

26

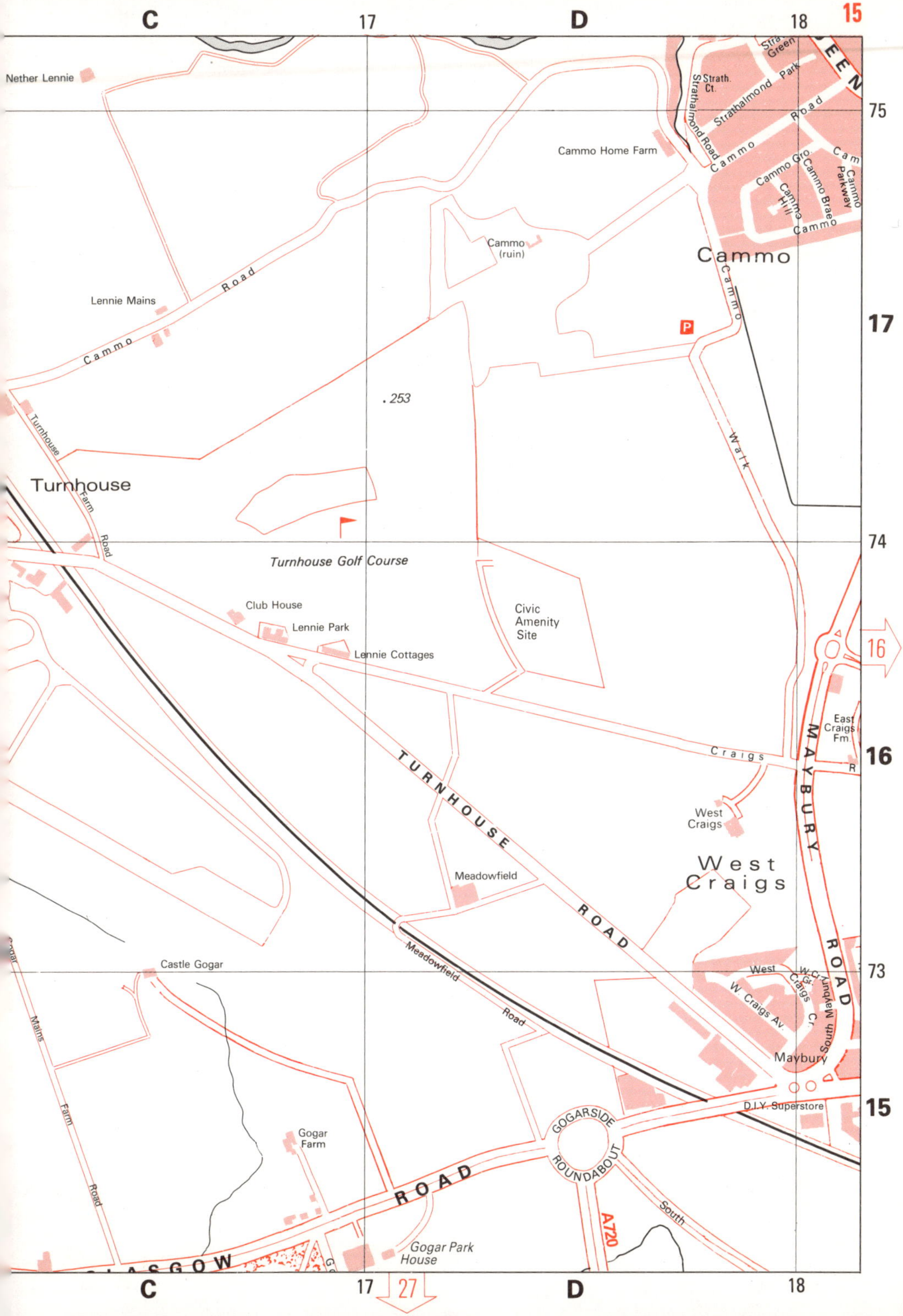

C
17
D
18
75
17
74
16
73
15
Nether Lennie
Cammo Home Farm
Strathalmond Road
Strath. Ct.
Strathalmond Park
Cammo Road
Cammo Gro.
Cammo Hill
Cammo Braes
Cammo Parkway
Cammo
(ruin)
Cammo
Cammo Walk
Lennie Mains
Cammo Road
.253
Turnhouse
Turnhouse Farm Road
Turnhouse Golf Course
Club House
Lennie Park
Lennie Cottages
Civic Amenity Site
16
East Craigs Fm.
Craigs
MAYBURY ROAD
TURNHOUSE ROAD
West Craigs
West Craigs
Meadowfield
Meadowfield Road
Castle Gogar
Mains Farm Road
West
W Craigs Av.
W Craigs Cr.
South Maybury
Maybury
D.I.Y. Superstore
GOGARSIDE ROUNDABOUT
Gogar Farm
ROAD
GLASGOW
A720
South
Gogar Park House
27

18
E
8
19
F
75
17
74
16
73
15
15
28
Barnton
Cammo
Drumbrae
Bughtlin
East Craigs
West Craigs
Gyle
Queensferry Road
Maybury Road
Drum Brae North
Drum Brae South
Glasgow Road
St. John's
Barnton Ct.
Barnton Gro.
Barnton Park Gdns.
Barnton Park Av.
Barnton Park Crescent
Barnton Park Wood
Cammo Crescent
Cammo Gardens
Cammo Grove
Cammo Gro.
Cammo Brae
Cammo Parkway
Cammo Hill
Cammo Bank
Cam. Pl.
Cammo Road
Cammo Walk
Strathalmond Park
Strath. Ct.
Strathalmond Green
Blackth. Ct.
Barntongate Av.
Barntongate Terr.
Barntongate Dr.
Birch Ct.
Blaeb. Gdns.
Bramble Dr.
Parkgrove Drive
Parkgrove Av.
Parkgrove Gdns.
Parkgrove Terrace
Parkgrove Crescent
Parkgrove Loan
Parkgrove Pl.
Parkgrove St.
Parkgrove Row
Parkgrove Bank
Parkgrove View
Parkgrove Neuk
Parkgrove Green
Parkgrove Road
Clermiston
Clermiston Road
Clermiston Park
Clermiston Loan
Drum Brae Park
Drum Brae Terrace
Drum Brae Cr.
D.B. Gro.
Drum Brae Drive
Drum Brae Av.
D.B. Neuk
Drum Brae Pl.
Drum Brae Park
Drum Brae Gdns.
258
Dochart Drive
Duart Cr.
Balfron Loan
Torrance Pk.
Morven St.
Glenure Loan
Ardshiel Av.
Durar Drive
Hoseason
Essendean Pl.
Essendean Terr.
N. B'rigg
F'burn Pk.
Fauldburn
N. B'field
North Bughtlinside
N.B. Neuk
N.B. Brae
N.B. Bank
N. Bughtlin Gate
North Bughtlin Road
N.B. Pl.
Maybury Dr.
Bughtlin Market
Bughtlin Park
B. Green
B. Drive
B. Gdns.
B. Loan
B. Place
Craigm. Av. N.
Crmt Court
Craigm. Bank
D.B. Walk
Craigm. Hill
Craigmount Brae
Craigmount Avenue North
Cr.mt. Way
East Craigs
Hayfield
Mearenside
Almond Green
Almond Square
Drive
Burnside
Maybury
Stuart Sq.
Stuart Pk.
Stuart Cr.
S. Wynd
Craigmount S. Gr.
Craigmount Loan
Craigmount Dr.
Craigmount Pl.
Craigmount Cr.
Craigmount View
Craigmount Gro. N.
Craigmount Gro.
Craigmount Terr.
Craigmount Gdns.
Craigmount Pk.
Craigmount Av.
Crmt. Appr.
Burnbrae
East Craigs Fm.
Seed Testing Station
Cr. Sq.
Craigievar Wynd
Craigs Road
Craigs Park
Craigs Drive
Craigmount
Craigs Crescent
Cr. Loan
Craigs Bank
Craigs Loan
Cr. Gro.
Craigs Gardens
Craigs Avenue
North Gyle Road
North Gyle Loan
N.G. Park
Dechmont Rd.
North Gyle Drive
North Gyle Av.
North Gyle Terrace
North Gyle Grove
N.G. Fm. Ct.
N.G. Fm. La.
North Gyle
W. Craigs Av.
West Craigs Cr.
South Maybury
D.I.Y. Superstore
Gyle Park Gdns.
The Gyle Park
Safeway Shopping Centre
Gylemuir Rd.
Gylemuir
W. Broom Pl.
Gyle Road
S. Gyle Gdns.
Meadow Pl. Rd.
Corstorphine Hill Cemetery
Clerw. Way
Clerw. Bk.
Clerwood
Clerw. Loan
Clerw. Row
Clerwood Gdns.
Caroline
D.B. Gdns.
Pearce Rd.
Pearce Av.
P'rce Gro.
Hillview
Hillview Drive
Bank Drive
Templeland
Cor. Bank Av.
Cor. Bank Terr.
Corstorphine Road
Tem. Gro.
Victor Pk. Terr.
Forrester
Mayfield Pl.
Featherhall Cr. N.
Featherhall Cr. S.
Featherhall Av.
Feath. Gro.
Feath. Rd.
Feath. Terr.
Ladywell Ho.
Ladywell Rd.
Corstorphine
Dunsmuir Ct.
Meadow Cotts.
Meadow
Court
Broomhall
Broomh. Pk.
Ladywell Gdns.
Ladywell Av.

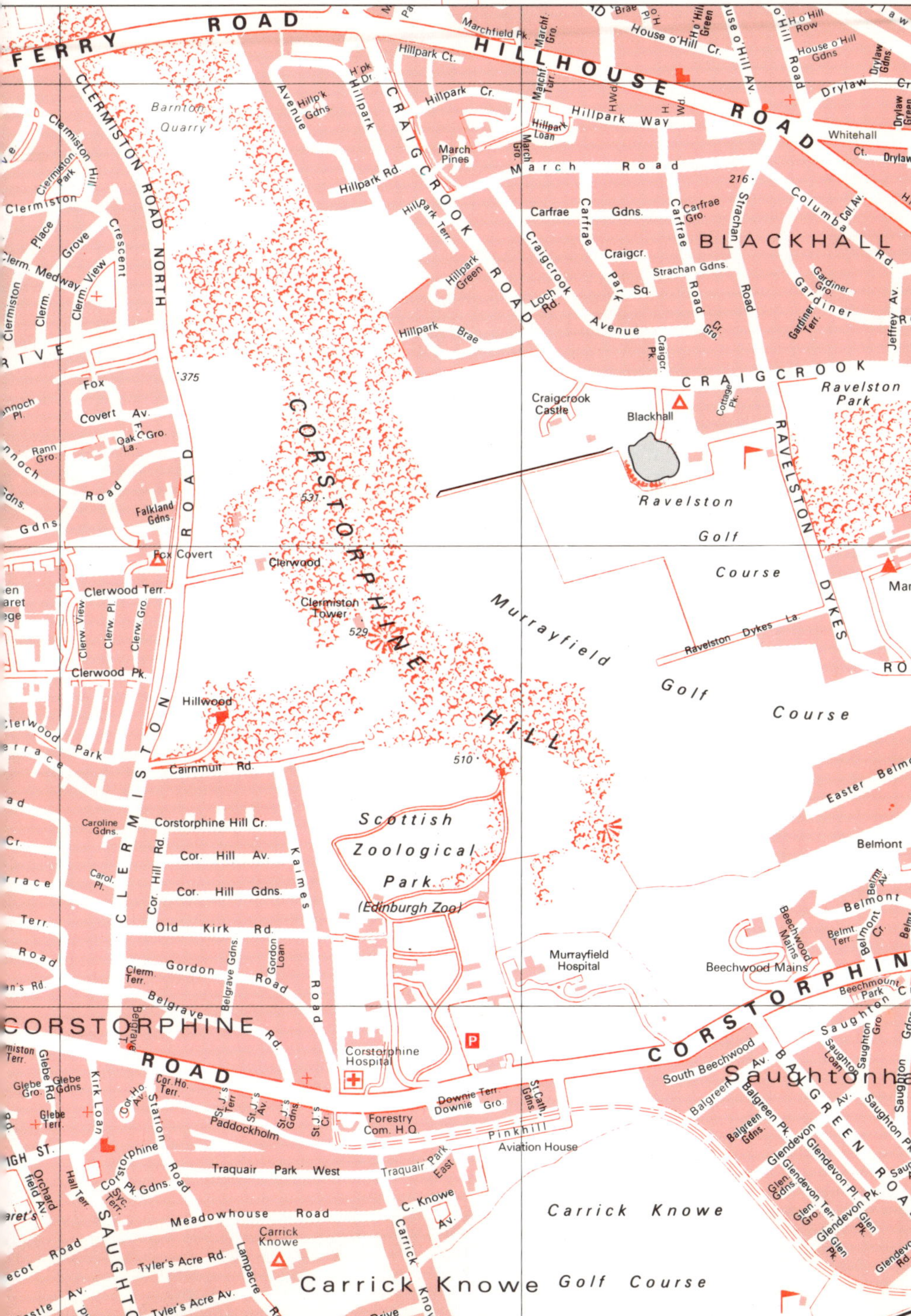


17
75
74
18
16
73
15

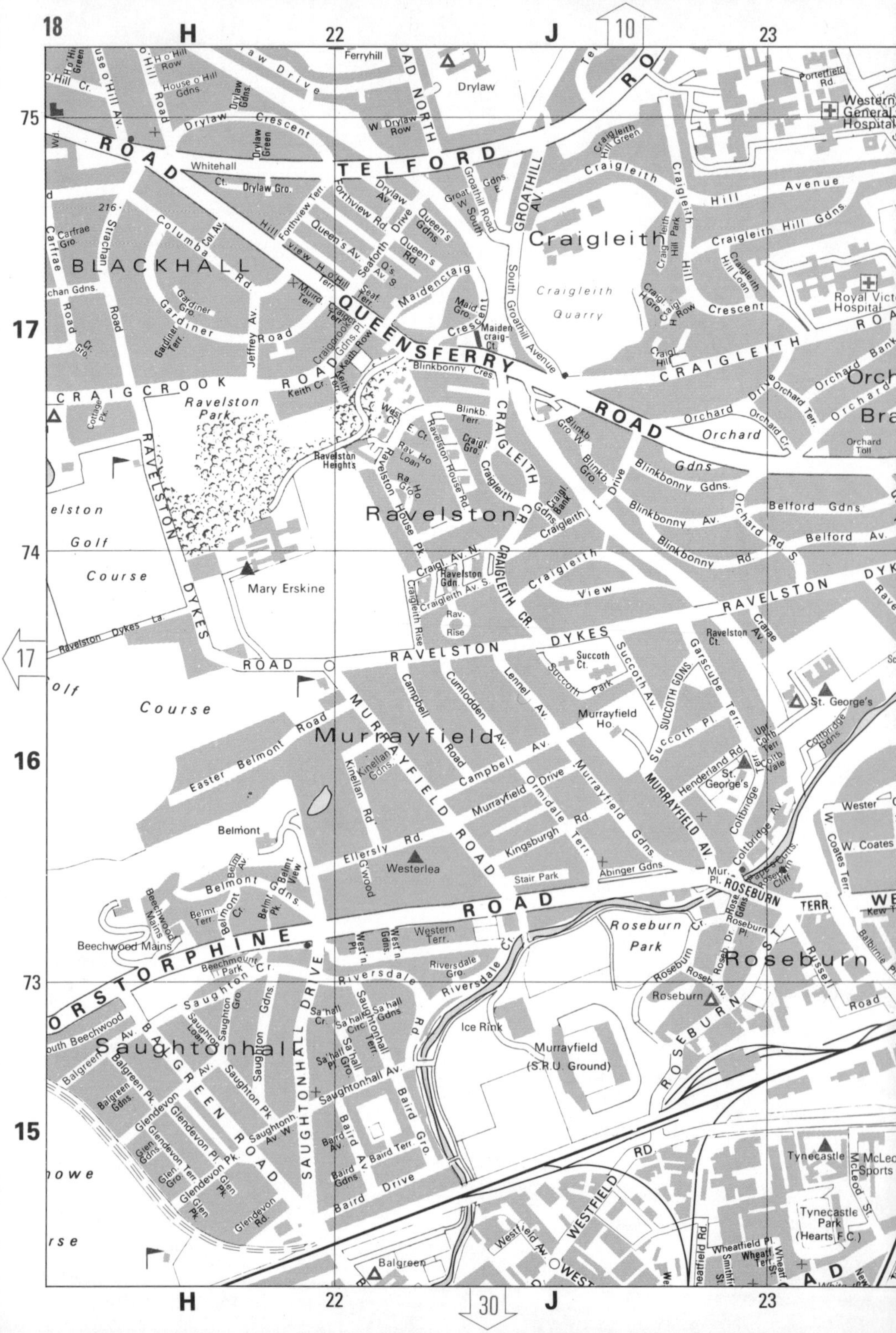
H
22
J
23
10
75
17
74
16
73
15
30
BLACKHALL
Craigleith
Craigleith Quarry
Ravelston
Ravelston Park
Ravelston Golf Course
Murrayfield
Saughtonhall
Roseburn
Roseburn Park
Drylaw
Ferryhill
Western General Hospital
Royal Victoria Hospital
Mary Erskine
Ravelston Heights
Westerlea
Belmont
Beechwood Mains
Ice Rink
Murrayfield (S.R.U. Ground)
Tynecastle Park (Hearts F.C.)
McLeod Sports
Balgreen
St. George's
Murrayfield Ho.
QUEENSFERRY ROAD
TELFORD ROAD
CRAIGLEITH ROAD
CRAIGCROOK ROAD
RAVELSTON DYKES ROAD
RAVELSTON DYKES
CORSTORPHINE ROAD
MURRAYFIELD ROAD
MURRAYFIELD AV.
GROATHILL AV.
CRAIGLEITH CR.
SAUGHTONHALL DRIVE
BALGREEN ROAD
ROSEBURN ST.
ROSEBURN TERR.
WESTFIELD RD
Drylaw Crescent
Whitehall Ct.
Drylaw Gro.
Columba Rd.
Gardiner Road
Strachan Road
Jeffrey Av.
Craigleith Hill Avenue
Craigleith Hill Gdns.
Craigleith Hill Crescent
South Groathill Avenue
Orchard Brae
Blinkbonny Gdns.
Blinkbonny Av.
Blinkbonny Rd.
Belford Gdns.
Belford Av.
Craigleith View
Campbell Av.
Cumlodden Av.
Lennel Av.
Succoth Av.
Succoth Pl.
Garscube Terr.
Murrayfield Drive
Ormidale Terr.
Kingsburgh Rd.
Abinger Gdns.
Stair Park
Ellersly Rd.
Kinellan Rd.
Easter Belmont Road
Belmont Gdns.
Riversdale Cr.
Riversdale Gro.
Western Terr.
Saughton Gdns.
Saughtonhall Av.
Baird Drive
Baird Av.
Baird Gro.
Glendevon Pl.
Glendevon Rd.
Coltbridge Av.
W. Coates
Westfield Av.
Wheatfield Pl.
McLeod St.

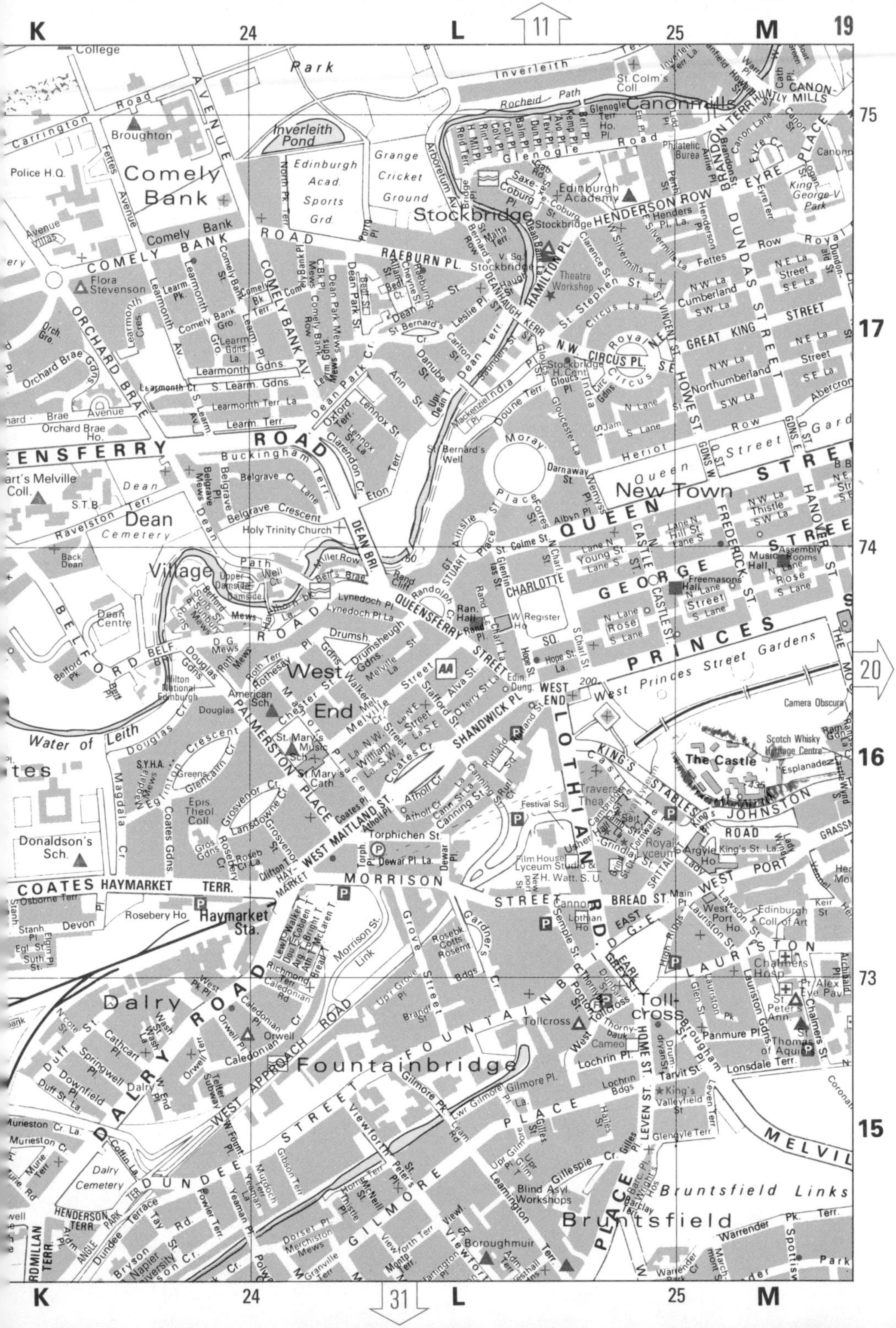
K
24
L
11
25
M
75
17
74
20
16
73
15
31
College
Park
Inverleith
St. Colm's Coll.
Canonmills
CANON MILLS
Rocheid Path
Carrington Road
Broughton
Inverleith Pond
Grange Cricket Ground
Edinburgh Acad. Sports Grd.
Glenogle Road
Police H.Q.
Comely Bank
Fettes Avenue
Avenue Villas
Comely Bank Road
Stockbridge
Edinburgh Academy
HENDERSON ROW
Philatelic Burea
BRANDON TERR.
EYRE PLACE
King George V Park
COMELY BANK
Flora Stevenson
Learmonth Cres.
COMELY BANK AV.
RAEBURN PL.
Dean Park St.
Theatre Workshop
HAMILTON PL.
DEANHAUGH ST.
Fettes Row
DUNDAS STREET
Royal
Cumberland
Great King Street
Orchard Brae
ORCHARD BRAE
Learmonth Gdns.
S. Learm. Gdns.
Learmonth Terr. La.
Learm. Terr.
Dean Park Cr.
Danube St.
Dean Terr.
N.W. CIRCUS PL.
Royal Circus
Stockbridge H. Cent.
ST. VINCENT ST.
HOWE ST.
Northumberland
Abercromby
Orchard Brae Ho.
QUEENSFERRY
ROAD
Buckingham Terr.
Clarendon Cr.
St. Bernard's Well
Moray Place
Darnaway St.
Heriot Row
Queen Street
Stuart's Melville Coll.
S.T.B.
Dean
Ravelston Terr.
Belgrave Crescent
Dean Cemetery
Holy Trinity Church
DEAN BRI.
Ainslie Place
Albyn Pl.
New Town
QUEEN STREET
Hill St.
Young St.
FREDERICK ST.
HANOVER ST.
Thistle St.
Assembly Rooms
Music Hall
Back Dean
Village
Path
Well Ct.
Miller Row
Bells Brae
Randolph Cr.
GT. STUART
CHARLOTTE SQ.
GEORGE STREET
Freemasons Hall
CASTLE ST.
Rose Street
Dean Centre
BELFORD
Lynedoch Pl.
QUEENSFERRY STREET
Ran. Hall
W. Register Ho.
PRINCES STREET
BELFORD BRI.
D.G. Mews
Drumsheugh Gdns.
Melville St.
Hope St.
West Princes Street Gardens
Belford Pk.
Hilton National Edinburgh
Douglas Gdns.
West End
Rothesay Pl.
AA
Alva St.
Edin. Dung.
WEST END
200
Camera Obscura
Douglas
American Sch.
PALMERSTON PLACE
Chester St.
Melville St.
Stafford St.
SHANDWICK PL.
LOTHIAN
Scotch Whisky Heritage Centre
Water of Leith
Douglas Cres.
Crescent
St. Mary's Music Sch.
William St.
Coates Cr.
Rutland Sq.
KING'S STABLES
The Castle
Esplanade
S.Y.H.A.
Glencairn Cr.
St. Mary's Cath.
Atholl Cr.
Canning St.
Traverse Thea.
435
JOHNSTON
Eglinton Cres.
Epis. Theol. Coll.
Grosvenor Cr.
Lansdowne Cr.
Coates Pl.
Festival Sq.
Royal Lyceum
Grindlay St.
KING'S
Magdala Cr.
Coates Gdns.
WEST MAITLAND ST.
Torphichen St.
Dewar Pl. La.
Film House
Lyceum Studio & H. Watt. S. U.
Argyle Ho.
King's St. La.
ROAD
GRASSMARKET
Donaldson's Sch.
Rosebery Cr.
HAYMARKET
MORRISON
SPITTAL
WEST PORT
COATES
HAYMARKET TERR.
Osborne Terr.
STREET
BREAD ST.
Main Pt.
Lawson St.
Edinburgh Coll. of Art
Keir St.
Rosebery Ho.
Haymarket Sta.
Devon Pl.
Morrison St. Link
Grove Street
Gardner's Cr.
Rosebk. Cotts
Semple St.
Lothian Ho.
EAST
West Port Ho.
Lauriston
LAURISTON
Chalmers Hosp.
Archibald Pl.
Richmond Terr.
Caledonian Rd.
Bdgs.
FOUNTAINBRIDGE
Ponton St.
Tollcross
Alex. Eye Pav.
Dalry
DALRY ROAD
Orwell
Tollcross
Thornybauk
Glen St.
Panmure Pl.
St. Peter's Ann.
St. Thomas of Aquin's
Chalmers St.
Caledonian Cr.
Orwell Terr.
WEST APPROACH ROAD
Fountainbridge
West Cameo
Lochrin Pl.
HOME ST.
Brougham
Lauriston Gdns.
Lonsdale Terr.
Cathcart Pl.
Springwell Pl.
Duff St.
Downfield Pl.
Duff St. La.
Dalry Pl.
Telfer Subway
Gilmore Pl.
Lochrin Bdgs.
Tarvit St.
King's
Valleyfield St.
Leven Terr.
Murieston Cr. La.
Murieston Cr.
Murie Terr.
DUNDEE STREET
Viewforth
Gilmore Pk.
PLACE
Leven St.
Glengyle Terr.
MELVILLE
Dalry Cemetery
Coffin La.
Gibson Terr.
St. Peter's Pl.
Upr. Gilmore Pl.
Gillespie Cr.
Bruntsfield Links
HENDERSON TERR.
ANGLE PARK TERR.
Dundee Terrace
Fowler Terr.
Yeaman Pl.
GILMORE
Leamington Terr.
Blind Asyl. Workshops
Bruntsfield
PLACE
Warrender Pk. Terr.
Spottiswoode
Park
Bryson Rd.
Napier University
Dorset Pl.
Merchiston Mews
Granville Terr.
Viewforth Terr.
Boroughmuir
Warrender
March. mont St.
ARDMILLAN TERR.
Polwarth
K
24
L
25
M

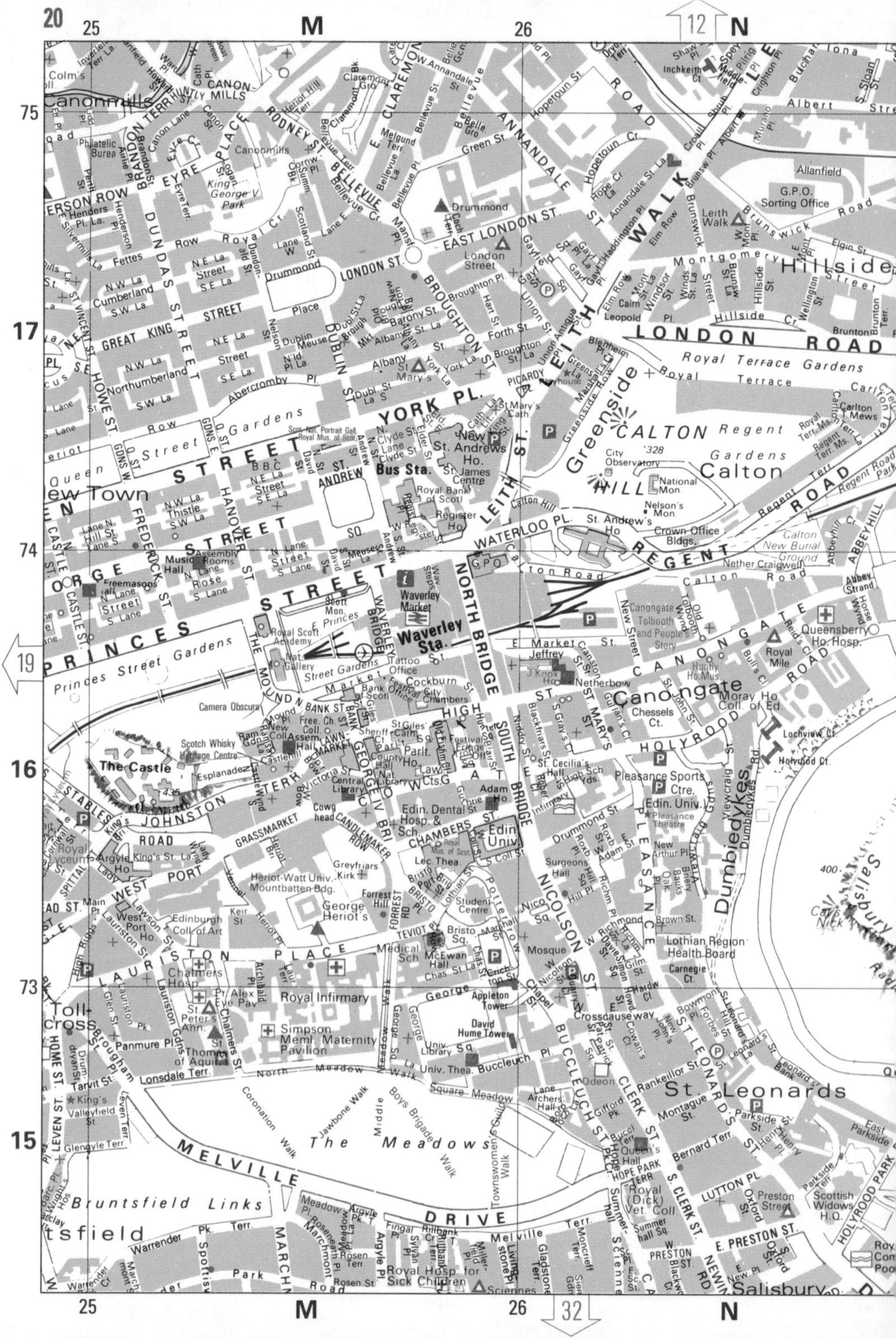
25
M
26
12
N
75
17
74
19
16
73
15
32
Canonmills
CANON MILLS
Philatelic Bureau
BRANDON TERR
EYRE PLACE
RODNEY ST
BELLEVUE
E. CLAREMONT
ANNANDALE ST
Canonmills
King George V Park
Drummond
EAST LONDON ST
London Street
Hopetoun Cr.
LEITH WALK
Leith Walk
Allanfield
G.P.O. Sorting Office
Brunswick Road
Hillside
Montgomery Street
Albert Street
Iona
Inchkeith Ct.
HENDERSON ROW
DUNDAS STREET
Royal Cr.
Fettes Row
Cumberland Street
GREAT KING STREET
Drummond Place
LONDON ST.
BROUGHTON ST
Barony St.
Albany St.
Forth St.
Broughton Pl.
Gayfield Sq.
Union St.
Leopold Pl.
Hillside Cr.
LONDON ROAD
Royal Terrace Gardens
Royal Terrace
Northumberland Street
Abercromby Pl.
Queen Street Gardens
YORK PL.
St. Mary's
Picardy Pl.
Playhouse
Greenside
CALTON HILL
Regent Gardens
Calton
City Observatory
National Mon.
Nelson's Mon.
St. Andrew's Ho.
Crown Office Bldgs.
REGENT ROAD
Calton New Burial Ground
Nether Craigwell
ABBEYHILL
Carlton Mews
New Town
QUEEN STREET
HANOVER ST
FREDERICK ST
ST. ANDREW SQ.
Bus Sta.
New St. Andrews Ho.
St. James Centre
Royal Bank of Scotl.
Register Ho.
LEITH ST.
WATERLOO PL.
Calton Road
G.P.O.
GEORGE STREET
Assembly Rooms
Music Hall
Freemasons Hall
Rose Street
PRINCES STREET
Princes Street Gardens
Scott Mon.
Royal Scott. Academy
Nat. Gallery
THE MOUND
WAVERLEY BRIDGE
Waverley Market
Waverley Sta.
NORTH BRIDGE
Market St.
Cockburn St.
City Chambers
Tattoo Office
Festival Office
Jeffrey St.
J. Knox Ho.
Netherbow
New Street
Canongate Tolbooth and People's Story
Huntly Ho. Mus.
CANONGATE
Canongate
Royal Mile
Queensberry Ho. Hosp.
Moray Ho. Coll. of Ed.
Chessels Ct.
HOLYROOD ROAD
Camera Obscura
Scotch Whisky Heritage Centre
The Castle
Esplanade
Castlehill
Assem. Hall
LAWNMARKET
BANK ST
HIGH ST.
St Giles' Cath
Parlt. Ho.
Law Cts.
County Hall
Nat. Library
SOUTH BRIDGE
St. Mary's St
St. Cecilia's Hall
Pleasance Sports Ctre. (Edin. Univ.)
Pleasance Theatre
Dumbiedykes
Lochview Ct.
Holyrood Ct.
JOHNSTON TERR
KING'S STABLES ROAD
GEORGE IV BRIDGE
Central Library
Cowgate
Victoria St
GRASSMARKET
CANDLEMAKER ROW
CHAMBERS ST.
Edin. Dental Hosp. & Sch.
Royal Mus. of Scot.
Edin. Univ.
Adam Ho.
Lec. Thea.
Greyfriars Kirk
Heriot-Watt Univ. Mountbatten Bdg.
George Heriot's
Forrest Hill
Student Centre
Bristo Sq.
Royal Lyceum
WEST PORT
Argyle Ho.
Surgeons Hall
Drummond St.
NICOLSON ST
PLEASANCE
Salisbury Crags
400
Cat's Nick
Edinburgh Coll. of Art
Keir St
LAURISTON PLACE
Chalmers Hosp.
Royal Infirmary
Medical Sch.
McEwan Hall
Appleton Tower
David Hume Tower
Mosque
Crosscauseway
Lothian Region Health Board
Carnegie Ct.
Tollcross
Simpson Meml. Maternity Pavilion
Univ. Library
Univ. Thea.
Buccleuch Pl.
ST. LEONARDS ST.
St. Leonards
Montague St.
Rankeillor St.
Odeon
Lonsdale Terr.
Meadow Walk
Jawbone Walk
Coronation Walk
Boys Brigade Walk
The Meadows
Townswomen's Guild Walk
BUCCLEUCH ST.
CLERK ST.
Queen's Hall
HOPE PARK TERR
Royal (Dick) Vet. Coll.
Bernard Terr.
Parkside St.
Scottish Widows H.Q.
HOLYROOD PARK
Preston Street
MELVILLE DRIVE
Bruntsfield Links
Bruntsfield
Warrender Pk. Terr.
MARCHMONT
Melville Terr.
Royal Hosp. for Sick Children
Sciennes
E. PRESTON ST.
NEWINGTON RD.
S. CLERK ST.
Salisbury
LEVEN ST.
King's
Valleyfield St.
Glengyle Terr
HOME ST.

13

27
O
28
P
75
17
74
16
73
15
D
Eastern Cemetery
Hawkhill Avenue
Easter Rd. Pk. (Hibernian F.C.)
Albion Road
Albion Pl.
Albion Terr.
Drum Terr.
Sunnyside
Bothwell St.
Edina Pl
Rossie Pl.
Norton Pk.
Maryfield Pl.
Alva Pl.
L.Menz.Pl.
Regent Pl.
Waver. Pl.
Carlyle Pl.
Salm. Pl.
Earlston Pl.
Norton Pl.
ROSE TERR.
Cadzow Pl.
Abbeyhill
Abbey La.
Lower London Rd.
LONDON ROAD
Meadowbank
Lane
Spring Gdns.
Milton St.
Waverley Park
Waverley Pk. Terr.
Clockmill La.
Royal Pk. Pl.
Royal Park Terr.
MEADOWBANK TERR.
Duke's Walk
Lochend Loch
Lochend Park
Lochend
Lochend Castle Barns
LOCHEND RD. SOUTH
SLEIGH DRIVE
Sleigh Gdns.
Lochend Gdns.
Lochend Drive
Lochend Quadrant
Lochend Gro.
Lochend Cr.
Lochend Pk.
Lochend Sq.
Lochend Av.
Hawkhill Ct.
Nisbet Ct.
RESTALRIG ROAD
RESTALRIG ROAD SOUTH
Restalrig Square
Restalrig Avenue
Restalrig Gdns.
Restalrig Ho.
Lochend Ho.
St. Ninian's
Restalrig Crescent
Restalrig Dr.
Loaning Road
Loaning Crescent
Craigentinny
CRAIGENTINNY
Golf Cour
(Public
Dalgety Rd.
Dalgety Av.
Dalgety St.
MARIONVILLE ROAD
Marionville Pk.
Marionville Cr.
Marionville Av.
Marionville Dr.
Mar. Gro.
Mar. Medwy.
Dean Cl.
Meadowbank Sports Centre (Meadowbank Thistle F.C.)
Wishaw Terr.
Camb. St.
Jock's Lodge
Piershill
Piershill Sq. W.
Piershill Sq. E.
Piersfield Gro.
Piersfield Terr.
Piershill Pl.
Piershill La.
Piershill Terr.
Baronsct. Rd.
Baronscourt Terr.
Loganlea Gdns.
Loganlea Drive
Loganlea Terr.
Loganlea Road
Loganlea Pl.
Loganlea Avenue
Loganlea Loan
Britwell
Restalrig
PORTOBELLO
Safeway Shopping Centre
Abercorn Gdns.
NORTH
The Royal High School
Parson's Grn. Terr.
Meadowbank Cr.
Meadowbank Av.
Queen's Park Av.
Scone Gdns.
Wolseley Terr.
Wolseley Cr.
Lismore Av.
Lismore Cr.
Wilf. T.
Lilyhill Terr.
Queen's Park Ct.
Abercorn Rd
Glenlee Av.
Glenlee Gdns.
Kenmure Av.
Willowbrae Gdns.
WILLOWBRAE
Willowbrae
Abercorn Gro.
Abercorn Av.
Abercorn Crescent
Abercorn Dr.
Ulster Drive
Ulster Crescent
Paisley Crescent
Paisley Gdns.
Paisley Terr.
Paisley Gro.
Paisley Avenue
Paisley Dr.
Northfield
Ulster Terr.
Ulster Gdns.
Ulst. Gro.
Parsons Green
Meadowfield Drive
Meadowfield Park
Meadowfield Terr
Meadowf. Gdns.
Mead Gdns
Lady Nairne Gro.
Lady Nairne Loan
Lady Nairne Pl.
Lady Nairne Cr.
St. Margaret's Loch
St. Anthony's Chapel (ruin)
QUEEN'S DRIVE
Haggis Knowe
HOLYROOD PARK
Hunter's Bog
The Dasses
Whinny Hill
584
Dunsapie Loch
369
Dunsapie Hill
Arthur's Seat
823
Gutted Haddie
Crow Hill
Nether Hill
Lion's Haunch
Windy Goule
Samson's Ribs
DRIVE
Pollock Halls of Residence
The Innocent
Nature Reserve
Duddingston Loch
Duddingston Village
OLD CHURCH LANE
The Causeway
DUDDINGSTON ROAD
Holy Rood
Cavalry Park Drive
27
O
28
P

22

33

13

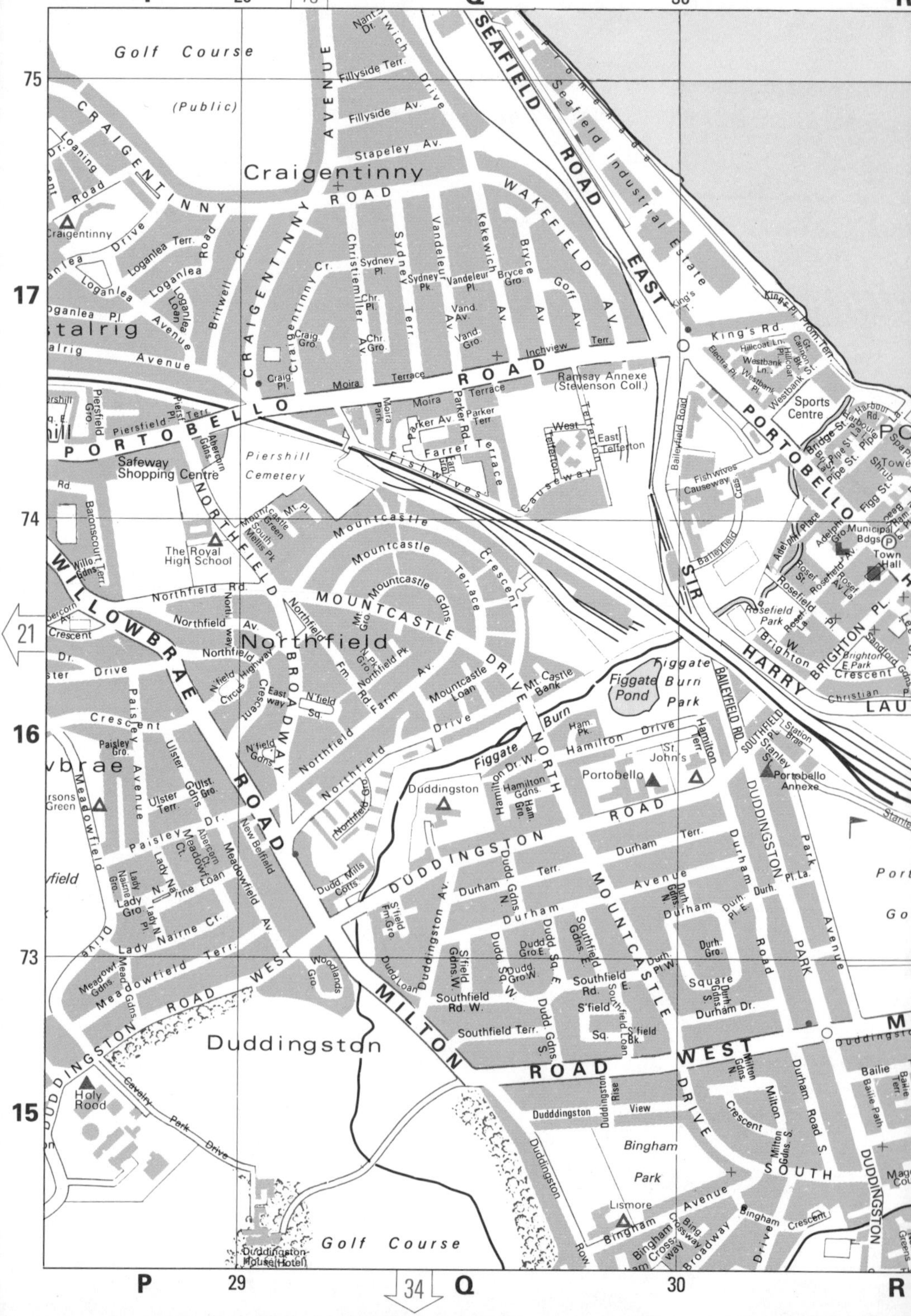
P
29
Q
30
R
75
17
74
16
73
15
Golf Course
(Public)
Craigentinny
CRAIGENTINNY ROAD
CRAIGENTINNY AVENUE
Fillyside Terr.
Fillyside Av.
Stapeley Av.
Nantwich Dr.
Nantwich Drive
SEAFIELD ROAD EAST
Seafield Industrial Estate
Promenade
WAKEFIELD AV.
Loaning Road
Loanlea Drive
Loganlea Terr.
Loganlea Road
Loganlea Avenue
Loganlea Loan
Loganlea Pl.
Restalrig
Restalrig Avenue
Britwell Cr.
Christiemiller Av.
Craigentinny Cr.
Craig. Gro.
Craig. Pl.
Sydney Pl.
Sydney Terr.
Sydney Pk.
Chr. Pl.
Chr. Gro.
Vandeleur Av.
Vandeleur Pl.
Vand. Av.
Vand. Gro.
Kekewich Av.
Bryce Av.
Bryce Gro.
Goff Av.
Inchview Terr.
King's T.
King's Pl.
Prom. Terr.
King's Rd.
Hillcoat Ln.
Hillcoat Pl.
Electra Pl.
Westbank Ln.
Westbank Pl.
Westbank St.
Gt. Canon Bk.
Sports Centre
Harbour Rd.
Harbour Pl.
Bridge St.
Pipe St.
Bath St.
Spa Pl.
Tower St.
Shrub Pl.
Figg St.
Beach La.
Ramsay Annexe (Stevenson Coll.)
PORTOBELLO ROAD
Moira Terrace
Moira Park
Parker Av.
Parker Rd.
Parker Terr.
Farrer Terrace
Farrer Gro.
West Telferton
East Telferton
Telferton
Fishwives Causeway
Baileyfield Road
Baileyfield Cres.
Piershill Gro.
Piershill Pl.
Piershill Terr.
Abercorn Gdns.
Safeway Shopping Centre
Piershill Cemetery
Baronscourt Terr.
Willo. Gdns.
NORTHFIELD BROADWAY
The Royal High School
Mountcastle Green
Mountcastle South Mellis Pk.
Mt. Pl.
Mountcastle Terrace
Mountcastle Crescent
Mountcastle Gdns.
MOUNTCASTLE DRIVE NORTH
Mt. Castle Bank
Mountcastle Loan
Northfield Rd.
Northfield Av.
Northfield Circus
Northfield Highway
Northfield Crescent
Northfield Pk.
Northfield Fm. Rd.
Northfield Farm Av.
Northfield Sq.
N'field Gdns.
Northfield Drive
Northfield Gro.
East way
Northfield
WILLOWBRAE ROAD
Abercorn Av.
Abercorn Crescent
Ulster Drive
Ulster Crescent
Ulster Avenue
Ulster Terr.
Ulster Gdns.
Ulst. Gro.
Paisley Crescent
Paisley Gro.
Paisley Dr.
Meadowfield Dr.
Meadowfield Av.
Meadowfield Ct.
Meadowfield Terr.
Meadowfield Gdns.
Lady Nairne Loan
Lady Nairne Gro.
Lady Nairne Pl.
Lady Nairne Cr.
New Belfield
Adelphi Place
Adelphi Gro.
Municipal Bdgs.
Town Hall
Rosefield Av.
Rosefield Av. La.
Rosefield St.
Rosefield Pl.
Rosefield Park
W Brighton Crescent
BRIGHTON PL.
Brighton E. Park
Sandford Gdns.
Lee Cr.
Christian
LAUD
SIR HARRY LAUDER ROAD
Figgate Pond
Figgate Burn Park
Figgate Burn
BAILEYFIELD RD.
Southfield Pl.
Station Brae
Stanley St.
Hamilton Drive
Hamilton Dr. W.
Hamilton Gdns.
Ham. Pk.
Ham. Gro.
Hamilton Terr.
St. John's
Portobello
Portobello Annexe
Duddingston
DUDDINGSTON ROAD
DUDDINGSTON PARK
Durham Terr.
Durham Avenue
Durham Sq.
Durham Pl. E.
Durham Pl. La.
Durham Gro.
Durham Gdns. N.
Durham Gdns. S.
Durham Dr.
Durham Road
Park Avenue
Duddingston Av.
Dudd. Gdns. N.
Dudd. Gdns. S.
Dudd. Sq. E.
Dudd. Sq. W.
Dudd. Gro. E.
Dudd. Gro. W.
Dudd. Loan
Dudd. Mills Cotts.
S'field Fm. Gro.
S'field Gdns. W.
Southfield Gdns. E.
Southfield Rd. W.
Southfield Rd. E.
Southfield Terr.
Southfield Sq.
Southfield Loan
S'field Bk.
MOUNTCASTLE DRIVE SOUTH
MILTON ROAD WEST
Woodlands Gro.
Meadowfield Gdns.
DUDDINGSTON ROAD WEST
Duddingston
Holy Rood
Cavalry Park Drive
Duddingston House (Hotel)
Golf Course
Duddingston Rise
Duddingston View
Duddingston Row
Bingham Park
Lismore
Bingham Avenue
Bingham Crossway
Bingham Cross.
Bingham Broadway
Bingham Drive
Bingham Crescent
Milton Gdns. N.
Milton Gdns. S.
Milton Crescent
Durham Road S.
Bailie Terr.
Bailie Path
Bailie
DUDDINGSTON
Duddingston
Port
Gol
M
Magd
Cou
21

34

31 S 32 T

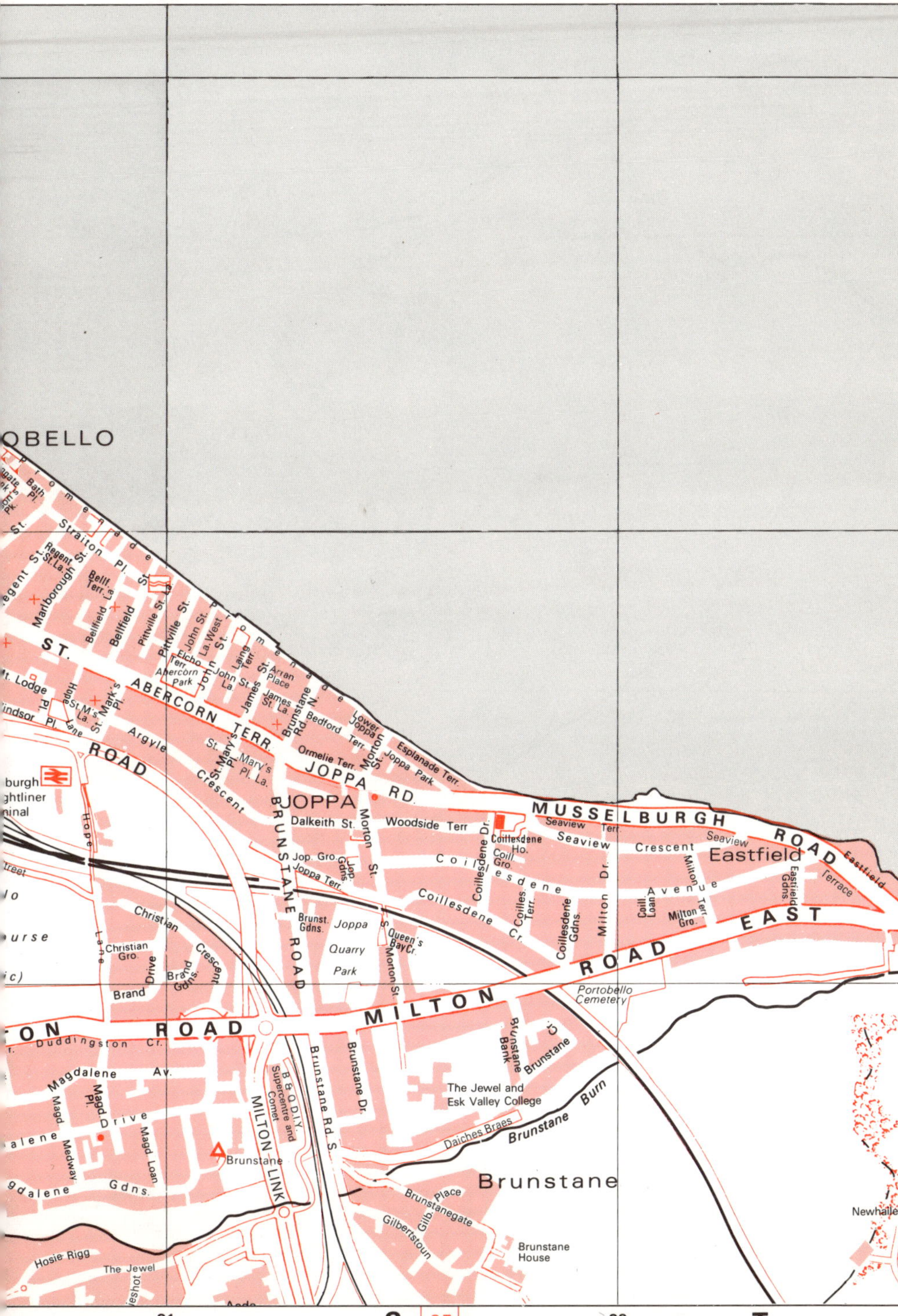


75
17
74
16
73
15

31 S 32 T

35

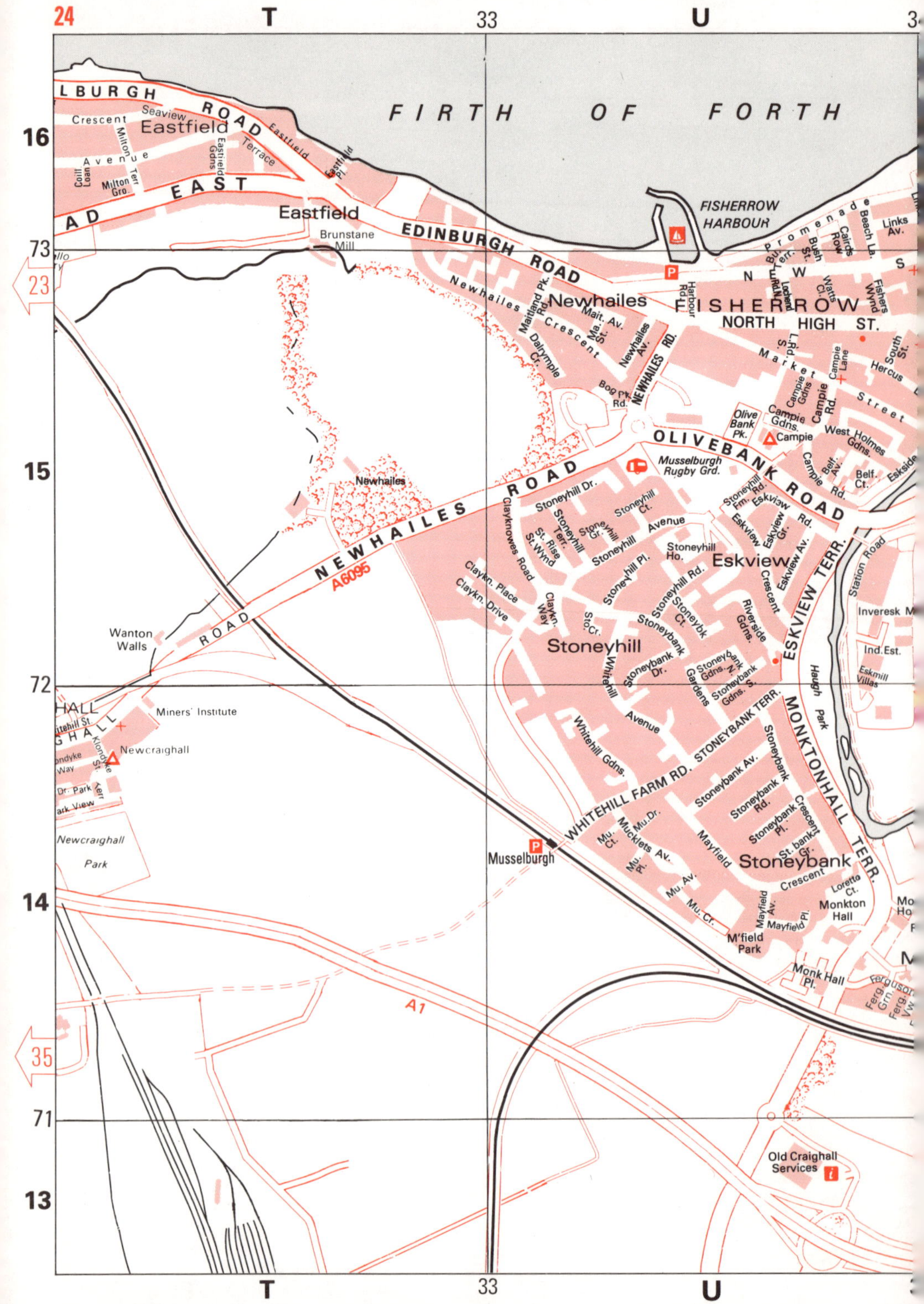

T
33
U
16
15
14
13
73
72
71
23
35
FIRTH OF FORTH
FISHERROW HARBOUR
Eastfield
Seaview
Crescent
Milton
Avenue
Eastfield Gdns.
Terrace
Eastfield Pl.
Coill. Loan
Milton Gro.
Terr
EAST
ROAD
Brunstane Mill
EDINBURGH ROAD
Newhailes
Newhailes Crescent
Maitland Pk. Rd.
Mait. Av.
Ma. St.
Dalrymple Ct.
Newhailes Av.
NEWHAILES RD.
Bog Pk. Rd.
Harbour Rd.
FISHERROW
NORTH HIGH ST.
Promenade
New St.
Bush St.
Bush Terr.
Lochend Rd. N.
Watts Cl.
Cairds Row
Beach La.
Fishers Wynd
Links Av.
L. Rd. S.
Market Street
Campie Lane
Campie Gdns.
Campie Rd.
South St.
Hercus
Olive Bank Pk.
Campie
West Holmes Gdns.
Belf. Av.
Belf. Ct.
Eskside
OLIVEBANK ROAD
Musselburgh Rugby Grd.
Stoneyhill Fm. Rd.
Eskview Rd.
Eskview Gr.
Eskview Av.
Eskview
ESKVIEW TERR.
Station Road
Inveresk
Ind. Est.
Eskmill Villas
Newhailes
NEWHAILES ROAD
A6095
Stoneyhill Dr.
Stoneyhill Ct.
Stoneyhill Gr.
Stoneyhill Avenue
Stoneyhill Terr.
St. Rise
St. Wynd
Claylnowes Road
Stoneyhill Ho.
Stoneyhill Pl.
Stoneyhill Rd.
Claykn. Place
Claykn. Drive
Claykn. Way
Sto. Cr.
Stoneybk Ct.
Stoneybank
Riverside Gdns.
Crescent
Stoneyhill
Wanton Walls
Stoneybank Dr.
Stoneyb Gdns. N.
Stoneybank Gdns. S.
Gardens
Whitehill
Avenue
Haugh Park
MONKTONHALL TERR.
HALL
Whitehill St.
Miners' Institute
Newcraighall
Klondyke St.
Way
Dr. Park
Terr
Park View
Whitehill Gdns.
STONEYBANK TERR.
WHITEHILL FARM RD.
Stoneybank Av.
Stoneybank Crescent
Stoneybank Rd.
Stoneybank Pl.
St. bank Gr.
Stoneybank
Newcraighall Park
Musselburgh
Mu. Ct.
Mu. Dr.
Mucklets Av.
Mu. Pl.
Mu. Av.
Mu. Cr.
Mayfield
Crescent
Loretto Ct.
Monkton Hall
Mayfield Av.
Mayfield Pl.
M'field Park
Monk Hall Pl.
Ferguson
Ferg. Grn.
Ferg. Vw.
A1
Old Craighall Services

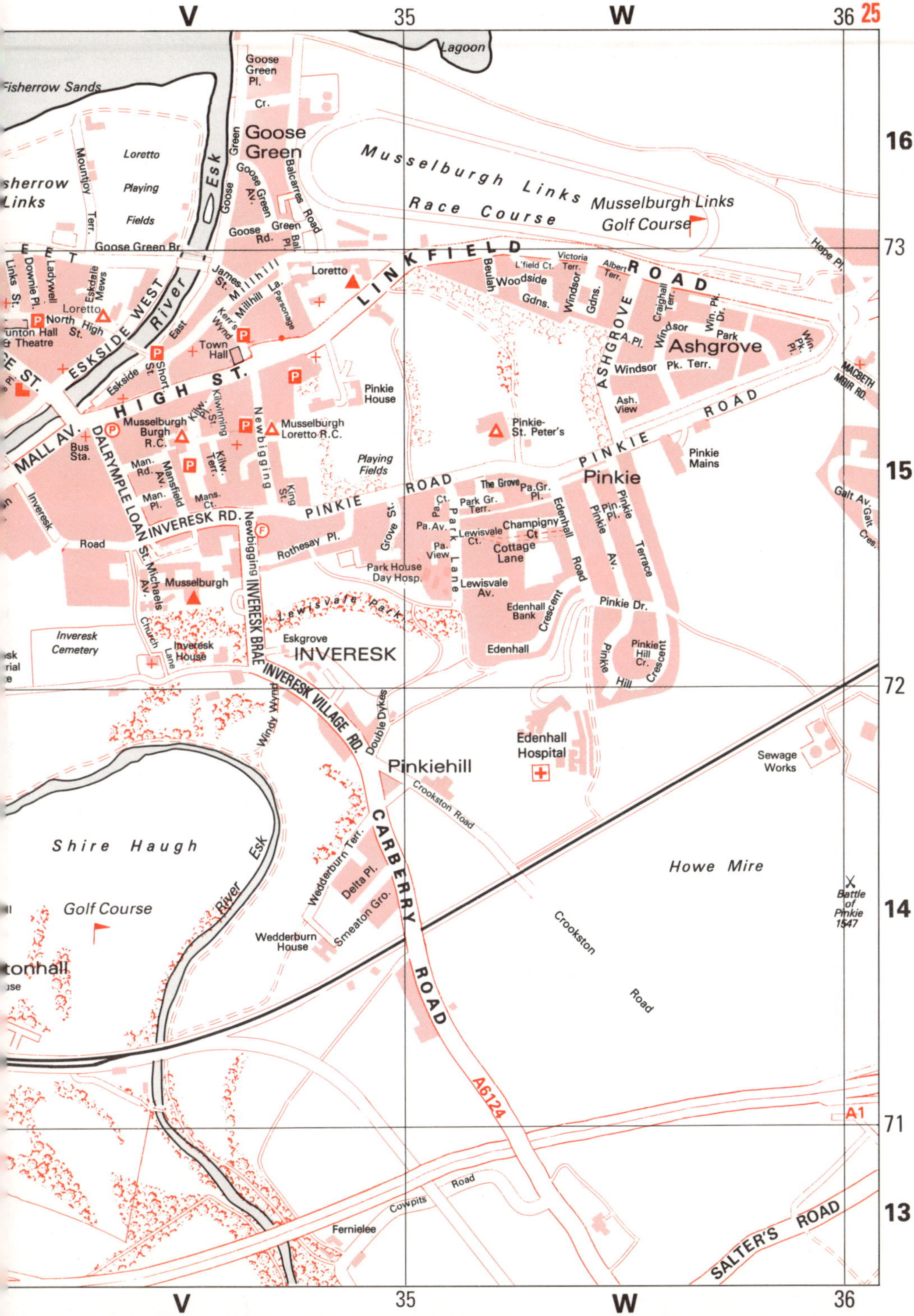

V
35
W
36
16
73
15
72
14
71
13
Lagoon
Fisherrow Sands
Fisherrow Links
Goose Green Pl.
Goose Green Cr.
Goose Green
Musselburgh Links Race Course
Musselburgh Links Golf Course
Mountjoy Terr.
Loretto Playing Fields
Esk
Goose Green Av.
Balcarres Road
Goose Green Rd.
Green Bal. Pl.
Goose Green Br.
LINKFIELD ROAD
Hope Pl.
Beulah
L'field Ct.
Victoria Terr.
Albert Terr.
Woodside Gdns.
Windsor Gdns.
Craighall Terr.
Win. Pk. Dr.
Loretto
Links St.
Dowie Pl.
Ladywell
Eskdale Mews
North High St.
Town Hall
Theatre
ESKSIDE WEST
River
ESKSIDE EAST
James St.
Millhill
Kerr's Wynd
La. Parsonage
Short St.
Eskside
ASHGROVE
A. Pl.
Windsor Park
Ashgrove
Win. Pk. Pl.
Windsor Pk. Terr.
MACBETH MOIR RD.
HIGH ST.
Pinkie House
Ash. View
PINKIE ROAD
MALL AV.
Bus Sta.
Musselburgh Burgh R.C.
Kilw. St.
Kilwinning St.
Newbigging
Musselburgh Loretto R.C.
Pinkie-St. Peter's
Pinkie Mains
DALRYMPLE LOAN
Man. Rd.
Mansfield Av.
Kilw. Terr.
Playing Fields
The Grove
Pa. Gr. Pl.
Pinkie
Man. Pl.
Mans. Ct.
King St.
Grove St.
Pa. Ct.
Park Gr. Terr.
Park Lane
Edenhall Road
Pinkie Pl.
Pinkie Av.
Pinkie Terrace
Galt Av.
Galt Cres.
Inveresk Road
INVERESK RD.
Pa. Av.
Lewisvale Ct.
Champigny Ct
Rothesay Pl.
Pa. View
Cottage Lane
St. Michaels Av.
Park House Day Hosp.
Lewisvale Av.
Musselburgh
Lewisvale Park
Edenhall Bank
Edenhall Crescent
Pinkie Dr.
Inveresk Cemetery
Church Lane
Inveresk House
INVERESK BRAE
Eskgrove
INVERESK
Edenhall
Pinkie Hill Cr.
Pinkie Hill Crescent
INVERESK VILLAGE RD.
Windy Wynd
Double Dykes
Edenhall Hospital
Sewage Works
Pinkiehill
Crookston Road
Shire Haugh
River Esk
CARBERRY ROAD
Wedderburn Terr.
Delta Pl.
Howe Mire
Golf Course
Smeaton Gro.
Wedderburn House
Battle of Pinkie 1547
A6124
A1
Road
Cowpits
Fernielee
SALTER'S ROAD

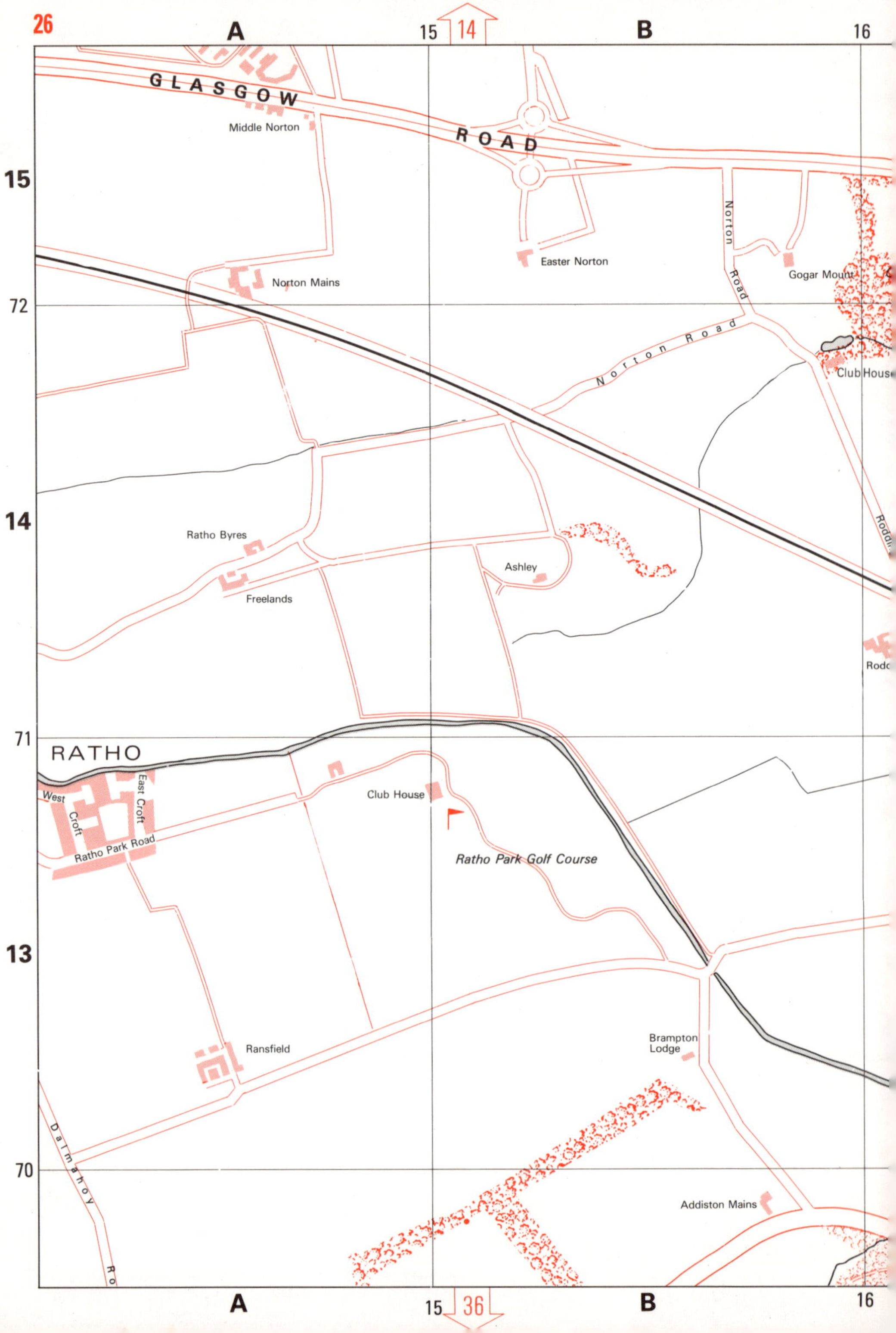
A
15
14
B
16
GLASGOW ROAD
Middle Norton
15
Easter Norton
Norton Road
Gogar Mount
Norton Mains
72
Norton Road
Club House
14
Ratho Byres
Ashley
Freelands
Rodd
71
RATHO
Club House
West Croft
East Croft
Ratho Park Road
Ratho Park Golf Course
13
Brampton Lodge
Ransfield
70
Dalmahoy Ro
Addiston Mains
A
15
36
B
16

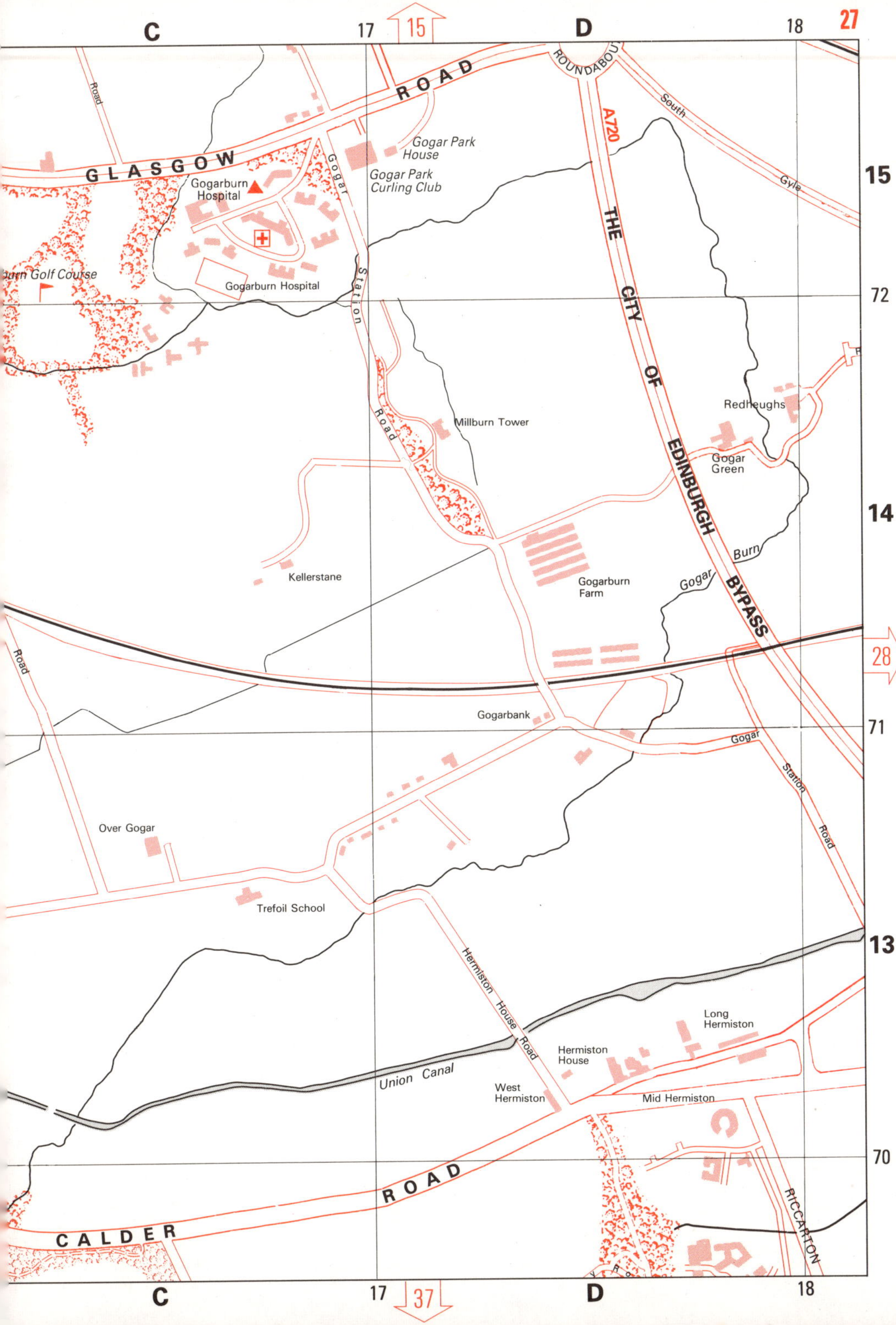
C
17
15
D
18
GLASGOW ROAD
ROUNDABOUT
South Gyle
A720
Gogar Park House
Gogar Park Curling Club
Gogarburn Hospital
Gogarburn Hospital
Gogar Station Road
Road
burn Golf Course
THE CITY OF EDINBURGH BYPASS
15
72
Redheughs
Millburn Tower
Gogar Green
14
Gogar Burn
Kellerstane
Gogarburn Farm
28
Road
Gogarbank
71
Gogar Station Road
Over Gogar
Trefoil School
13
Hermiston House Road
Long Hermiston
Hermiston House
West Hermiston
Union Canal
Mid Hermiston
70
CALDER ROAD
RICCARTON
C
17
37
D
18

18
E
16
19
F
15
72
14
71
13
70
27
38
South Gyle
South Gyle Sta.
Gylemuir
W. Broom Pl.
S. Gyle Gdns.
South Gyle Road
W. B. Gro.
W. B. Gdns.
Wester Broom Av.
Wester Broom Terr.
W. Broom
Wester Broom Drive
MEADOW PLACE ROAD
Broomhall Drive
Broomhall Terr.
Broomh. Pk.
Broomhall
Broomh. Loan
Broomhall Gdns.
B'h. Bank
Broomhall
Broomh. Pl.
Court
Ladywell Gdns.
Ladywell
Gyle Broadway
Gogarloch Rd.
South Gyle Ln.
S. G. Park
South Gyle Broadway
South Gyle
Mains
South Gyle Wynd
South Gyle Access
South Gyle Cres.
Redheughs Rigg
Redheughs Ave.
Redheughs Muir
Redheughs
Gogar Green
Burn
BYPASS
160
Cultins Road
H.M.S.O.
BANKHEAD DRIVE
St. Augustine's
Forrester
BROOMH
F.Pk.Gdns.
Sighthill
Park
Stevenson College
Bankhead
Crossway N.
Bankhead Medway
Broadway
Sighthill
Terrace
Bankhead
Crossway S.
Bankhead
Industrial
Estate
Bankhead Way
Bankhead St.
Bankhead Place
H.M. Govt. Offices
Bankhead Loan
BANKHEAD AVENUE
Cultins
Road
Drive
Napier University (Former Poly.)
Hermiston Ct.
Sighthill Ct.
Sighthill Health Centre
SIGHTH
Mid New Cultins
Gogar Station Road
Union Canal
East Hermiston
CALDER RD.
Calder View
Calder Pk.
Calder Ct.
Calder Gdns.
Cobbinshaw Ho.
Medwin Ho.
Dunsyre Ho.
Sighthill
Calder Pl
Calder Cr.
Calder Drive
Calder Gro.
Murrayburn
Wester Hailes Education Centre
WESTER HAILES ROAD
Sighthill
Sighth. Neuk
Sighthill
Westburn
Sighthill
Sighth. Rise
M'burn Appr.
Drive
Larbour
Long Hermiston
Murray Burn
RICCARTON
Westburn Gdns.
Westburn Middlefield
Avenue
W'burn Pk.
Wester Hailes Centre

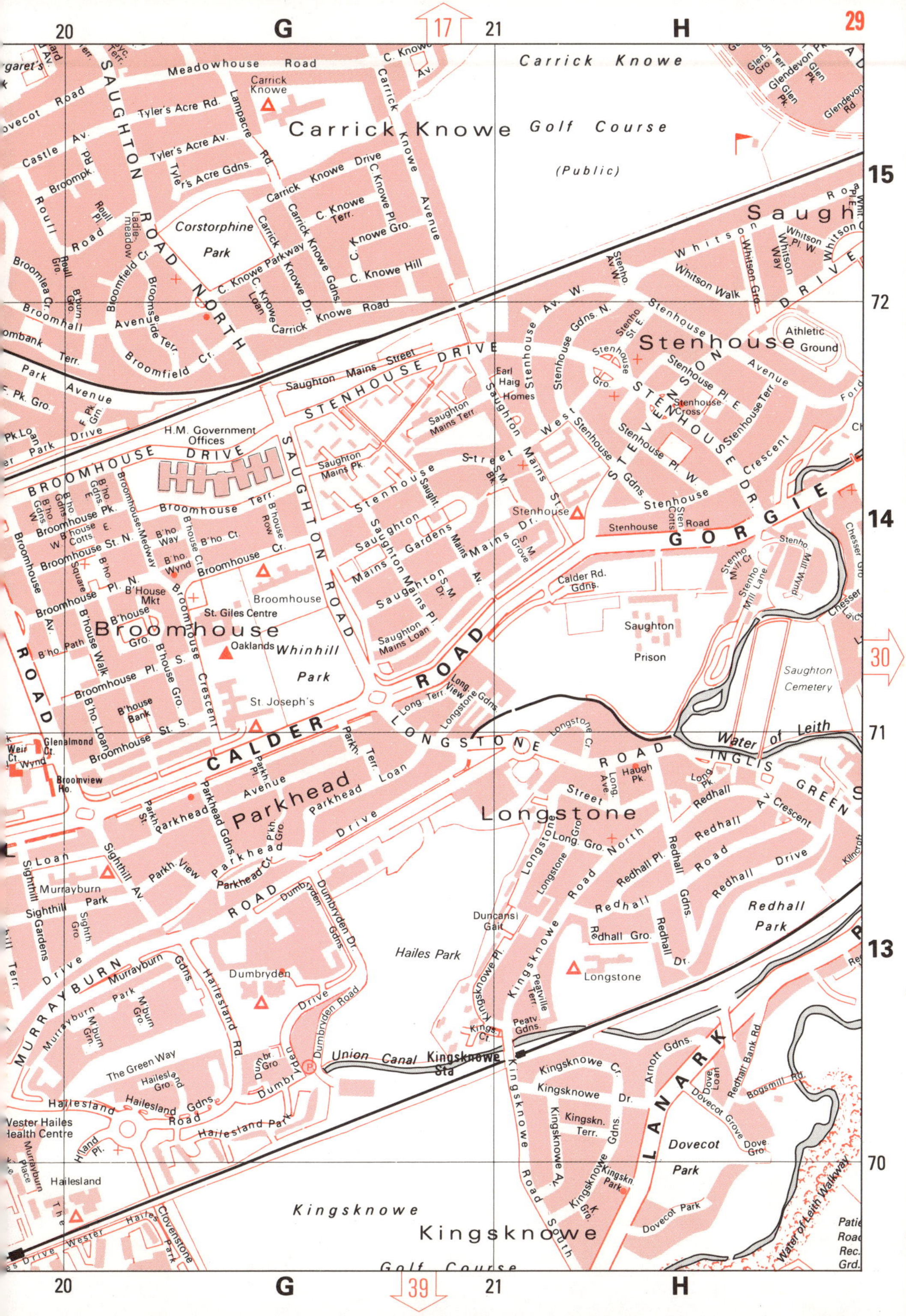

20
G
17
21
H
15
72
14
30
71
13
70
39
Carrick Knowe
Carrick Knowe Golf Course
(Public)
Meadowhouse Road
Carrick Knowe Av.
Carrick Knowe Avenue
Carrick Knowe Drive
Carrick Knowe Road
Carrick Knowe Parkway
Carrick Knowe Gdns.
C. Knowe Terr.
C. Knowe Pl.
C. Knowe Gro.
C. Knowe Hill
C. Knowe Loan
Carrick Knowe Dr.
Tyler's Acre Rd.
Tyler's Acre Av.
Tyler's Acre Gdns.
Lampacre Rd.
Corstorphine Park
Saughton Road North
Dovecot Road
Castle Av.
Broompk. Rd
Broomhall Avenue
Broomhall Terr.
Broomfield Cr.
Broomside Terr.
Broomlea Cr.
Ladiemeadow
Roull Road
Roull Pl.
Roull Gro.
Park Avenue
Pk. Gro.
Pk. Loan
Park Drive
Saughton
Whitson Road
Whitson Walk
Whitson Gro.
Whitson Pl. W.
Whitson Way
Whitson Drive
Glendevon Pk.
Glendevon Rd.
Glen Pk.
Glen Gro.
Stenhouse
Stenhouse Av. W.
Stenhouse Gdns. N.
Stenhouse St. E.
Stenhouse Gro.
Stenhouse Pl. E.
Stenhouse Pl. W.
Stenhouse Cross
Stenhouse Terr.
Stenhouse Drive
Stenhouse Crescent
Stenhouse Avenue
Stenhouse Road
Stenhouse Cotts
Stevenson
Athletic Ground
Earl Haig Homes
Saughton Mains Street
Stenhouse Drive
Saughton Mains Terr.
Saughton Mains Pk.
Saughton Mains Gardens
Saughton Mains Dr.
Saughton Mains Av.
Saughton Mains Pl.
Saughton Mains Loan
Saughton Mains Grove
West Saughton Mains St.
H.M. Government Offices
Broomhouse Drive
Broomhouse Terr.
Broomhouse Pk.
Broomhouse Cotts
Broomhouse Medway
Broomhouse Way
Broomhouse Ct.
Broomhouse Wynd
Broomhouse Cr.
Broomhouse Row
Broomhouse St. N.
Broomhouse St. S.
Broomhouse Square
Broomhouse Pl. N.
Broomhouse Pl. S.
Broomhouse Mkt
Broomhouse Gro.
Broomhouse Path
Broomhouse Walk
Broomhouse Loan
Broomhouse Bank
Broomhouse Crescent
Broomhouse Av.
Broomhouse
St. Giles Centre
Oaklands
Whinhill Park
St. Joseph's
Calder Road
Calder Rd. Gdns.
Saughton Prison
Saughton Cemetery
Gorgie Road
Stenhouse Mill Cr.
Stenhouse Mill Lane
Stenhouse Mill Wynd
Chesser Gro.
Water of Leith
Inglis Green Road
Longstone Road
Longstone Terr.
Longstone View
Longstone Gdns.
Longstone Cr.
Longstone Street
Longstone Av.
Longstone Gro.
Longstone
Haugh Pk.
Long. Pk.
Redhall Crescent
Redhall Av.
Redhall Road
Redhall Drive
Redhall Gdns.
Redhall Pl.
Redhall Gro.
Redhall Dr.
Redhall Park
Glenalmond Ct.
Weir Ct.
Wynd
Broomview Ho.
Parkhead
Parkhead Avenue
Parkhead Loan
Parkhead Terr.
Parkhead Pl.
Parkhead St.
Parkhead Gdns.
Parkhead Gro.
Parkhead Drive
Parkhead Cr.
Parkhead View
Sighthill Loan
Sighthill Av.
Sighthill Gdns.
Sighthill Gardens
Murrayburn Park
Murrayburn Road
Murrayburn Gdns.
Murrayburn Gro.
Murrayburn Place
Sighthill Drive
Dumbryden Road
Dumbryden Dr.
Dumbryden Gdns.
Dumbryden Gro.
Dumbryden Drive
Dumbryden
Hailes Park
Hailesland Rd.
Hailesland Gro.
Hailesland Gdns.
Hailesland Road
Hailesland Park
Hailesland
The Green Way
Vester Hailes Health Centre
Duncans Gait
Kingsknowe Pl.
Kingsknowe Ct.
Kingsknowe Road
Kingsknowe Av.
Kingsknowe Gdns.
Kingsknowe Terr.
Kingsknowe Dr.
Kingsknowe Park
Kingsknowe Gro.
Kingsknowe Sta
Kingsknowe Road South
Kingsknowe Golf Course
Peatville Terr.
Peatville Gdns.
Union Canal
Lanark Road
Arnott Gdns.
Dovecot Loan
Dovecot Grove
Dovecot Park
Dove Gro.
Redhall Bank Rd
Bogsmill Rd.
Water of Leith Walkway
Patie Road Rec. Grd.
Clovenstone Park
Wester Hailes Drive

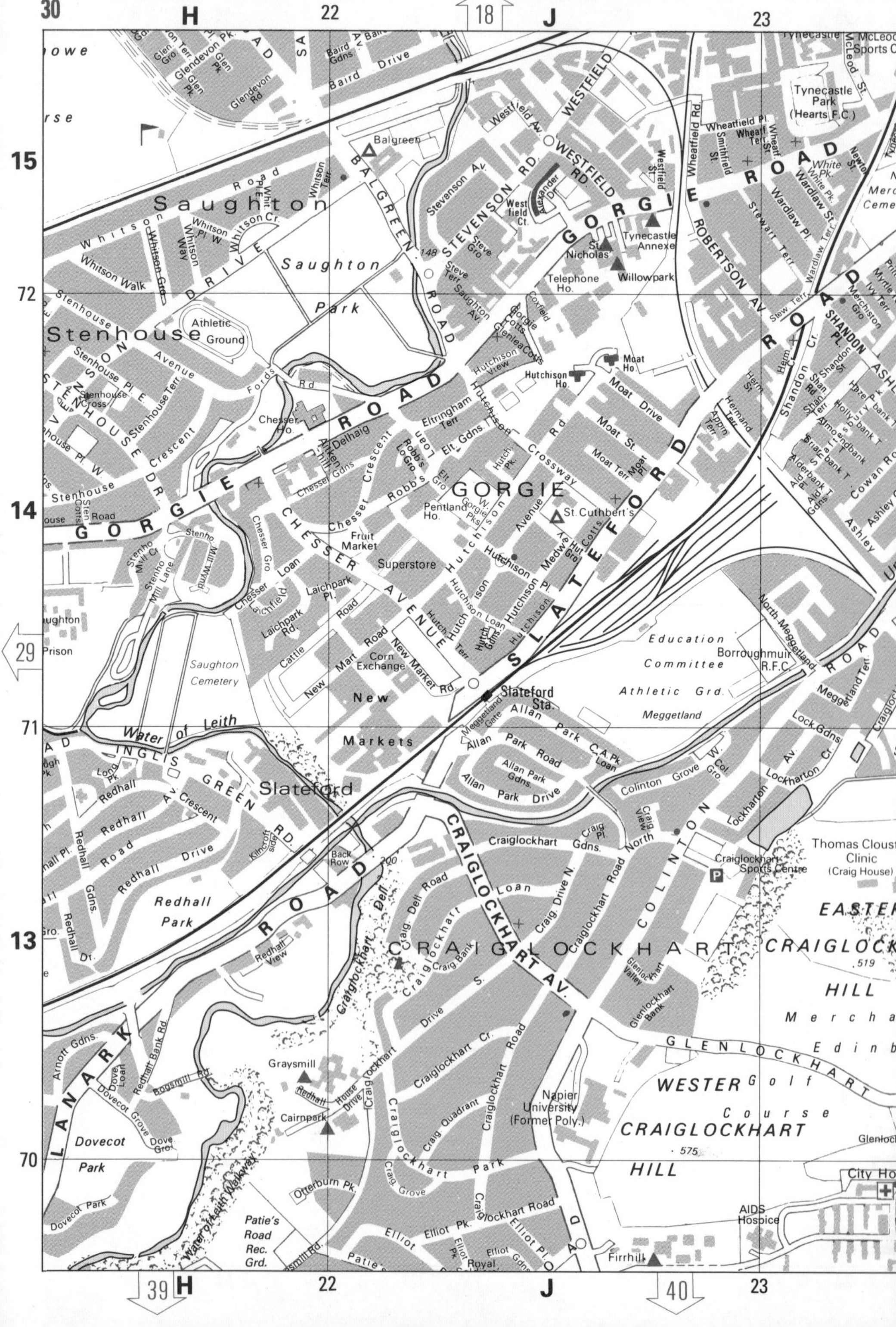
H
22
18
J
23
15
72
14
71
13
70
29
39
40
Saughton
Stenhouse
Saughton Park
Athletic Ground
Balgreen
BALGREEN ROAD
STEVENSON RD.
WESTFIELD RD.
GORGIE ROAD
ROBERTSON AV.
Tynecastle Park (Hearts F.C.)
McLeod St. Sports Ctr.
Tynecastle Annexe
St. Nicholas'
Willowpark
Telephone Ho.
Moat Ho.
Hutchison Ho.
GORGIE
St. Cuthbert's
Chesser Ho.
Fruit Market
Superstore
Pentland Ho.
CHESSER AVENUE
SLATEFORD ROAD
Corn Exchange
New Markets
Slateford Sta.
Education Committee Athletic Grd.
Meggetland
Borroughmuir R.F.C.
Saughton Cemetery
Saughton Prison
Water of Leith
INGLIS GREEN RD.
Slateford
Redhall Park
CRAIGLOCKHART AV.
CRAIGLOCKHART
COLINTON ROAD
Craiglockhart Sports Centre
Thomas Clouston Clinic (Craig House)
EASTER CRAIGLOCKHART HILL
WESTER CRAIGLOCKHART HILL
GLENLOCKHART ROAD
Golf Course
Napier University (Former Poly.)
Graysmill
Cairnpark
LANARK ROAD
Dovecot Park
Patie's Road Rec. Grd.
Water of Leith Walkway
Firrhill
AIDS Hospice
City Hosp.
.575
.519

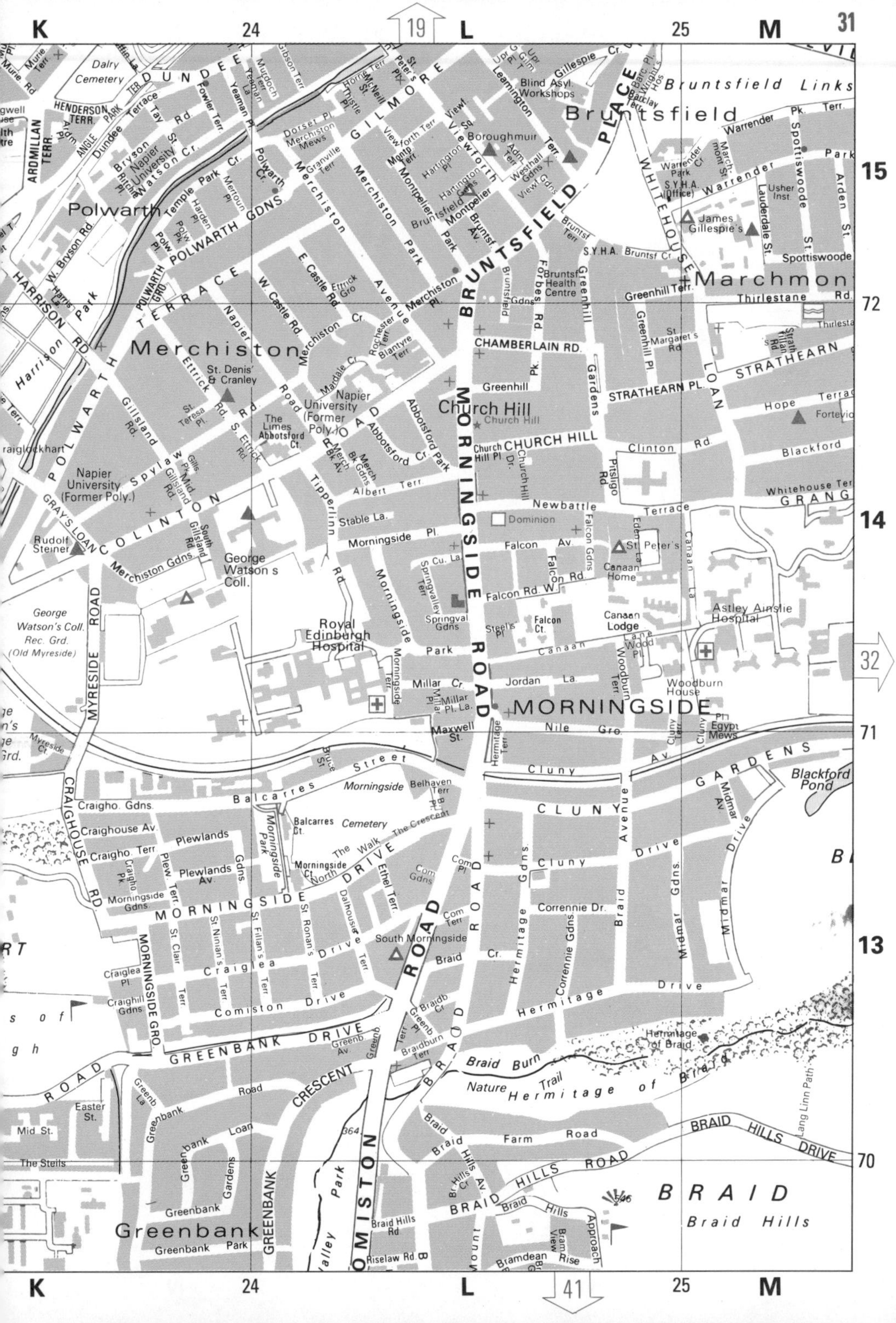
K
24
19
L
25
M
15
72
14
32
71
13
70
41
Dalry Cemetery
DUNDEE TERRACE
HENDERSON TERR.
ARDMILLAN TERR.
Dundee Terrace
Bryson Rd.
Napier University
Watson Cr.
Polwarth
POLWARTH GDNS.
POLWARTH TERRACE
HARRISON RD
Harrison Park
Merchiston
GILMORE PL.
Merchiston Park
Montpelier Park
Viewforth
Boroughmuir
Blind Asyl. Workshops
Gillespie Cr.
Leamington Terr.
Bruntsfield
BRUNTSFIELD PLACE
Bruntsfield Links
WHITEHOUSE LOAN
Warrender Pk. Terr.
Warrender Park Rd.
Spottiswoode St.
S.Y.H.A. (Office)
Usher Inst.
James Gillespie's
Lauderdale St.
Arden St.
Marchmont
Thirlestane Rd.
Greenhill Terr.
Bruntsf. Health Centre
CHAMBERLAIN RD.
STRATHEARN PL.
STRATHEARN RD.
Hope Terrace
Blackford
Whitehouse Terr.
GRANGE
Church Hill
CHURCH HILL
Clinton Rd.
Pitsligo Rd.
Newbattle Terrace
Dominion
Falcon Av.
St. Peter's
Canaan Home
Canaan Lodge
Canaan La.
Astley Ainslie Hospital
Woodburn House
MORNINGSIDE ROAD
MORNINGSIDE
Merchiston Cr.
St. Denis' & Cranley
Napier University (Former Poly.)
The Limes Abbotsford Ct.
COLINTON ROAD
Rudolf Steiner
George Watson's Coll.
George Watson's Coll. Rec. Grd. (Old Myreside)
MYRESIDE ROAD
Royal Edinburgh Hospital
Morningside Pl.
Tipperlinn Rd.
Jordan La.
Nile Gro.
Maxwell St.
Egypt Mews
Cluny Av.
Cluny Gardens
Blackford Pond
Balcarres Street
Morningside Cemetery
CRAIGHOUSE RD.
Craighouse Av.
Plewlands Gdns.
MORNINGSIDE DRIVE
Cluny Drive
Midmar Drive
Midmar Gdns.
Braid Avenue
Hermitage Gdns.
Correnie Dr.
South Morningside
Braid Cr.
Craiglea Drive
Comiston Drive
Hermitage Drive
Hermitage of Braid
GREENBANK DRIVE
GREENBANK CRESCENT
Braid Burn
Nature Trail
Braid Farm Road
BRAID HILLS DRIVE
BRAID HILLS ROAD
Lang Linn Path
BRAID
Braid Hills
COMISTON ROAD
Valley Park
Greenbank
Greenbank Park
Greenbank Gardens
Greenbank Loan
Easter St.
Mid St.
The Steils
Riselaw Rd.
Mount
Braid Hills Approach
Bramdean
364
546

25
M
26
N
20
31
41
42
15
72
14
71
13
70
Bruntsfield Links
Melville Drive
Warrender Park Road
Warrender Park Terr.
Spottiswoode St.
Spottiswoode Rd.
Arden St.
Marchmont Road
Marchmont Crescent
Marchmont St.
Lauderdale St.
Usher Inst.
S.Y.H.A. (Office)
James Gillespie's
Whitehouse Loan
Marchmont
Thirlestane Rd.
Thirlestane La.
Napier University (Former Poly.)
Royal Hosp. for Sick Children
Sciennes Road
Sciennes
Hatton Pl.
Chalmers Cr.
Lovers' Loan
Mansionhouse Rd.
Lauder Road
Tantallon Pl.
Gladstone Terr.
Sciennes Gdns.
Causewayside
Nat. Library
Royal (Dick) Vet. Coll.
Newington
Salisbury
Salisbury Rd.
Salisbury Pl.
Longmore Hosp.
Synagogue
Preston Street
E. Preston St.
Scottish Widows H.Q.
Royal Comm. Pool
Holyrood Park
Minto Street
Blacket Pl.
Grange Road
Grange Cemetery
Beaufort Rd.
Strathearn Rd.
Strathearn Pl.
Kilgraston Rd.
Kilgraston Ct.
Mount Grange
St. Margaret's Rd.
Greenhill Pl.
Greenhill Terr.
Hope Terrace
Forteviot
Blackford Rd.
Grange
Dick Place
Carlton Cricket Grd.
Grange Loan
Grange Terr.
Whitehouse Terr.
Monkwood Ct.
Esdaile
Cumin Pl.
Seton Pl.
Findhorn Place
Kittle Yards
Ratcliffe Terr.
Dalrymple Cr.
Lauder Rd.
Masson Hall
Fountainhall Road
South Lauder Road
St. Alban's Road
Mayfield Gdns.
Mayfield Terr.
W. Mayfield
Bright's Cr.
Mentone Terr.
Royal Blind Sch.
Savile Terr.
Astley Ainslie Hospital
Canaan La.
Woodburn House
Oswald Rd.
Oswald Ct.
South Oswald Rd.
St. Raphael's
Dun-ard Gdns.
British Geological Survey
St. Thomas Road
Relugas Road
W. Relugas Rd.
Blackford Av.
Mortonhall Rd.
West Savile Terrace
MacDowall Rd.
Ross Gardens
St. Crispin's
Langton Road
Egypt Mews
Charterhall Rd.
Blackford
Blackford Pond
Midmar Gardens
Midmar Drive
Midmar Av.
Blackford Av.
Ladysmith Rd.
Rankin Rd.
Rankin Av.
Rankin Drive
West Mains Road
Observatory Rd.
Murchison House B.G.S.
Blackford Hill
Royal Observatory
Corbie's Craig
Craigmillar Park
Scottish Agricultural Coll.
King's Buildings (Univ. of Edin.)
West Mains
Golf Course
Blackford Quarry
Hermitage of Braid
Blackford Glen
Lang Linn Path
Howe Dean
Braid Hills Drive
Braid
Braid Hills
539
218
425

27 O 21 28 P

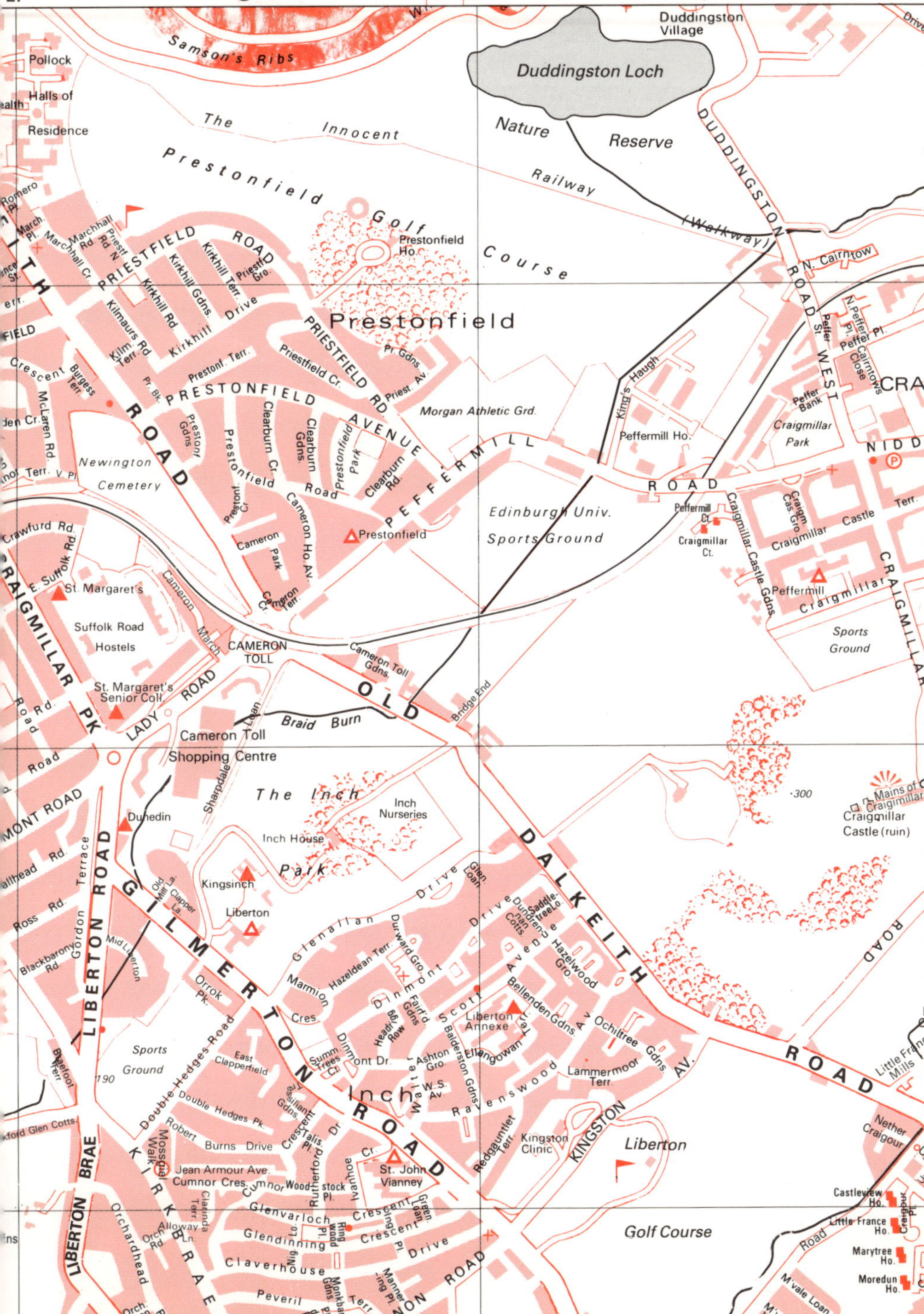


27 O 28 P 43

P
29
Q
22
30
R
15
14
13
72
71
70
33
43
Golf Course
Duddingston House (Hotel)
Braid Burn
Bingham Park
Lismore
Bingham Avenue
Bingham Crossway
Bingham Broadway
Bingham Drive
Bingham Crescent
Bingham Way
Bingham Medway
Bingham Pl.
Duddingston Row
SOUTH
DUDDINGSTON
PARK
Jewel Park
Magdalene Court
North Greens
The Parrotshot
Milton Gdns.
N. Cairntow
Niddrie Mains Terrace
Niddrie Mill Cr.
Niddrie Mill Dr.
Niddrie Mill Av.
N. Mill Pl.
N. Mill Gro.
N. Mill Terr.
CRAIGMILLAR
NIDDRIE
Peffer St.
N. Peffer Pl.
Peffer Pl.
Cairntows Close
Peffer Bank
Craigmillar Park
Harewood Dr.
Harewood Road
Harewood Cr.
Craigmillar
Niddrie Mains Road
Niddrie Mains Terr.
Wauchope Pl.
Wauchope Av.
Wauchope Cr.
Wauchope Terr.
Wauchope Sq.
Hay Road
Hay Pl.
Hay Terr.
Hay Drive
Hay Av.
N. Mains Ct.
St. Francis
Craigmillar Castle Terr.
Craigmillar Castle Loan
Craigmillar Castle Avenue
Craigm. Cas. Gro.
Craigmillar Castle Gdns.
Peffermill
Niddrie Farm Gro.
Queen's Walk
Chapel Ct.
W. Court
Thistle Foundation
Greendykes Av.
Greendykes Road
Greendykes Dr.
Greendykes Terr.
Greendykes Gdns.
Greend. Loan
Greendykes
N. Mar. Gdns.
N. Mar. Loan
N. Mar. St.
Niddrie Marischal Pl.
Niddrie Marischal Rd.
Niddrie Marischal Cr.
Niddrie Marischal Dr.
Niddrie Marischal Green
N. Mar. Gro.
N. House Pk.
N. Ho. Sq.
Niddrie House Dr.
N. House Gro.
N. Ho. Av.
N. House Gdns.
Niddrie Burn
J. Kane Centre
Niddrie Policies
Wauchope Ho.
Greendykes Ho.
Bankfield
Sports Ground
Castlebrae School
CRAIGMILLAR CASTLE ROAD
300
Mains of Craigmillar
Craigmillar Castle (ruin)
THE WISP
Little France Caravan Park
Little France Mills
Little France
ROAD
Nether Craigour
Upper Craigour
Up. Cr. Wy.
Craigour Pl.
Craigour Grn.
Craigour Cr.
Craigour Drive
Castleview Ho.
Little France Ho.
Marytree Ho.
Moredun Ho.
M'vale Loan
Pentecox
Edmonstone Cottage
Edmonstone Mains

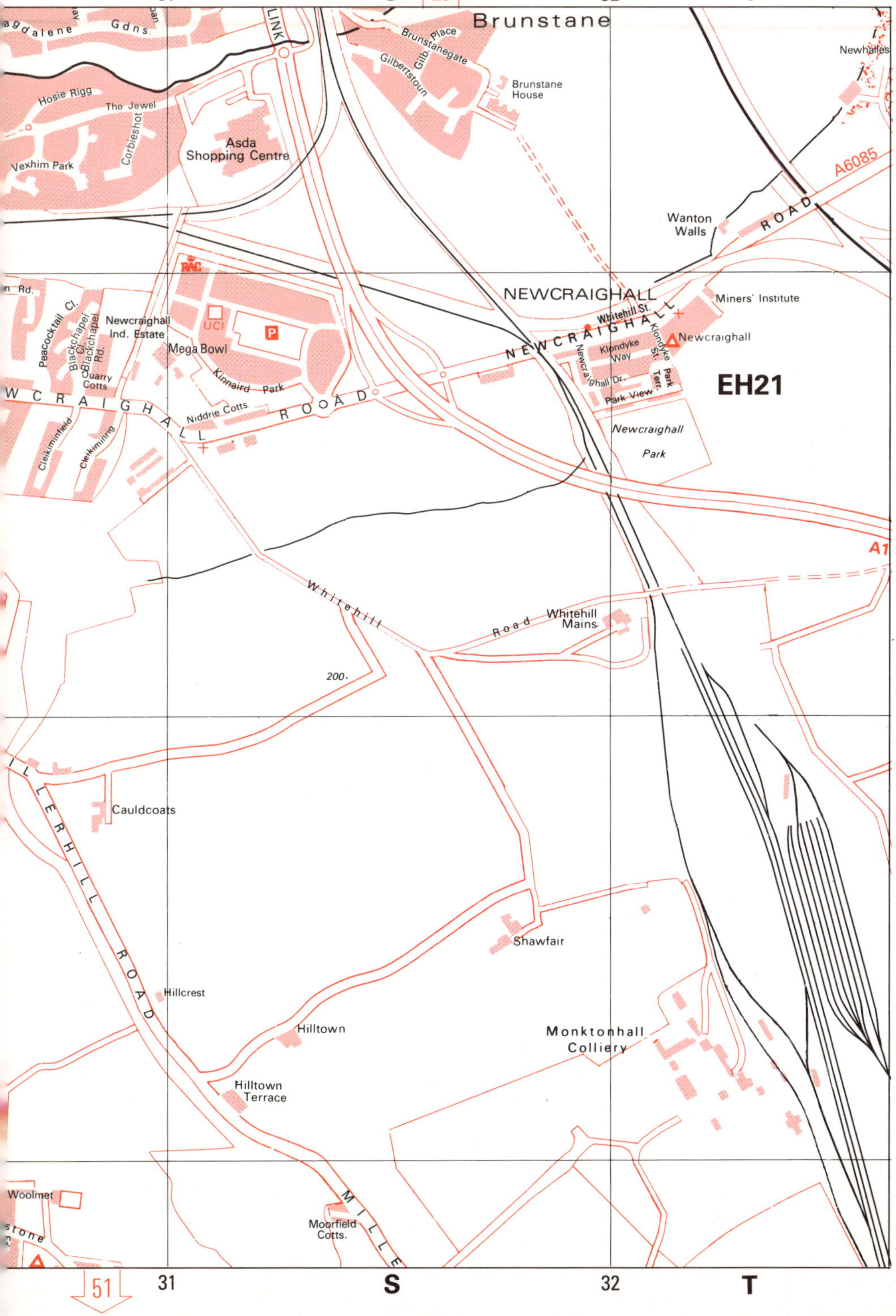
31
S
23
32
T
Brunstane
Magdalene Gdns.
LINK
Brunstane Place
Brunstanegate
Gilb.
Gilbertstoun
Brunstane House
Newhailes
Hosie Rigg
The Jewel
Corbieshot
Vexhim Park
Asda Shopping Centre
15
A6085
Wanton Walls
ROAD
72
RAC
Peacocktail Cl.
Blackchapel Cl.
Blackchapel Rd.
Newcraighall Ind. Estate
Mega Bowl
UCI
P
NEWCRAIGHALL
Whitehill St.
Miners' Institute
Newcraighall
NEWCRAIGHALL
Klondyke Way
Klondyke St.
Park Terr.
Newcraighall Dr.
Park View
EH21
Quarry Cotts
Kinnaird Park
Niddrie Cotts.
ROAD
WCRAIGHALL
Cleikiminfield
Cleikiminrig
Newcraighall Park
14
A1
Whitehill
Road
Whitehill Mains
200
71
Cauldcoats
MILLERHILL ROAD
13
Shawfair
Hillcrest
Hilltown
Monktonhall Colliery
Hilltown Terrace
70
Woolmet
Moorfield Cotts.
MILLE
51
31
S
32
T

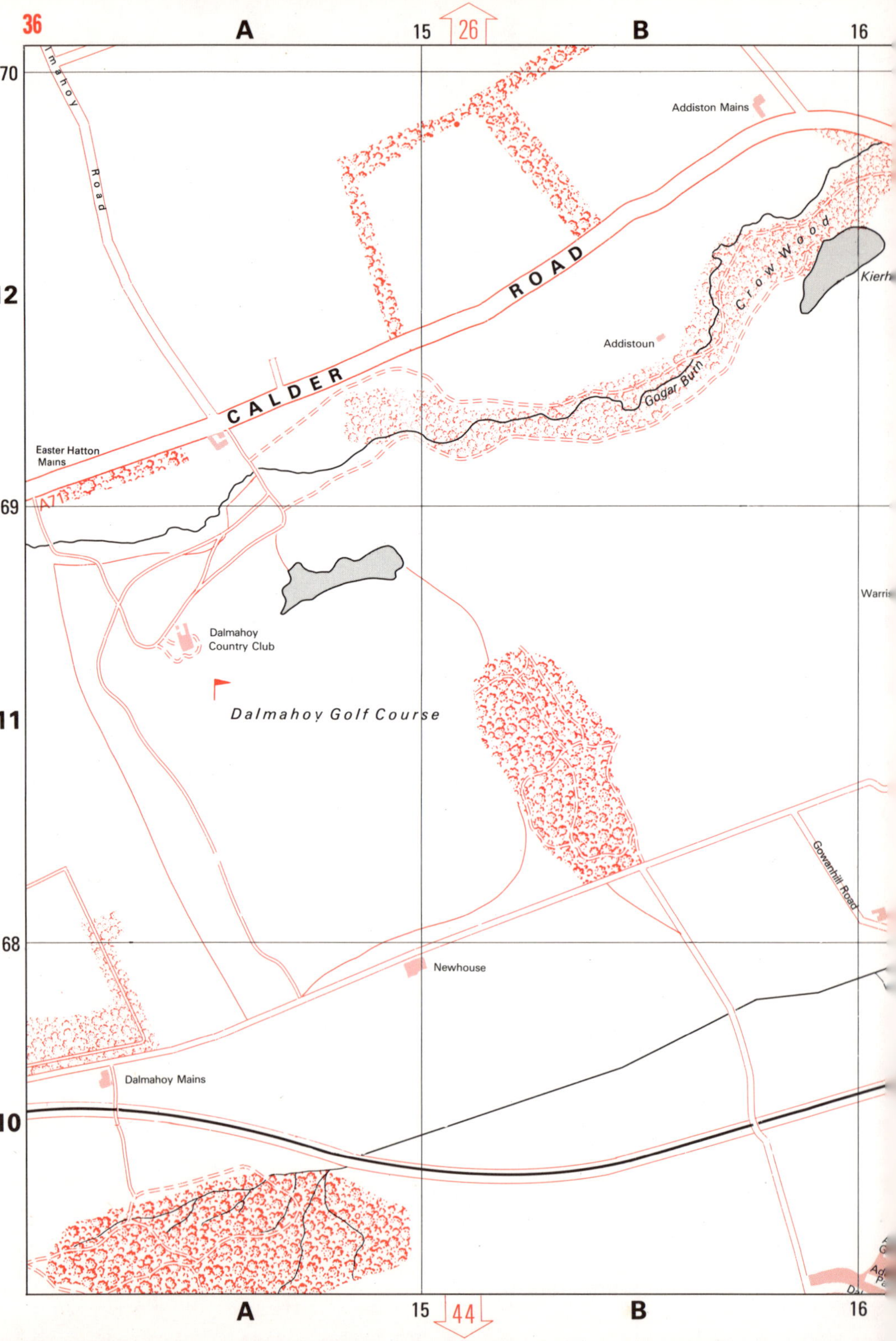
A
15
26
B
16
70
Imahoy Road
Addiston Mains
CALDER ROAD
Crow Wood
Kierh
12
Addistoun
Gogar Burn
Easter Hatton Mains
A71
69
Warris
Dalmahoy Country Club
Dalmahoy Golf Course
11
Gowanhill Road
68
Newhouse
Dalmahoy Mains
10
A
15
44
B
16

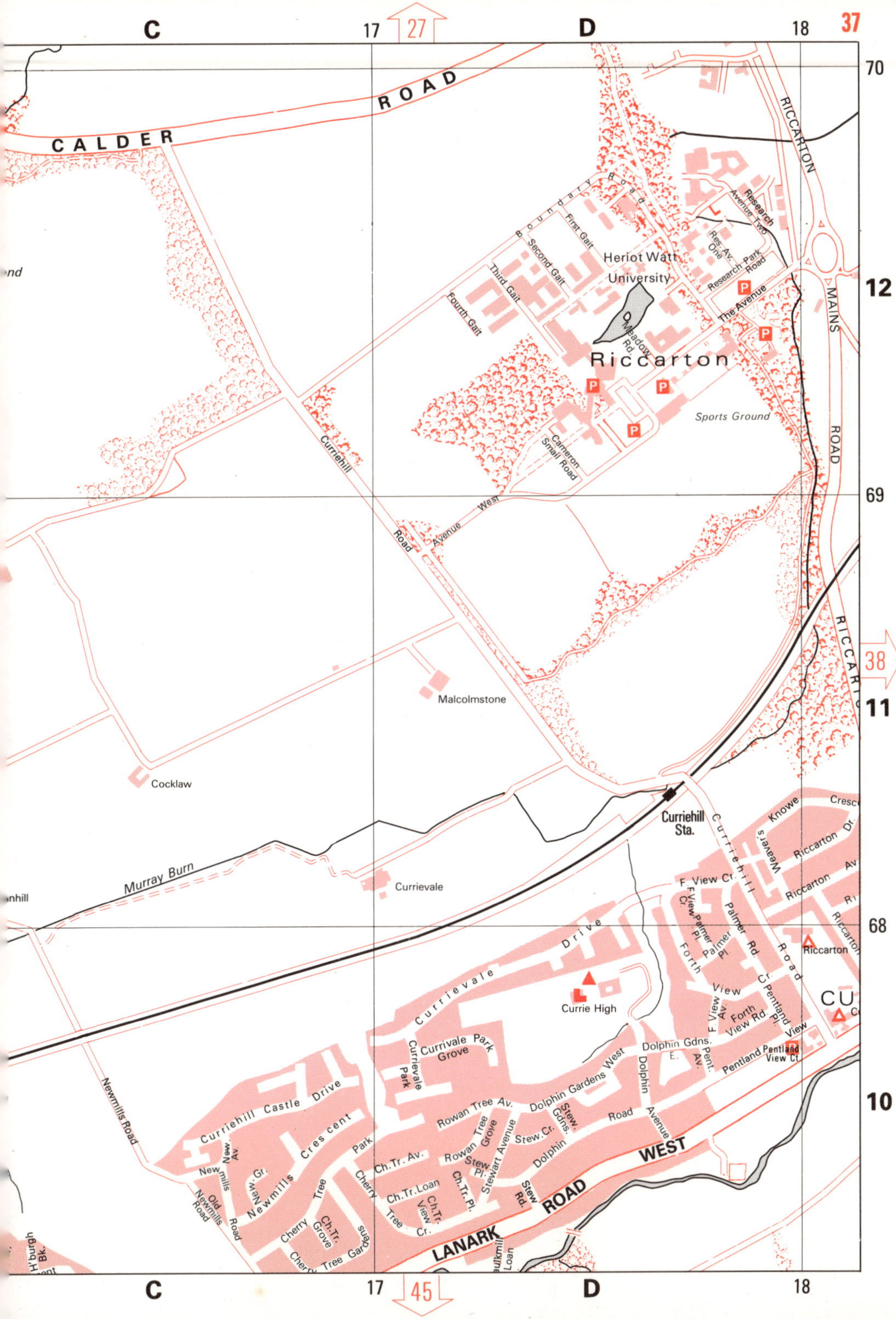
C
17
27
D
18
70
CALDER ROAD
RICCARTON
MAINS ROAD
RICCARTON
Boundary Road
Research Avenue Two
Research
First Gait
Second Gait
Third Gait
Fourth Gait
Res. Av. One
Research Park Road
Heriot Watt University
The Avenue
Meadow Rd.
Riccarton
Sports Ground
Cameron Small Road
Avenue West
Curriehill Road
12
69
38
11
Malcolmstone
Cocklaw
Curriehill Sta.
Curriehill Road
Murray Burn
Currievale
Weaver's Knowe
Cresc
Riccarton Dr.
Riccarton Av.
F. View Cr.
F. View Cr.
Forth View Palmer Pl.
Palmer Pl.
Palmer Rd.
Riccarton
68
Currievale Drive
Currie High
Forth View Av.
F. View Av.
Forth View Rd.
Pentland View Pl.
Pentland View Ct.
Pentland View Ct.
CU
Currivale Park Grove
Currievale Park
Dolphin Gdns. E.
Pent. Av.
Dolphin Gardens West
Dolphin Avenue
Dolphin Road
Newmills Road
Curriehill Castle Drive
New. Av.
Newmills Crescent
New. Gr.
Newmills Road
Old Newmills Road
Rowan Tree Av.
Rowan Tree Grove
Stew. Gdns.
Stew. Cr.
Stewart Avenue
Stew. Pl.
Stew. Rd.
Cherry Tree Park
Ch.Tr. Av.
Ch.Tr. Loan
Ch.Tr. Pl.
Ch.Tr. View
Cherry Tree Cr.
Cherry Tree Grove
Ch.Tr. Grove
Cherry Tree Gardens
LANARK ROAD WEST
Faulkmill Loan
H'burgh Bk.
10
C
17
45
D
18

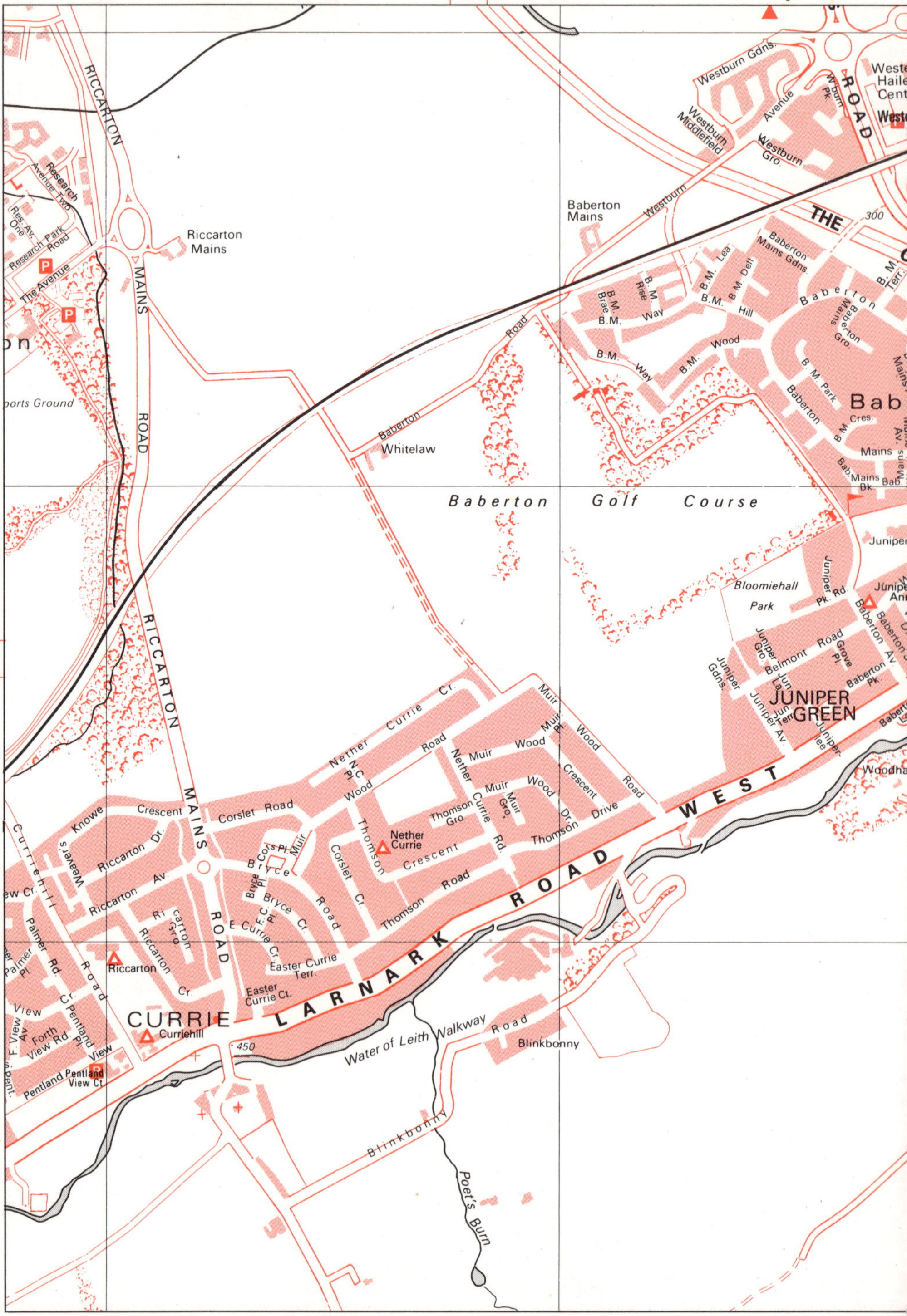
18
E
28
19
F
70
12
69
11
68
10
37
Riccarton
Riccarton Mains Road
Riccarton Mains
Research Avenue Two
Res. Av. One
Research Park Road
The Avenue
Sports Ground
Westburn Gdns.
Westburn Middlefield
Westburn Avenue
Westburn Gro.
Westburn
W.burn Pk.
Road
Wester Hailes Centre
The
300
Baberton Mains
Baberton Mains Gdns.
B.M. Lea
B.M. Dell
B.M. Brae
B.M. Rise
B.M. Way
B.M. Hill
B.M. Wood
Baberton Mains Gro.
B.M. Park
Baberton
B.M. Cres.
Mains
Bab. Mains Bk.
B.M. Terr.
Baberton Whitelaw
Baberton Golf Course
Juniper
Bloomiehall Park
Juniper Pk. Rd.
Juniper Gro.
Belmont Road
Grove Pl.
Juniper Gdns.
Jun. La.
Baberton Pk.
Baberton Av.
Juniper Av.
Jun. Terr.
Juniperlee
JUNIPER GREEN
Woodhall
Lanark Road West
Nether Currie Cr.
N.C. Pl.
Nether Currie Road
Nether Currie Rd.
Muir Wood Road
Muir Wood Pl.
Muir Wood Crescent
Muir Wood Gro.
Muir Wood Dr.
Muir Wood Drive
Thomson Gro.
Thomson Drive
Thomson Crescent
Thomson Road
Nether Currie
Corslet Road
Corslet Cr.
Crescent
Knowe
Weavers
Riccarton Dr.
Riccarton Av.
Riccarton Gro.
Riccarton Cr.
Cross Pl.
Bryce
Bryce Pl.
Bryce Cr.
F.C. Pl.
E. Currie Cr.
Easter Currie Terr.
Easter Currie Ct.
Curriehill Road
Palmer Rd.
Palmer Pl.
Pentland View Cr.
Pentland View Pl.
Forth View Rd.
F. View Av.
Pentland View Ct.
CURRIE
Curriehill
450
Water of Leith Walkway
Blinkbonny Road
Blinkbonny
Poet's Burn

20
G
29
21
H
70
69
68
12
11
10
40
Kingsknowe
Kingsknowe Golf Course
Dovecot Park
Dovecot Park
Dove Gro.
Kingsknowe South Road
Kingsknowe Gro.
Kingskn. Park
Wester Hailes
Hailesland
Murrayburn Place
Hailes Drive
Wester Hailes Drive
Clovenstone Park
Clovenstone Road
Clovenstone Green
Clovenstone Way
Clovenstone Gardens
Clovenstone
Clovenstone Park
Clovenstone Drive
WESTER HAILES RD.
A720
EDINBURGH BYPASS
OF
LANARK ROAD
Hailes
Hailes Terr
Hailes Gro.
Hailes Cr.
Hailes Av.
Hailes Park
Hailes Gardens
Hailes Bk.
Hailes Appr.
Spylaw Bank Road
Spylaw Park
Spylaw Av.
Pentland Rd.
Pentland Av.
Viewfield Rd.
Muirend Av.
Mains Loan
Baberton Crescent
Foulis Cr.
Woodhall Av
Woodhall Millbrae
GILLESPIE ROAD
Water of Leith Walkway
COLINTON
BRIDGE RD.
Spylaw Ho.
Spylaw St.
Spylaw Park
Colinton Dell
Redhall Mill
250
Water of Leith Walkway
Colinton Castle Sports Club
Merchiston Castle
Colinton Castle (ruin)
Dell Rd
Bonaly Annex
Westgarth Av.
Dreghorn Loan
Barnshot Road
West Mill Road
Campbell Park
Woodfield Avenue
Woodfield Park
Grant Avenue
Harelaw Rd.
Castlelaw Rd.
Carnethy Av.
Campbell Park Cr.
Campbell Pk. Dr.
Woodhall Gro.
Woodhall Bank
Woodhall Road
Capelaw Rd.
Allermuir Rd.
W. Carnethy Av.
Bonaly Road
Fernielaw Avenue
Munro Drive
Bonaly Steading
Bonaly Farm Cotts
Bonaly Drive
Bonaly Terr.
Bonaly Avenue
Bonaly Gdns.
Bonaly
Bonaly Grove
Bonaly Wester
Bonaly Brae
Bonaly Rise
Laverockdale Cr.
Laver. Loan
Laverockdale Crescent
Laverockdale Pk.
Water of Leith
Woodhall Road
Woodhall
Woodhall Mains
Torphin Road
627 · Corbie Hill
Torphin
Torphin Hill Golf Course
Torphin Hill
Closed to Vehicles
Torduff Reservoir
Torduff Hill
Torduff Road
Bonaly Tower
Scout Hostel
Bonaly Burn
White Hill
1044 ·

22 30 J 23 K

70 12 69 11 68 10 39

22 J 23 K

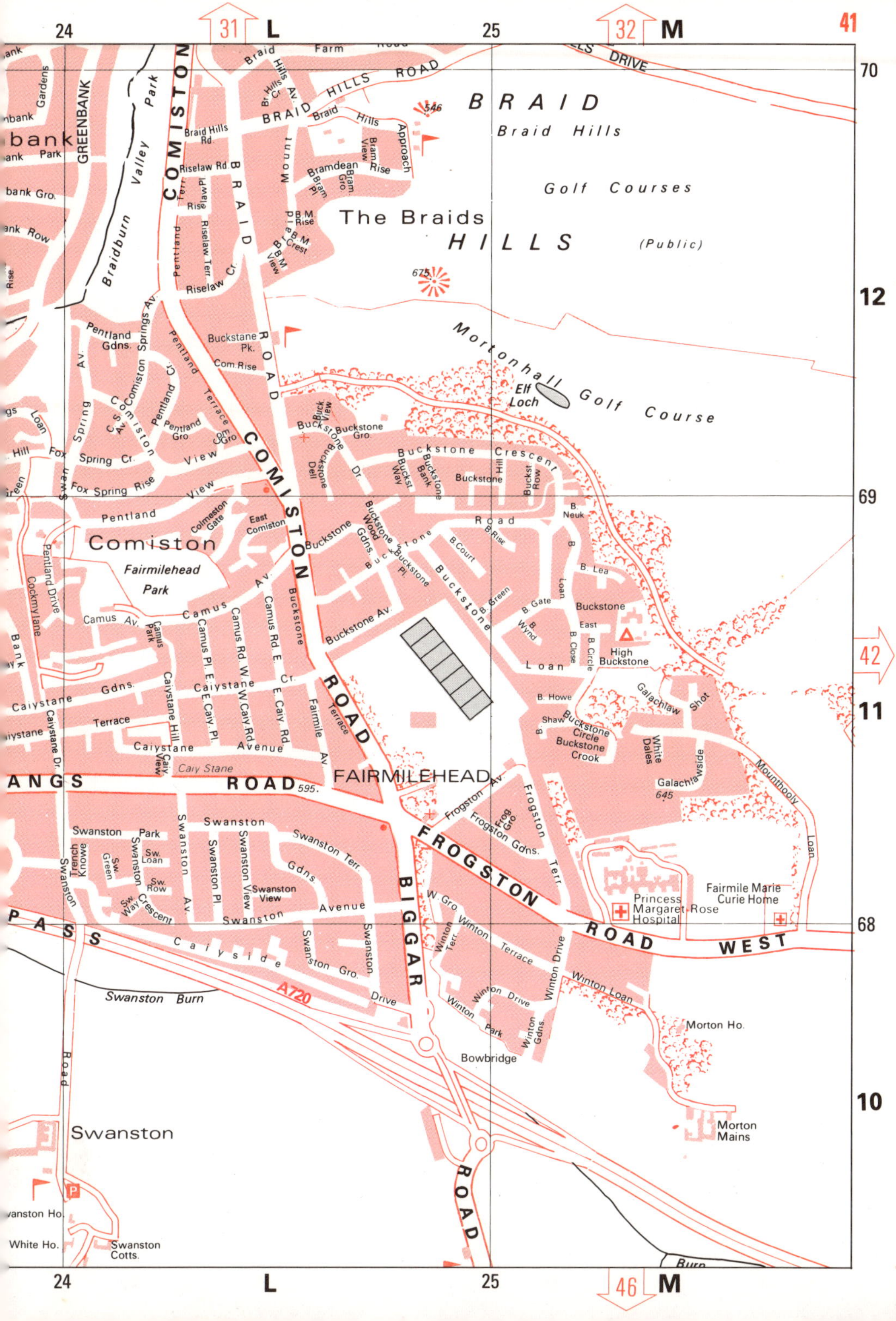
24
31
L
25
32
M
70
12
69
11
42
68
10
46
BRAID
Braid Hills
Golf Courses
The Braids
HILLS
(Public)
546
675
Mortonhall Golf Course
Elf Loch
DRIVE
Braid Hills Road
Farm
Braid Hills Av.
Br. Hills Cr.
Braid Hills Approach
Bram View
Bramdean Rise
Bramdean Pl.
Bram. Gro.
Mount
Braid Hills Rd.
Riselaw Rd.
Riselaw Pl.
Riselaw Terr.
Riselaw Cr.
Pentland Terr.
B.M. Rise
B.M. Crest
B.M. View
Braid Rise
BRAID ROAD
COMISTON
COMISTON ROAD
Greenbank Gardens
GREENBANK
bank Park
bank Gro.
bank Row
Braidburn Valley Park
Pentland Gdns.
Springs Av.
Pentland Cr.
Pentland Terrace
Pentland Gro.
Pentland View
Pentland Drive
Pentland
Buckstane Pk.
Com. Rise
Com. Gro.
Comiston Av.
Comiston View
C.S. Av.
Spring Av.
Spring Cr.
Fox Spring Rise
Fox Spring
Swan
Loan
Hill
Comiston
Colmestone Gate
East Comiston
Fairmilehead Park
Camus Av.
Camus Park
Camus Pl. E.
Camus Rd. W.
Camus Rd. E.
Caiystane Gdns.
Caiystane Terrace
Caiystane Dr.
Caiystane Hill
Caiystane Cr.
Caiystane View
Caiystane Avenue
E. Caiy. Pl.
W. Caiy. Rd.
E. Caiy. Rd.
Caiy Stane
Cockmylane
Bank
Buckstone
Buckstone Gro.
Buck View
Buckstone Dell
Buckstone Dr.
Buckstone Crescent
Buckst. Way
Buckstone Bank
Buckst. Row
Buckstone Hill
Buckstone Road
B. Neuk
B. Rise
B. Court
Buckstone Wood
Buckstone Gdns.
Buckstone Pl.
Buckstone Av.
B. Green
B. Gate
B. Wynd
B. Lea
B. Loan
Buckstone East
B. Close
B. Circle
High Buckstone
Buckstone Loan
B. Howe
B. Shaw
Buckstone Circle
Buckstone Crook
Galachlaw Shot
White Dales
Galachlawside
645
Mounthooly Loan
Fairmile Av.
Fairmile Terrace
FAIRMILEHEAD
ANGS ROAD
595
Frogston Av.
Frog. Gro.
Frogston Gdns.
Frogston Terr.
FROGSTON ROAD WEST
Princess Margaret Rose Hospital
Fairmile Marie Curie Home
Swanston Park
Swanston
Swanston Av.
Swanston Pl.
Swanston View
Swanston Terr.
Swanston Gdns.
Swanston Avenue
Swanston Gro.
Swanston Drive
Swanston Crescent
Trench Knowe
Sw. Green
Sw. Loan
Sw. Row
Sw. Way
BIGGAR ROAD
W. Gro.
Winton Gro.
Winton Terr.
Winton Terrace
Winton Drive
Winton Loan
Winton Park
Winton Gdns.
PASS
Caiyside
A720
Swanston Burn
Bowbridge
Morton Ho.
Morton Mains
Swanston Road
Swanston
Swanston Ho.
White Ho.
Swanston Cotts.
P
Burn

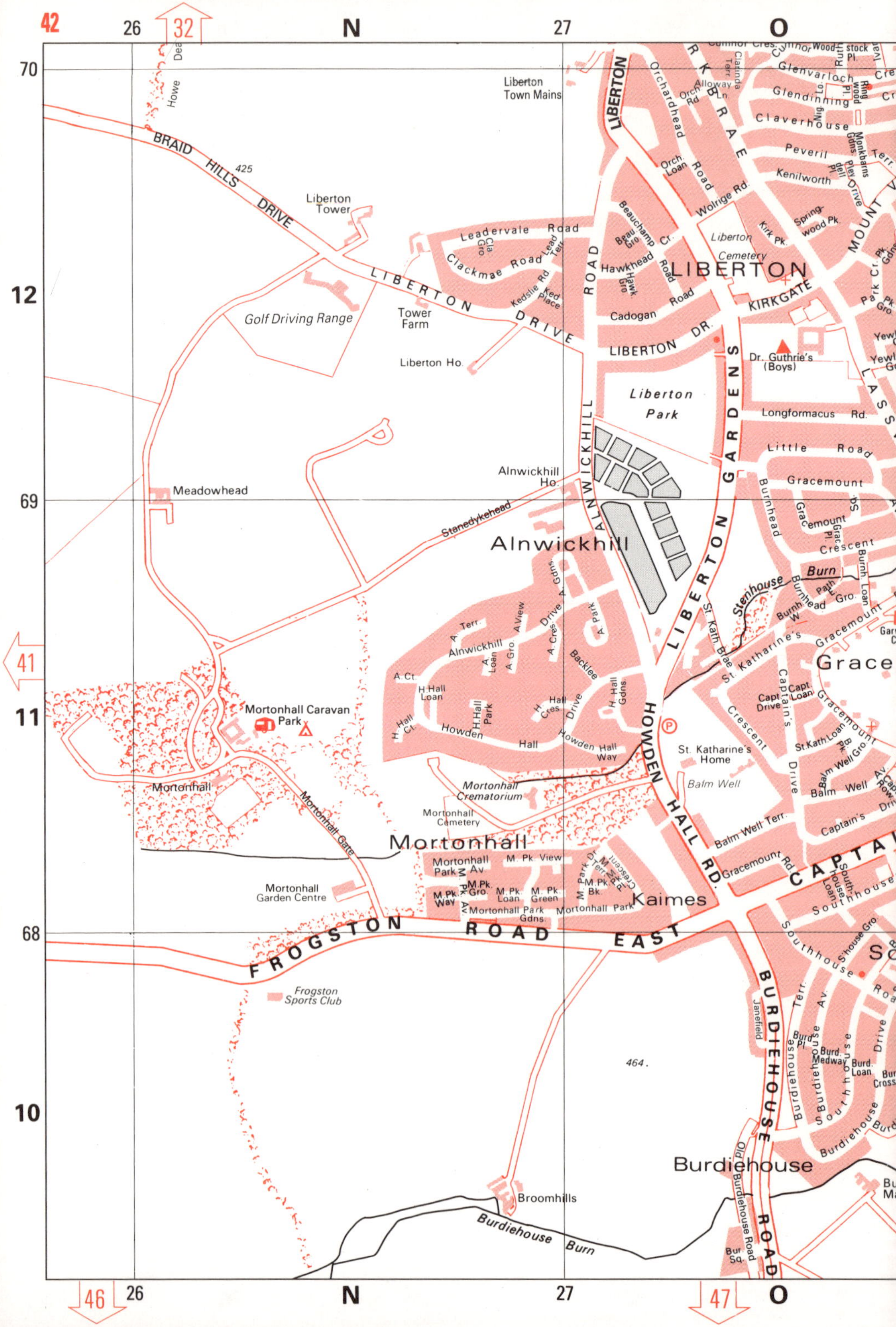

26
32
N
27
O
70
12
69
11
68
10
41
46
47
Howe
Dean
BRAID HILLS DRIVE
425
Liberton Tower
LIBERTON DRIVE
Golf Driving Range
Tower Farm
Liberton Ho.
Liberton Town Mains
LIBERTON
Orchardhead Road
Orch. Rd
Orch. Loan
Alloway Ln.
Claremont Terr.
Cumnor Cres.
Cumnor Wood
Ruth
Woodstock Pl.
Glenvarloch Cres.
Glendinning Cres.
Claverhouse
Peveril Terr.
Kenilworth
Monkbarns Gdns.
Mount Vernon
Wolrige Rd.
Leadervale Road
Clackmae Road
Cla Gro.
Lead Terr.
Kedslie Rd.
Ked Place
Beauchamp Road
Beau Gro.
Hawkhead Cr.
Hawk Gro.
Cadogan Road
ROAD
Liberton Cemetery
LIBERTON
KIRKGATE
Kirk Pk.
Springwood Pk.
Park Cr.
Pk. Gdns.
Pk. Gro.
Yewlands Cres.
Yewlands Gdns.
LIBERTON DR.
Dr. Guthrie's (Boys)
Liberton Park
LIBERTON GARDENS
Longformacus Rd.
Little Road
Gracemount
Burnhead
Gracemount Pl.
Grac Crescent
Burnh. Loan
Burn
Stenhouse
Burnhead Path
Burnh. W.
Gro.
Gracemount
Garvald Ct
Gracemount
Alnwickhill Ho.
ALNWICKHILL ROAD
Meadowhead
Stanedykehead
Alnwickhill
LIBERTON
St. Kath. Brae
St. Katharine's
Captain's Drive
Capt. Drive
Capt. Loan
Crescent
A. Gdns.
A. Terr.
A. View
Drive
A. Park
Alnwickhill
A. Loan
A. Gro.
A. Cres.
Backlee
A. Ct.
H. Hall Loan
H. Hall Park
H. Hall Ct.
Howden Hall
H. Cres.
Drive
H. Hall Gdns.
Howden Hall Way
HOWDEN HALL RD.
St. Katharine's Home
Balm Well
St. Kath. Loan
B. Pk.
Balm Well Gro.
Balm Well Av.
Capt. Row
Drive
Captain's
Mortonhall Caravan Park
Mortonhall
Mortonhall Gate
Mortonhall Crematorium
Mortonhall Cemetery
Mortonhall
Balm Well Terr.
Gracemount Rd
CAPTAIN'S
Southhouse Loan
Southhouse
Mortonhall Park Av.
M. Pk. View
M. Park Dr.
M. Pk. Terr.
M. Pk. Pl.
Crescent
M. Pk. Av.
M. Pk. Way
M. Pk. Gro.
M. Pk. Loan
M. Pk. Green
M. Pk. Bk.
Mortonhall Park Gdns.
Mortonhall Park
Kaimes
Mortonhall Garden Centre
FROGSTON ROAD EAST
Frogston Sports Club
Southhouse Gro.
S'house Gro.
Southhouse Road
Janefield
Terr.
Av.
Burd. Pl.
Burd. Medway
Burd. Loan
Burdiehouse Crossway
Burdiehouse
Drive
Southhouse
BURDIEHOUSE ROAD
464.
Burdiehouse
Old Burdiehouse Road
Broomhills
Burdiehouse Burn
Bur. Sq.
Burdiehouse Mains

33
28
P
29
34
Q
70
69
68
12
11
10
51
48
Golf Course
Castleview Ho.
Little France Ho.
Marytree Ho.
Moredun Ho.
Craigour Pl.
Craigour Grn.
Craigour Cr.
Craigour Gro.
Craigour Loan
Craigour Drive
Craigour Terr.
Craigour Av.
Cr. Gdns.
Green Park (N.C.B.)
Liberton
Greenend Gardens
Gardens Road
Green. Gro.
Moredun
M'vale Loan
M'vale Way
M'vale Green
M'vale Gro.
M'vale Pk.
M'vale Bank
M'vale View
M'vale Pl.
Moredunvale Road
Forteviot Ho.
Moncrieffe Ho.
Edinburgh Southern Harriers'
Old Dalkeith Rd.
Fernieside Dr.
Fernieside Av.
Fernieside Crescent
Fernieside Gro.
Fernieside
Fernieside Gdns.
FERNIEHILL RD.
GILMERTON ROAD
MOREDUN PARK ROAD
Moredun Park Gardens
M. Pk. Ct.
Moredun Pk. Dr.
M. Pk. Loan
Park St.
M. Pk. Way
Moredun Park View
St. Barnabas Court
Gilmerton Park
Moredun Inst.
Ellen's Glen
Stennis Gdns.
Glen
Protein Frac. Centre
St. Alvernia Convent
Southfield Hospital
Liberton Hospital
Ellen's
Murray Home
The Pillars
M. Pk. Green
M. Pk. Walk
Moredun Pk. Gro.
Ferniehill
Ferniehill Road
Ferniehill Way
Fern. Gro.
Ferniehill St.
Ferniehill Gdns.
Ferniehill Pl.
FERNIEHILL DRIVE
Fern. Terr.
Ferniehill Av.
Fern. Sq.
Drum Pl.
Drum Av.
Drum Crescent
Candlemaker's Park
Candle. Cres.
East Farm of Gilmerton
The Spinney
Hyvot Gro.
Hyvot Loan
Gilmerton
Dykes Rd.
Hyvots Bank Av.
Hyvots Bank
Hyvot Av.
Hyvot Gdns.
Hyvot Pk.
Hyvot Terr.
Moredun Dykes
Drive Park Valley
Dykes Av.
Dykes Crescent
Gilmerton Dykes
G. D. Gdns.
G. Dykes Pl.
G. Dykes Gro.
Burdiehouse Burn
Burdiehouse Burn Park
Lockerby Gro.
Lockerby Cres.
Lockerby Cotts.
Soutra Ct.
Fala Ct.
Gracemount
Kaimes Sch.
Gracemount Park
St. Catherines R.C.
Gracemount Leisure Centre
GILMERTON DYKES ST.
NEWTOFT ST.
DRUM ST.
GILMERTON
Hawthorne Pl.
Burghtoft
Ravenscroft St.
Ravenscroft Gdns.
Drum Cotts.
New St.
Ravenscr. Pl.
Hyvot Grn.
Hyvot Ct.
Hyvot View
Gilmerton Pl.
G.D. View
Gilmerton G. Dykes Terr.
G. Dykes Loan
G. Dykes Dr.
Gilmerton
Hyvots Bank
Lasswade Gro.
Lasswade Bank
ROAD
S'house Terr.
S'house Paths
Medway
Crescent
Park
Muirhouse
S'house Sq.
Southhouse
Burdiehouse
Burdiehouse Burn
The M Brae
The Murrays
LASSWADE ROAD
G. Dykes Road
Gilmerton
Station Road
Gilmerton Station
476
West Edge Farm
Langloan
Road
THE CI

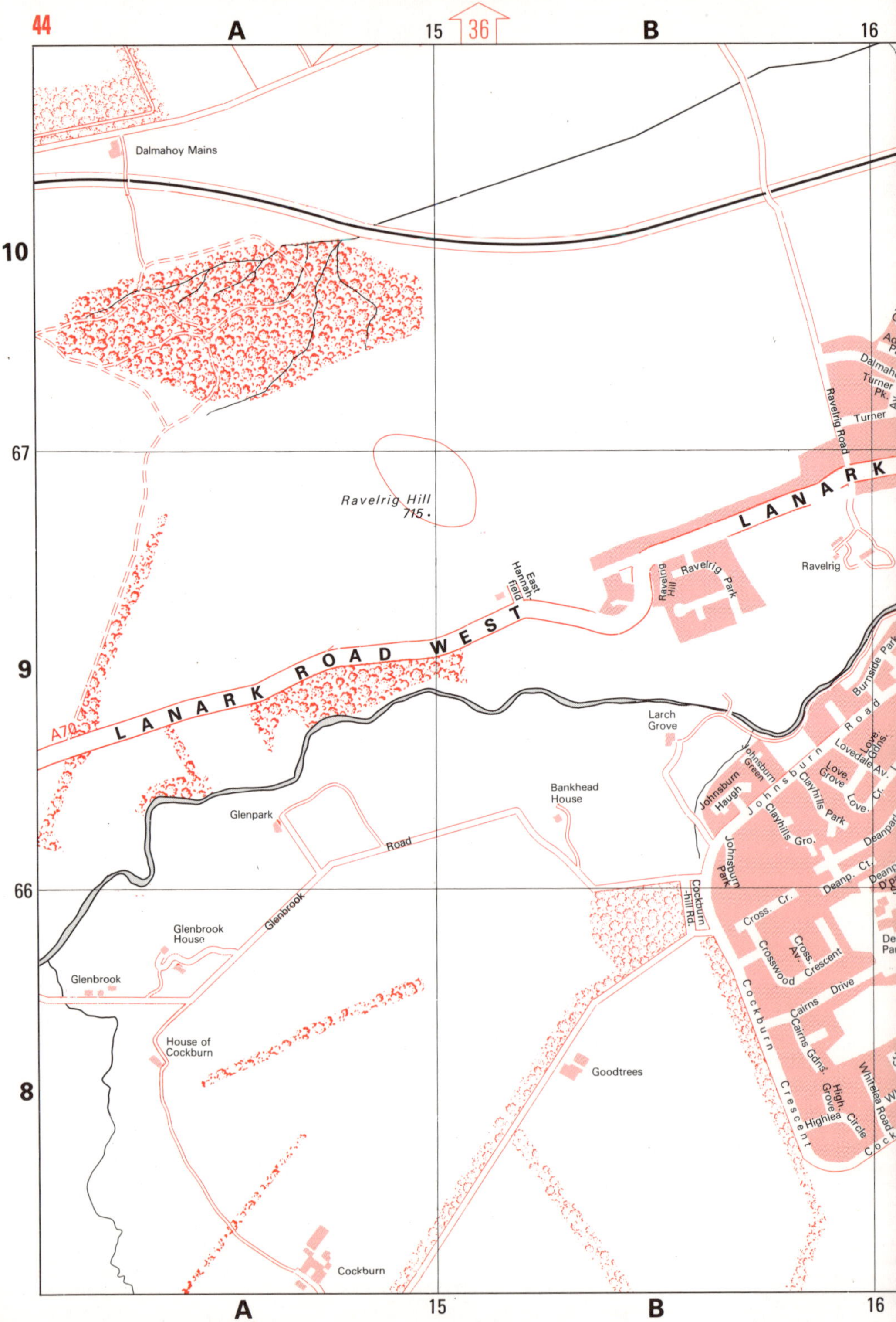
A
15
36
B
16
10
67
9
66
8
Dalmahoy Mains
Ravelrig Hill
715
East Hannah-field
LANARK ROAD WEST
A70
LANARK
Ravelrig Hill
Ravelrig Park
Ravelrig
Ravelrig Road
Turner Pk.
Turner
Av.
Dalmahoy
Larch Grove
Bankhead House
Glenpark
Road
Glenbrook
Glenbrook House
Glenbrook
House of Cockburn
Cockburn
Goodtrees
Cockburn -hill Rd.
Burnside Park
Johnsburn Road
Johnsburn Green
Johnsburn Haugh
Johnsburn Park
Lovedale Av.
Love. Gdns.
Love. Grove
Love. Cr.
Clayhills Park
Clayhills Gro.
Deanpark
Deanp. Ct.
Cross. Cr.
Cross. Av.
Crosswood Crescent
Cairns Drive
Cairns Gdns.
Cockburn Crescent
High. Grove
Highlea Circle
Whitelea Road
A
15
B
16

37

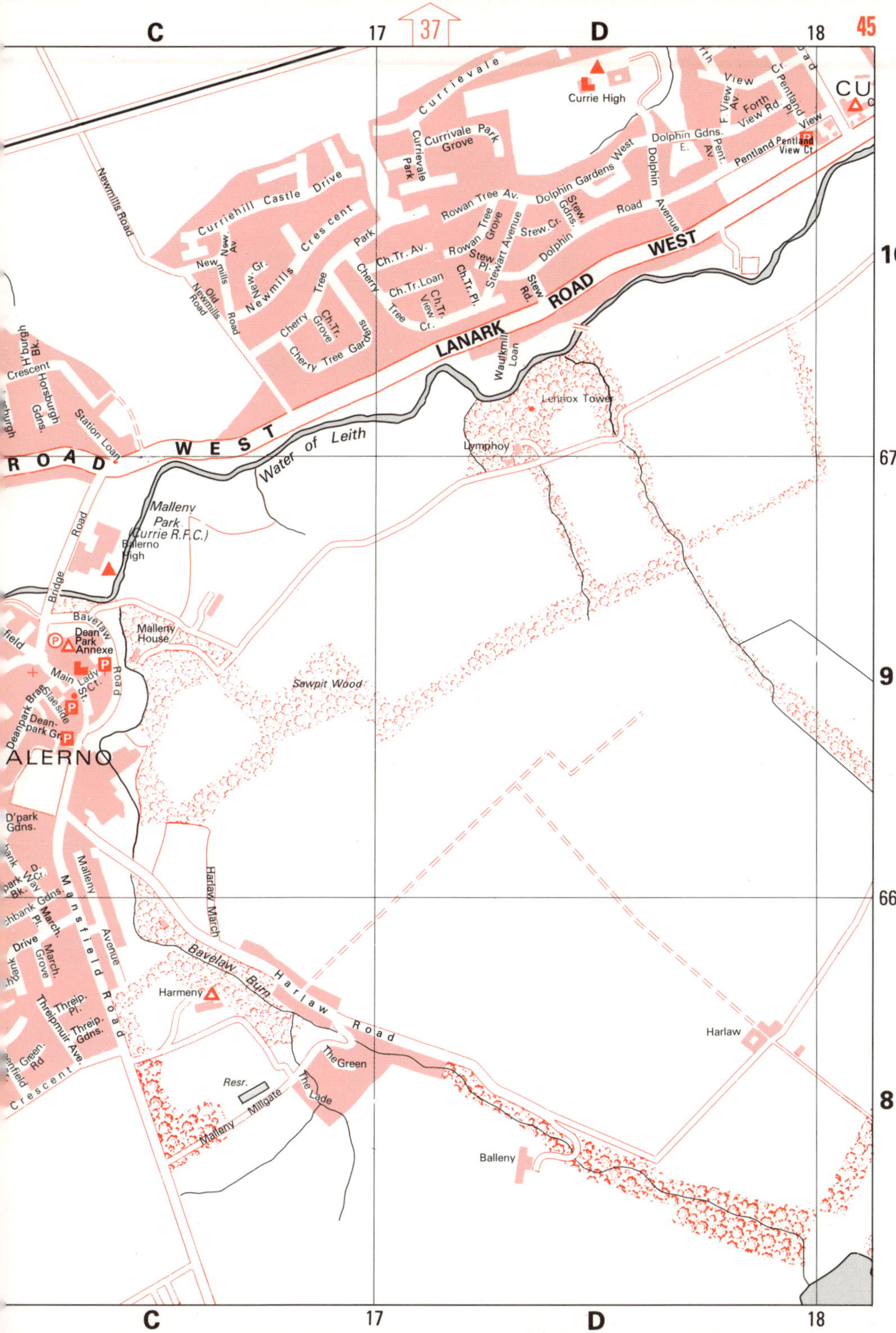
C
17
D
18
10
67
9
66
8
Currievale
Currie High
View
Forth View Rd.
F. View Av.
Pentland Pl.
Pentland View Ct.
Dolphin Gdns. E.
Pent. Av.
Pentland View
Currivale Park Grove
Currievale Park
Dolphin Gardens West
Dolphin Avenue
Dolphin Road
Rowan Tree Av.
Rowan Tree Grove
Stewart Avenue
Stew. Gdns.
Stew. Cr.
Stew. Pl.
Stew Rd.
Curriehill Castle Drive
Cres cent
Park
Cherry
Ch. Tr. Av.
Ch. Tr. Loan
Ch. Tr. View
Ch. Tr. Pl.
Tree Cr.
Cherry Tree
Ch. Tr. Grove
Cherry Tree Gardens
Newmills Road
New. Av.
New Mills
New. Gr.
Newmills
Old Newmills Road
Road
LANARK ROAD WEST
Waulkmill Loan
Lennox Tower
Lymphoy
Water of Leith
H'burgh Bk.
Crescent
Horsburgh Gdns.
Station Loan
ROAD WEST
Malleny Park (Currie R.F.C.)
Balerno High
Bridge Road
Bavelaw Road
Dean Park Annexe
Malleny House
Main St.
Lady Ct.
Deanpark Brae
Glaeside
Deanpark Gr.
ALERNO
Sawpit Wood
D'park Gdns.
Malleny Avenue
Mansfield Road
March. Grove
Drive
Threip. Pl.
Threip. Gdns.
Threipmuir Ave.
Green Rd
Crescent
Harlaw March
Bavelaw Burn
Harlaw Road
Harmeny
Resr.
The Green
The Lade
Malleny Millgate
Harlaw
Balleny
C
17
D
18

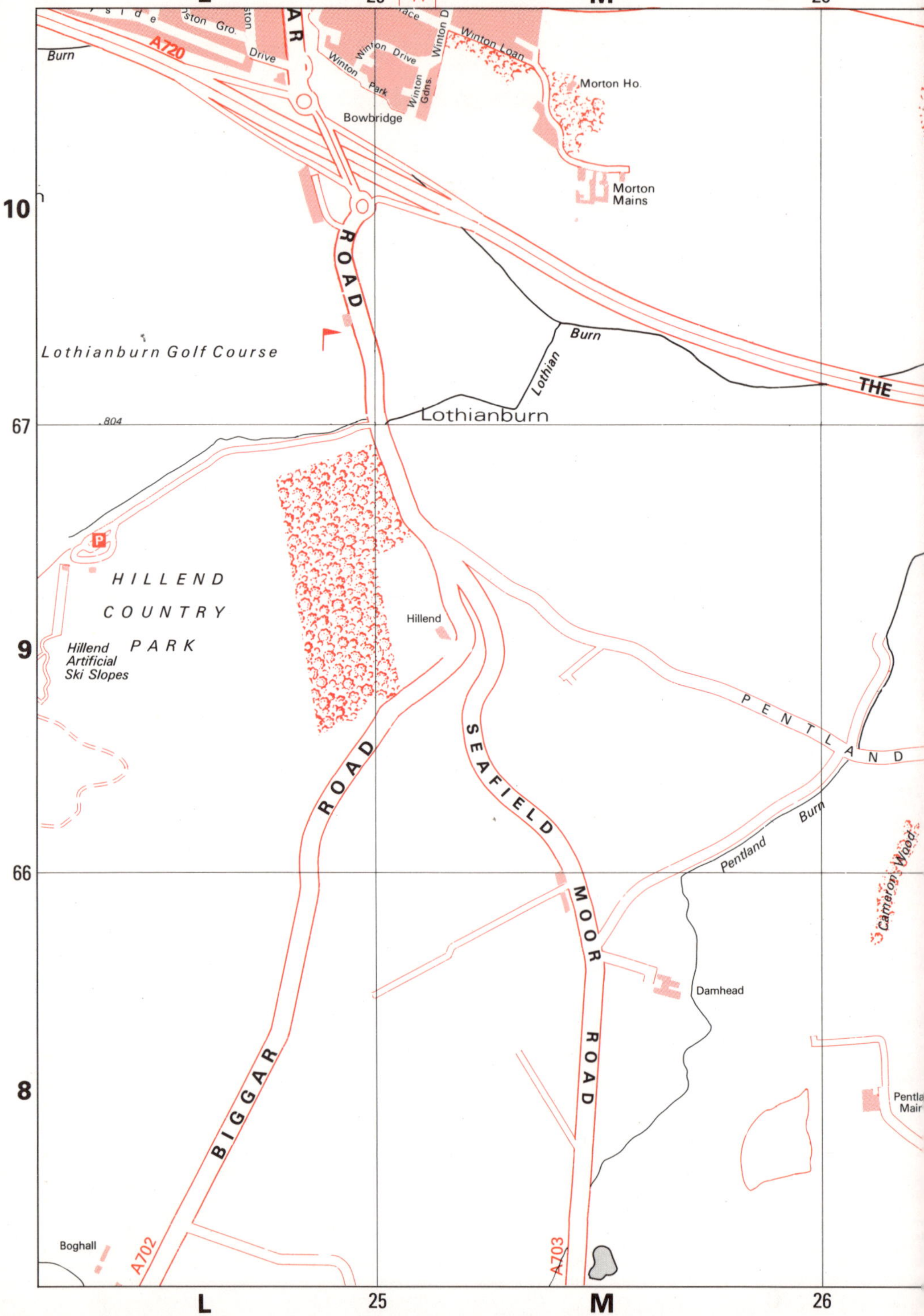
L
25
41
M
26
10
67
9
66
8
Burn
A720
Drive
Winton Drive
Winton Park
Winton Gdns.
Winton Loan
Morton Ho.
Bowbridge
Morton Mains
ROAD
Lothianburn Golf Course
Burn
Lothian
THE
Lothianburn
804
HILLEND COUNTRY PARK
Hillend
Hillend Artificial Ski Slopes
SEAFIELD
ROAD
PENTLAND
Pentland Burn
Cameron Wood
MOOR ROAD
Damhead
BIGGAR ROAD
Boghall
A702
A703

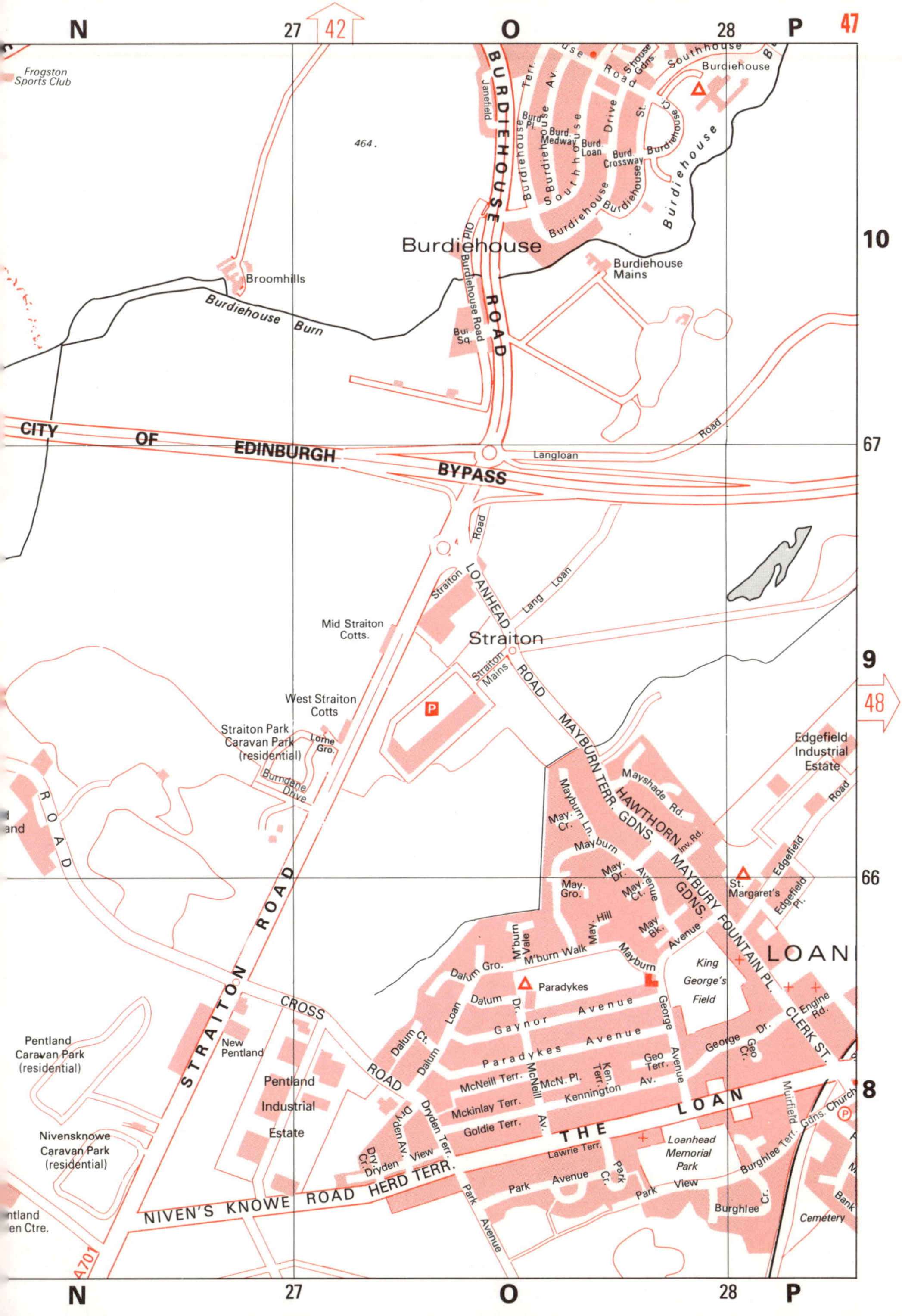

N
27
42
O
28
P
10
67
9
48
66
8
Frogston Sports Club
464.
Burdiehouse
Broomhills
Burdiehouse Burn
BURDIEHOUSE ROAD
Janefield
Old Burdiehouse Road
Burd. Sq.
Burdiehouse Terr.
Burd. Pl.
Burdiehouse Av.
Burd. Medway
Burd. Loan
Southhouse Drive
Burd. Crossway
Burdiehouse Burdiehouse
Southhouse Road
Southhouse Gdns.
Southhouse
Burdiehouse St.
Burdiehouse Cr.
Burdiehouse
Burdiehouse Mains
CITY OF EDINBURGH BYPASS
Langloan Road
Loanhead Road
Straiton
Lang Loan
Straiton
Mid Straiton Cotts.
West Straiton Cotts
Straiton Mains
P
Straiton Park Caravan Park (residential)
Lorne Gro.
Burndane Drive
ROAD
STRAITON ROAD
MAYBURN TERR.
HAWTHORN GDNS.
Mayshade Rd.
Inv. Rd.
MAYBURY GDNS.
FOUNTAIN PL.
Mayburn Ln.
May. Cr.
Mayburn
May. Dr.
May. Ct.
Mayburn Avenue
May. Gro.
May. Hill
May. Bk.
M'burn Vale
M'burn Walk
Dalum Gro.
Paradykes
Mayburn
Avenue
King George's Field
St. Margaret's
Edgefield Industrial Estate
Edgefield Road
Edgefield Dr.
Edgefield Pl.
LOAN
CLERK ST.
Engine Rd.
CROSS ROAD
New Pentland
Pentland Industrial Estate
Dalum Dr.
Dalum Loan
Dalum Ct.
Dalum
Gaynor Avenue
Paradykes Avenue
George Avenue
George Dr.
Geo Cr.
Geo Terr.
McNeill Terr.
McNeill Av.
McN. Pl.
Ken. Terr.
Kennington Av.
Mckinlay Terr.
Goldie Terr.
Dryden Av.
Dryden Terr.
Dry. Cr.
Dryden View
THE LOAN
Muirfield Gdns.
Church
Loanhead Memorial Park
Lawrie Terr.
Park Avenue
Park Cr.
Park View
Burghlee Terr.
Burghlee Cr.
Bank
Cemetery
Park Avenue
HERD TERR.
NIVEN'S KNOWE ROAD
Pentland Caravan Park (residential)
Nivensknowe Caravan Park (residential)
ntland en Ctre.
and
A701

P 29 43 Q 30

P 29 Q 30

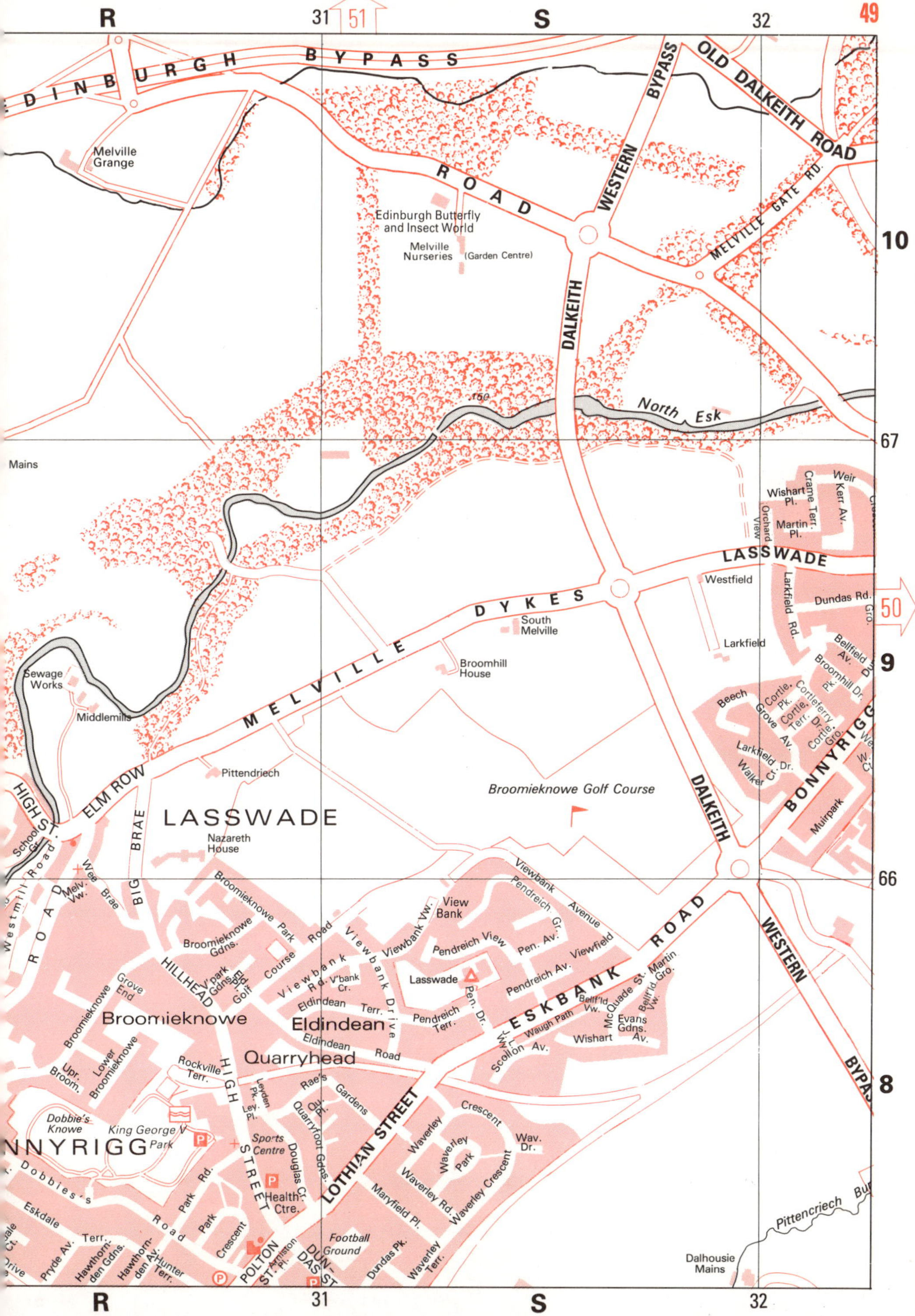
R
31
51
S
32
EDINBURGH BYPASS
OLD DALKEITH ROAD
WESTERN BYPASS
Melville Grange
ROAD
Edinburgh Butterfly and Insect World
Melville Nurseries (Garden Centre)
MELVILLE GATE RD.
10
DALKEITH
North Esk
150
67
Mains
Wishart Pl.
Crame Terr.
Weir
Kerr Av.
Orchard View
Martin Pl.
LASSWADE
Westfield
Larkfield Rd.
Dundas Rd.
50
MELVILLE DYKES
South Melville
Larkfield
Broomhill House
Bellfield Av.
Broomhill Dr.
9
Sewage Works
Middlemills
Beech Grove Av.
Cortle. Pk.
Cortleferry Dr.
Cortle. Terr.
Cortle. Gro.
Larkfield Dr.
Walker Ct.
BONNYRIGG
Pittendriech
Broomieknowe Golf Course
DALKEITH
Muirpark
HIGH ST.
ELM ROW
BRAE
LASSWADE
Nazareth House
School Gr.
Westmill Road
ROAD
Wee Brae
Melv. Vw.
BIG
Broomieknowe Park
Viewbank
Pendreich Gr.
Avenue
View Bank
Broomieknowe Gdns.
Course
Road
Viewbank Vw.
Pendreich View
Pen. Av.
Viewfield
66
ESKBANK ROAD
WESTERN
HILLHEAD
V'park Gdns.
Eld. Pl.
Golf
Viewbank Rd.
V'bank Cr.
Viewbank Drive
Lasswade
Pen. Dr.
Pendreich Av.
St. Martin Gro.
Grove End
Broomieknowe
Eldindean Terr.
Pendreich Terr.
Bellf'ld Vw.
McQuade St.
Bellf'ld Vw.
Broomieknowe
Eldindean
Waugh Path
J. L. Vw.
Evans Gdns.
Wishart Av.
Lower Broomieknowe
Upr. Broom.
Rockville Terr.
Eldindean Road
Quarryhead
Scollon Av.
HIGH STREET
Leyden Pk.
Ley. Pl.
Rae's Gardens
Qu. Pl.
Quarryfoot Gdns.
LOTHIAN STREET
Crescent
BYPASS
8
Dobbie's Knowe
King George V Park
Sports Centre
Douglas Cr.
Waverley
Waverley Park
Wav. Dr.
NNYRIGG
Dobbie's Road
Park Rd.
Health Ctre.
Maryfield Pl.
Waverley Rd.
Waverley Crescent
Pittencriech Burn
Eskdale
Pryde Av. Terr.
Hawthorn-den Gdns.
Hawthorn-den Av.
Hunter Terr.
Park Crescent
POLTON ST.
Arniston Pl.
DUNDAS ST.
Football Ground
Dundas Pk.
Waverley Terr.
Dalhousie Mains
R
31
S
32

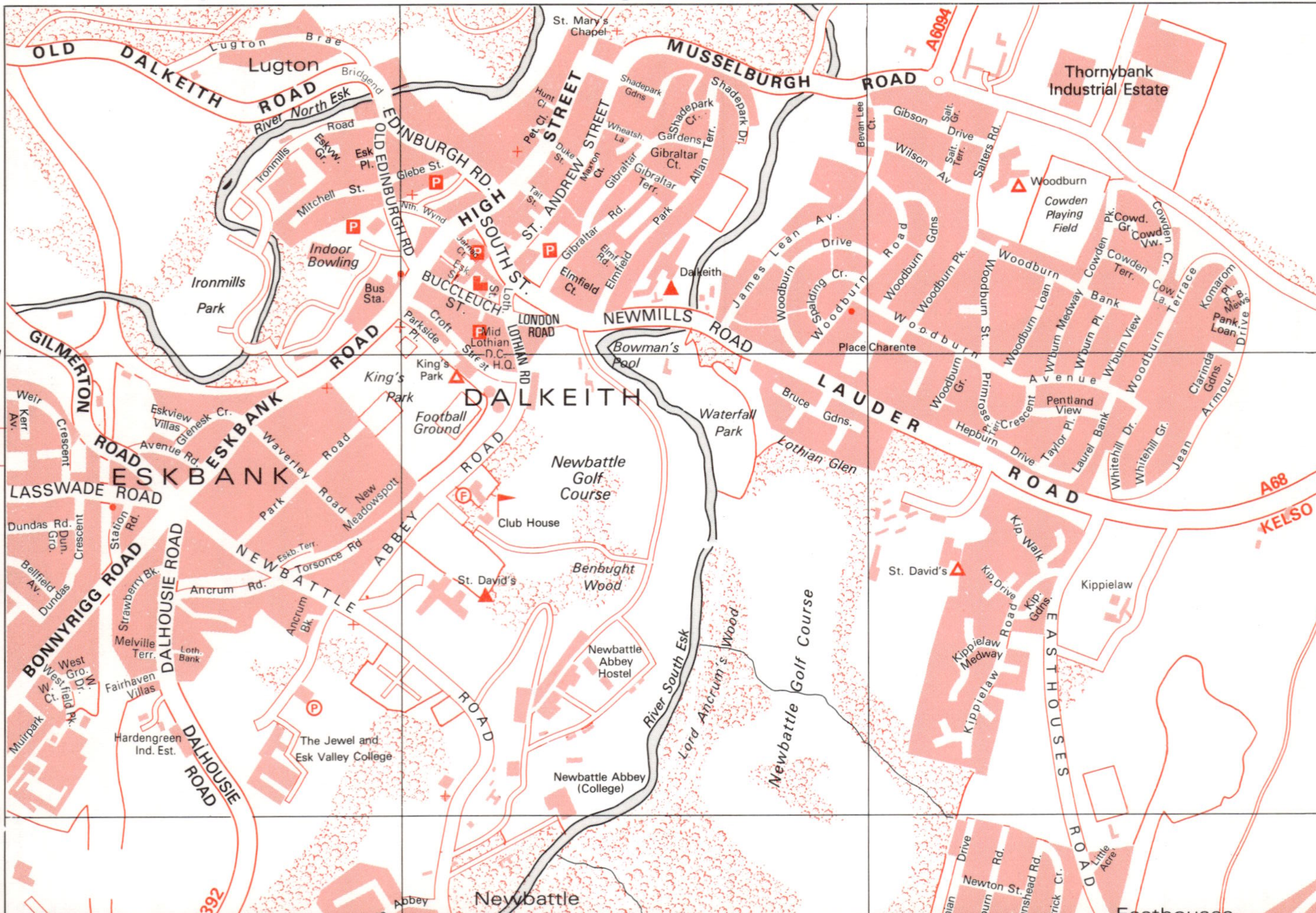

T
33
U
34
V
10
67
9
66
8
DALKEITH
ESKBANK
Lugton
Newbattle
Easthouses
Thornybank Industrial Estate
OLD DALKEITH ROAD
Lugton Brae
Bridgend
River North Esk
MUSSELBURGH ROAD
A6094
HIGH STREET
ST. ANDREW STREET
EDINBURGH RD.
OLD EDINBURGH RD
SOUTH ST.
BUCCLEUCH ST.
LONDON ROAD
LOTHIAN RD
NEWMILLS ROAD
LAUDER ROAD
A68
KELSO
GILMERTON ROAD
ESKBANK ROAD
LASSWADE ROAD
BONNYRIGG ROAD
DALHOUSIE ROAD
ABBEY ROAD
NEWBATTLE ROAD
EASTHOUSES ROAD
St. Mary's Chapel
Ironmills Park
Indoor Bowling
Bus Sta.
King's Park
Football Ground
Mid Lothian D.C. H.Q.
Bowman's Pool
Waterfall Park
Lothian Glen
Newbattle Golf Course
Club House
Benbught Wood
St. David's
Newbattle Abbey Hostel
Newbattle Abbey (College)
The Jewel and Esk Valley College
Hardengreen Ind. Est.
River South Esk
Lord Ancrum's Wood
Woodburn
Cowden Playing Field
Place Charente
Kippielaw
Dalkeith


49

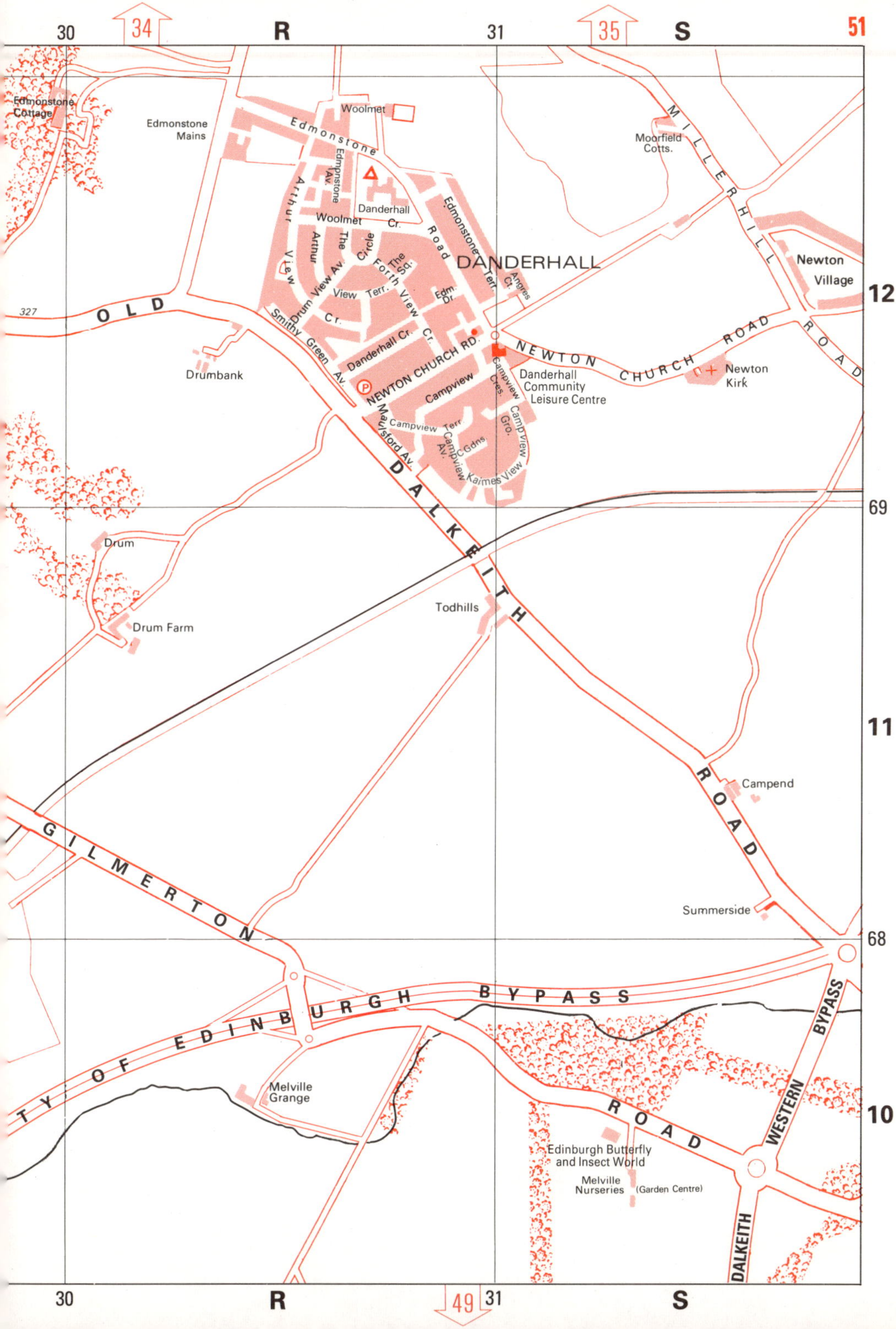
30
34
R
31
35
S
Edmonstone Cottage
Edmonstone Mains
Woolmet
Edmonstone
Edmonstone Av.
Arthur View
Danderhall
Woolmet Cr.
Arthur
The Circle
Edmonstone Road
Edmonstone Terr.
The Sq.
Forth View Cr.
Drum View Av.
View Terr.
Cr.
Edm. Dr.
Angres Ct.
DANDERHALL
Moorfield Cotts.
MILLERHILL ROAD
Newton Village
327
OLD
Smithy Green Av.
Danderhall Cr.
NEWTON CHURCH RD.
Campview
Campview Cres.
NEWTON CHURCH ROAD
Newton Kirk
Danderhall Community Leisure Centre
Drumbank
Maulsford Av.
Campview Terr.
Campview Gro.
Campview Av.
C.Gdns.
Kaimes View
Campview
12
69
Drum
DALKEITH ROAD
Todhills
Drum Farm
11
Campend
GILMERTON
Summerside
68
CITY OF EDINBURGH BYPASS
WESTERN BYPASS
Melville Grange
ROAD
10
Edinburgh Butterfly and Insect World
Melville Nurseries
(Garden Centre)
DALKEITH
30
R
49
31
S

**Abbreviations**
Acad.-Academy
Appr.-Approach
Av.-Avenue
Bdgs.-Buildings
Bdwy.-Broadway
Bk.-Bank
Cem.-Cemetery
Cl.-Close
Coll.-College
Cotts.-Cottages
Cr.-Crescent
Crem.-Crematorium
Ct.-Court
Dalk.-Dalkeith
Dr.-Drive
E.-East
Er.-Easter
Fm.-Farm
Gall.-Gallery
Gdn.-Garden
Gdns.-Gardens
Gr.-Green
Grd.-Ground
Gro.-Grove
Ho.-House
Hosp.-Hospital
Ind.-Industrial
La.-Lane
Ln.-Loan
Lo.-Lodge
Mem.-Memorial
Muss.-Musselburgh
N.-North
Pav.-Pavilion
Pk.-Park
Pl.-Place
Pt.-Port
Qt.-Quadrant
Rd.-Road
S.-South
Sch.-School
Sq.-Square
St.-Saint, Street
Sta.-Station
Terr.-Terrace
Vw.-View
W.-West
Wr.-Wester
Wy.-Way
An asterisk in the index indicates a street too small to show on the plan and an equals sign refers to the nearest street name.

| | | |
|---|---|---|
| Abbey La. | 21 | O17 |
| Abbey Rd., Dalk. | 50 | T9 |
| Abbey St. | 21 | O17 |
| Abbey Strand | 7 | N16 |
| Abbeyhill | 7 | N16 |
| Abbeyhill Cr. | 7 | N17 |
| Abbeyhill Sch. | 21 | O17 |
| Abbeymount | 7 | N17 |
| Abbotsford Ct. | 31 | L14 |
| Abbotsford Cr. | 31 | L14 |
| Abbotsford Pk. | 31 | L14 |
| Abercorn Av. | 21 | P16 |
| Abercorn Cotts.* =The Causeway | | |
| Abercorn Ct. | 21 | P16 |
| Abercorn Cr. | 21 | P16 |
| Abercorn Dr. | 21 | P16 |
| Abercorn Gdns. | 22 | P17 |
| Abercorn Gro. | 21 | P16 |
| Abercorn Park | 23 | S16 |
| Abercorn Rd. | 21 | P16 |
| Abercorn Terr. | 23 | R16 |
| Abercromby Pl. | 6 | M17 |
| Abinger Gdns. | 18 | J16 |
| Academy La. | 48 | P8 |
| Academy St. | 12 | O18 |
| Adam Ho. | 7 | M16 |
| Adelphi Gro. | 22 | R16 |
| Adelphi Pl. | 22 | R16 |
| Addiston Cr. | 45 | C10 |
| Addiston Gr. | 44 | C10 |
| Addiston Mains | 36 | B12 |
| Addiston Pk. | 44 | C10 |
| Admiral Terr. | 31 | L22 |
| Admiralty St. | 12 | N19 |
| Advocates Cl.*=High St. | | |
| Affleck Ct.* =Craigievar Wynd | | |
| Afton Pl. | 11 | L19 |
| Afton Terr. | 11 | L19 |
| Agnew Terr.* =Connaught Pl. | | |
| AIDS Hospice | 40 | J12 |
| Ainslie Park Recreation Centre | 10 | K19 |
| Ainslie Park Sch. | 6 | J19 |
| Ainslie Pl. | 6 | L17 |
| Air Terminal | 7 | M16 |
| Airlie Pl. | 19 | M17 |
| Aitchison's Pl.* =Figgate St. | | |
| Aitkenhill | 30 | H14 |
| Alan Breck Gdns. | 16 | F17 |
| Albany La. | 7 | M17 |
| Albany St. | 7 | M17 |
| Albany St. La. | 7 | M17 |
| Albert Pl. | 20 | N17 |
| Albert Rd. | 13 | O19 |
| Albert St. | 12 | N18 |
| Albert Terr. | 31 | L14 |
| Albert Terr., Muss. | 25 | W15 |
| Albion Pl. | 21 | O17 |
| Albion Rd. | 21 | O17 |
| Albion Terr. | 21 | O17 |
| Albyn Pl. | 6 | L17 |
| Alderbank Gdns. | 30 | K14 |
| Alderbank Pl. | 30 | K14 |
| Alderbank Terr. | 30 | K14 |
| Alexander Dr. | 30 | J15 |
| Alfred Pl. | 32 | N14 |
| Allan Park Cr. | 30 | J14 |
| Allan Park Dr. | 30 | J13 |
| Allan Park Gdns. | 30 | J13 |
| Allan Park Ln. | 30 | J13 |
| Allan Park Rd. | 30 | J13 |
| Allan St. | 19 | L17 |
| Allandale*=Spylaw St. | | |
| Allanfield | 20 | N17 |
| Allan Terr., Dalk. | 50 | U10 |
| Allermuir Ct. | 40 | K12 |
| Allermuir Rd. | 39 | H11 |
| Alloway Ln. | 42 | O12 |
| Almond Av. | 14 | A16 |
| Almond Bank Cotts.* =Whitehouse Rd. | | |
| Almond Ct. | 8 | E18 |
| Almond Gr. | 16 | E16 |
| Almond Rd. | 14 | A16 |
| Almond Sq. | 16 | E16 |
| Almondbank Terr. | 30 | K14 |
| Alnwickhill Cr. | 42 | N11 |
| Alnwickhill Ct. | 42 | N11 |
| Alnwickhill Dr. | 42 | N11 |
| Alnwickhill Gdns. | 42 | O11 |
| Alnwickhill Gro. | 42 | N11 |
| Alnwickhill Ln. | 42 | N11 |
| Alnwickhill Pk. | 42 | O11 |
| Alnwickhill Rd. | 42 | O12 |
| Alnwickhill Terr. | 42 | N11 |
| Alnwickhill Vw. | 42 | N11 |
| Alva Pl. | 21 | O17 |
| Alva St. | 6 | L16 |
| Alvanley Terr.* =Whitehouse Loan | | |
| American Sch., The | 19 | L16 |
| Anchorfield* =Lindsay Rd. | | |
| Ancrum Bk., Dalk. | 50 | T9 |
| Ancrum Rd., Dalk. | 50 | T9 |
| Anderson Pl. | 12 | N19 |
| Andrew Wood Ct. | 11 | M19 |
| Angle Park Terr. | 19 | K15 |
| Angres Ct. | 51 | S12 |
| Ann St. | 6 | L17 |
| Annandale St. | 20 | M18 |
| Annandale St. La. | 20 | N17 |
| Annfield | 12 | M19 |
| Annfield St. | 12 | M19 |
| Antigua St. | 7 | N17 |
| Anworth Villas* =Saughton Rd. N. | | |
| Appin Terr. | 30 | J14 |
| Appleton Tower | 7 | M15 |
| Arboretum Av. | 19 | L17 |
| Arboretum Pl. | 11 | L18 |
| Arboretum Rd. | 11 | L18 |
| Arbuthnot Rd. | 48 | P8 |
| Archer's Hall | 7 | N15 |
| Archibald Pl. | 6 | M16 |
| Arden St. | 32 | M15 |
| Ardmillan Pl. | 31 | K15 |
| Ardmillan Terr. | 31 | K15 |
| Ardmillan Terr. La.* =Ardmillan Terr. | | |
| Ardshiel Av. | 16 | F17 |
| Argyle Cr. | 23 | R16 |
| Argyle Ho. | 6 | M16 |
| Argyle Park Terr. | 20 | M15 |
| Argyle Pl. | 20 | M15 |
| Argyle St. | 12 | N19 |
| Argyll Terr. | 19 | L16 |
| Arniston Pl. | 49 | R8 |
| Arnott Gdns. | 29 | H13 |
| Arran Pl.*=James St. | | |
| Arran Pl. | 23 | S16 |
| Arthur Pl.*=Arthur St. | | |
| Arthur St. | 12 | N18 |
| Arthur View Cr. | 51 | R12 |
| Arthur View Terr. | 51 | R12 |
| Arthur's Seat | 21 | O15 |
| Asda Shopping Centre | 23 | S15 |
| Ashgrove, Muss. | 25 | W15 |
| Ashgrove Pl., Muss. | 25 | W15 |
| Ashgrove Vw., Muss. | 25 | W15 |
| Ashley Dr. | 30 | K14 |
| Ashley Gdns. | 30 | K14 |
| Ashley Gro. | 30 | K14 |
| Ashley Pl. | 12 | N18 |
| Ashley Terr. | 30 | K14 |
| Ashton Gro. | 33 | O13 |
| Ashton Villas* =Brunstane Rd. | | |
| Ashville Terr. | 13 | O18 |
| Assembly Hall | 6 | M16 |
| Assembly Rooms | 6 | M16 |
| Assembly St. | 12 | O19 |
| Astley Ainslie Hosp. | 31 | M14 |
| Atholl Cr. | 6 | L16 |
| Atholl Cr. La. | 6 | L16 |
| Atholl Pl. | 6 | L16 |
| Atholl Terr. | 19 | L16 |
| Auchingane | 40 | K11 |
| Auchinleck Ct. | 11 | M19 |
| Auchinleck's Brae* =Main St. | | |
| Avenue Rd. | 50 | T9 |
| Avenue, The | 37 | D12 |
| Avenue Villas | 19 | K17 |
| Avenue W. | 37 | D11 |
| Aviation Ho. | 17 | G15 |
| Avon Gr. | 8 | E18 |
| Avon Pl. | 8 | E18 |
| Avon Rd. | 8 | E18 |
| Avondale Pl. | 19 | L17 |
| Baberton Av. | 38 | F11 |
| Baberton Cr. | 39 | F11 |
| Baberton Golf Course | 38 | E11 |
| Baberton Ln. | 38 | F11 |
| Baberton Mains | 38 | F12 |
| Baberton Mains Av. | 38 | F12 |
| Baberton Mains Bk. | 38 | F12 |
| Baberton Mains Brae | 38 | F12 |
| Baberton Mains Ct. | 38 | G12 |
| Baberton Mains Cr. | 38 | F12 |
| Baberton Mains Dell | 38 | F12 |
| Baberton Mains Dr. | 38 | F12 |
| Baberton Mains Gdns. | 38 | F12 |
| Baberton Mains Gr. | 38 | F12 |
| Baberton Mains Gro. | 38 | F12 |
| Baberton Mains Hill | 38 | F12 |
| Baberton Mains Lea | 38 | F12 |
| Baberton Mains Ln. | 39 | G12 |

| | | |
|---|---|---|
| Baberton Mains Pk. | 38 | F12 |
| Baberton Mains Pl. | 38 | F12 |
| Baberton Mains Rise | 38 | F12 |
| Baberton Mains Row | 38 | F12 |
| Baberton Mains Terr. | 38 | F12 |
| Baberton Mains Vw. | 39 | G12 |
| Baberton Mains Way | 38 | F12 |
| Baberton Mains Wood | 38 | F12 |
| Baberton Mains Wynd | 38 | F12 |
| Baberton Pk. | 38 | F11 |
| Baberton Rd. | 38 | E12 |
| Baberton Sq. | 38 | F11 |
| Back Dean | 19 | K17 |
| Backlee | 42 | O11 |
| Back Row | 30 | J13 |
| Back Station Rd.* =Peffer St. | | |
| Baileyfield Cr. | 22 | R16 |
| Baileyfield Rd. | 22 | R16 |
| Bailie Gro. | 23 | R15 |
| Bailie Path | 22 | R15 |
| Bailie Pl. | 23 | R15 |
| Bailie Terr. | 22 | R15 |
| Baird Av. | 18 | J15 |
| Baird Dr. | 18 | J15 |
| Baird Gdns. | 18 | J15 |
| Baird Gro. | 18 | J15 |
| Baird Terr. | 18 | J15 |
| Baker's Pl.*=Kerr St. | | |
| Balbirnie Pl. | 18 | K16 |
| Balcarres Ct. | 31 | L13 |
| Balcarres Pl., Muss. | 25 | V16 |
| Balcarres Rd., Muss. | 25 | V16 |
| Balcarres St. | 31 | K13 |
| Balderston Gdns | 33 | O13 |
| Balerno High Sch. | 45 | C9 |
| Balfour Pl. | 12 | N18 |
| Balfour St. | 12 | N18 |
| Balfron Ln. | 16 | F17 |
| Balgreen Av. | 17 | H15 |
| Balgreen Gdns. | 17 | H15 |
| Balgreen Pk. | 17 | H15 |
| Balgreen Rd. | 18 | H15 |
| Balgreen Sch. | 30 | J15 |
| Ballantyne La.* =Ballantyne Rd. | | |
| Ballantyne Rd. | 12 | N19 |
| Ballantyne La. | 12 | N19 |
| Balm Well Av. | 42 | O11 |
| Balm Well Gro. | 42 | O11 |
| Balm Well Pk. | 42 | O11 |
| Balm Well Terr. | 42 | O11 |
| Balmoral Pl. | 19 | L17 |
| Baltic St. | 12 | O19 |
| Bangholm Av. | 11 | L19 |
| Bangholm Bower Av. | 11 | L19 |
| Bangholm Gro. | 11 | M19 |
| Bangholm Ln. | 11 | M19 |
| Bangholm Pk. | 11 | L19 |
| Bangholm Pl. | 11 | L30 |
| Bangholm Rd. | 11 | L19 |
| Bangholm Terr. | 11 | L18 |
| Bangholm Vw. | 11 | M19 |
| Bangholm Villas* =Ferry Rd. | | |
| Bangor Rd. | 12 | N19 |
| Bank of Scotland | 7 | M16 |
| Bank St. | 7 | M16 |
| Bankhead Av. | 28 | F14 |
| Bankhead Bdwy. | 28 | E14 |
| Bankhead Crossway N. | 28 | E14 |
| Bankhead Crossway S. | 28 | E13 |
| Bankhead Dr. | 28 | E14 |
| Bankhead Ho. | 44 | B9 |
| Bankhead Ln. | 28 | F13 |
| Bankhead Medway | 28 | F14 |
| Bankhead Pl. | 28 | F14 |
| Bankhead St. | 28 | F13 |
| Bankhead Terr. | 28 | E13 |
| Bankhead Way | 28 | E13 |
| Barclay Pl. | 19 | M15 |
| Barclay Terr. | 31 | L15 |
| Barnballoch Ct.* =Craigievar Wynd | | |
| Barnshot Rd. | 39 | H11 |
| Barnton Av. | 8 | F18 |
| Barnton Av. W. | 8 | E18 |
| Barnton Brae | 8 | E18 |
| Barnton Ct. | 16 | E18 |
| Barnton Gdns. | 9 | G18 |
| Barnton Gro. | 16 | E18 |
| Barnton Ln. | 9 | G18 |
| Barnton Pk. | 9 | G18 |
| Barnton Park Av. | 8 | F18 |
| Barnton Park Cr. | 16 | F18 |
| Barnton Park Dell | 8 | F18 |
| Barnton Park Dr. | 16 | F18 |
| Barnton Park Gdns. | 16 | F18 |
| Barnton Park Gro. | 8 | F18 |
| Barnton Park Pl. | 8 | F18 |
| Barnton Park Vw. | 16 | F18 |
| Barnton Park Wood | 16 | E17 |
| Barntongate Av. | 16 | E17 |
| Barntongate Dr. | 16 | E17 |
| Barntongate Terr. | 16 | E17 |
| Baronscourt Rd. | 21 | P17 |
| Baronscourt Terr. | 21 | P17 |
| Barony Pl. | 7 | M17 |
| Barony St. | 7 | M17 |
| Barony Terr. | 16 | F16 |
| Bath Pl. | 23 | R17 |
| Bath Rd. | 13 | O19 |
| Bath St. | 22 | R16 |
| Bath St. La.*=Bath St. | | |
| Bathfield | 12 | N19 |
| Baxter's Bdgs.* =Holyrood Rd. | | |
| Baxter's Pl.*=Leith Walk | | |
| Bavelaw Gdns.* =Bavelaw Rd. | | |
| Bavelaw Rd. | 45 | C9 |
| Beach Lane | 22 | R17 |
| Beach La., Muss. | 24 | U16 |
| Beauchamp Gro. | 42 | O12 |
| Beauchamp Rd. | 42 | O12 |
| Beaufort Rd. | 32 | M14 |
| Beaverbank Pl. | 11 | M18 |
| Beaverhall Rd. | 12 | M18 |
| Bedford Cr. | 19 | L17 |
| Bedford Ct. | 19 | L17 |
| Bedford St. | 19 | L17 |
| Bedford Terr. | 23 | S16 |
| Beech Grove Av. | 49 | S9 |
| Beechmount Pk. | 17 | H16 |
| Beechwood Mains | 17 | H16 |
| Beechwood Terr. | 13 | O18 |
| Belfield Av., Muss. | 24 | U15 |
| Belfield Ct., Muss. | 24 | U15 |
| Belfield Av. | 50 | T9 |
| Belford Av. | 19 | K17 |
| Belford Bridge* =Belford Rd. | | |
| Belford Gdns. | 19 | K17 |
| Belford Mews | 19 | K16 |
| Belford Pk. | 19 | K16 |
| Belford Pl. | 19 | K16 |
| Belford Rd. | 19 | K16 |
| Belford Terr.* =Belford Rd. | | |
| Belgrave Cr. | 19 | K17 |
| Belgrave Cr. La. | 19 | K17 |
| Belgrave Gdns. | 17 | G16 |
| Belgrave Mews | 19 | K17 |
| Belgrave Pl. | 19 | K17 |
| Belgrave Rd. | 17 | G16 |
| Belgrave Terr. | 17 | G15 |
| Belhaven Pl. | 31 | L13 |
| Belhaven Terr. | 31 | L13 |
| Bell Pl. | 19 | L17 |
| Bellenden Gdns. | 33 | P13 |
| Bellevue | 20 | M17 |
| Bellevue Cr. | 20 | M17 |
| Bellevue Gdns. | 20 | M18 |
| Bellevue Gro. | 20 | M17 |
| Bellevue La. | 20 | M17 |
| Bellevue Pl. | 20 | M17 |
| Bellevue Rd. | 20 | M17 |
| Bellevue St. | 20 | M17 |
| Bellevue Terr. | 20 | M17 |
| Bellfield Av. | 50 | T9 |
| Bellfield Av., Muss. | 24 | U15 |
| Bellfield Ct., Muss. | 24 | U15 |
| Bellfield La. | 23 | R16 |
| Bellfield St. | 23 | R16 |
| Bellfield Terr. | 23 | R16 |
| Bellfield Vw. | 49 | S8 |
| Bells Brae | 19 | L16 |
| Bell's Mills*=Belford Rd. | | |
| Bell's Wynd*=High St. | | |
| Belmont Av. | 17 | H16 |
| Belmont Cr. | 17 | H16 |
| Belmont Gdns. | 17 | H16 |
| Belmont Pk. | 17 | H16 |
| Belmont Rd. | 38 | F11 |
| Belmont Terr. | 17 | H16 |
| Belmont Vw. | 18 | H16 |
| Belvedere Pk. | 11 | M19 |
| Beresford Av. | 11 | M19 |
| Beresford Gdns. | 11 | M19 |
| Beresford Pl. | 11 | L19 |
| Beresford Terr. | 11 | M19 |
| Bernard St. | 12 | O19 |
| Bernard Terr. | 20 | N15 |
| Berry Sq.* =Figgate St. | | |
| Beulah, Muss. | 25 | W15 |
| Bevan Lee Ct., Dalk. | 50 | U10 |
| Big Brae | 49 | R8 |
| Biggar Rd. | 46 | L8 |
| Bilston Glen Colliery | 47 | O8 |
| Bingham Av. | 22 | Q15 |
| Bingham Bdwy. | 34 | Q15 |
| Bingham Cr. | 34 | R15 |
| Bingham Crossway | 34 | Q15 |
| Bingham Dr. | 34 | Q15 |
| Bingham Medway | 34 | Q15 |
| Bingham Pk. | 22 | Q15 |
| Bingham Pl. | 34 | Q15 |
| Bingham St. | 34 | Q15 |
| Bingham Way | 34 | Q15 |
| Birch Ct. | 16 | E17 |
| Birnies Ct. | 9 | H19 |
| Blacket Av. | 32 | N15 |
| Blacket Pl. | 32 | N15 |
| Blackbarony Rd. | 33 | O13 |
| Blackchapel Cl. | 35 | R14 |
| Blackchapel Rd. | 35 | R14 |
| Blackford Av. | 32 | M14 |
| Blackford Bk. | 32 | M14 |
| Blackford Glen Rd. | 32 | N13 |
| Blackford Hill | 32 | M13 |
| Blackford Hill Gro. | 32 | M13 |
| Blackford Hill Rise | 32 | M13 |
| Blackford Hill Vw. | 32 | M13 |
| Blackford Rd. | 32 | M14 |
| Blackfriars St. | 7 | N16 |
| Blackhall Sch. | 17 | H17 |
| Blackie Rd. | 13 | O18 |
| Blackthorn Ct. | 16 | E17 |
| Blackwood Cr. | 32 | N15 |
| Blaeberry Gdns. | 16 | E17 |
| Blair St. | 20 | M16 |
| Blantyre Terr. | 31 | L14 |
| Bleachfield | 12 | M19 |
| Blenheim Pl. | 7 | N17 |
| Blinkbonny Av. | 18 | J17 |
| Blinkbonny Cr. | 18 | J17 |
| Blinkbonny Gdns. | 18 | J17 |
| Blinkbonny Gro. | 18 | J17 |
| Blinkbonny Gro. W. | 18 | J17 |
| Blinkbonny Rd. | 18 | J17 |
| Blinkbonny Rd., Currie | 38 | E10 |
| Blinkbonny Terr. | 18 | J17 |
| Bloomiehall Pk. | 38 | F11 |
| Boat Gr. | 11 | M18 |
| Boghall | 46 | L8 |
| Bog Park Rd., Muss. | 24 | U15 |
| Bogsmill Rd. | 29 | H13 |
| Bonaly Annexe | 39 | H12 |
| Bonaly Av. | 39 | H11 |
| Bonaly Brae | 39 | H11 |
| Bonaly Cr. | 39 | H11 |
| Bonaly Dr. | 39 | H11 |
| Bonaly Farm Cotts. | 39 | H11 |
| Bonaly Gdns. | 39 | H11 |
| Bonaly Gro. | 39 | H11 |
| Bonaly Rise | 39 | H11 |
| Bonaly Rd. | 39 | H11 |
| Bonaly Sch. | 39 | H10 |
| Bonaly Sch. Annexe | 39 | H12 |
| Bonaly Steading | 39 | H11 |

| | | |
|---|---|---|
| Bonaly Terr. | 39 | H11 |
| Bonaly Tower | 39 | H10 |
| Bonaly Wester | 39 | H11 |
| Bonar Pl. | 12 | M19 |
| Bonnington Av. | 12 | M19 |
| Bonnington Gro. | 12 | M19 |
| Bonnington Rd. | 12 | N18 |
| Bonnington Rd. La. | 12 | N18 |
| Bonnington Sch. | 12 | N18 |
| Bonnington Sch. Annexe | 12 | N19 |
| Bonnington Terr. | 12 | M19 |
| Bonnyhaugh | 12 | M18 |
| Bonnyhaugh La. | 12 | M18 |
| Bonnyrigg Rd. | 50 | T9 |
| Boothacre Cotts.* =Seafield Pl. | | |
| Boothacre La. | 13 | P18 |
| Boroughloch Bdgs.* =Boroughloch Sq. | | |
| Boroughloch La. | 7 | N15 |
| Boroughloch Sq.* =Boroughloch La. | | |
| Boroughmuir Sch. | 19 | L15 |
| Boroughmuir Sch. Annexe | 19 | L15 |
| Borroughmuir R.F.C. | 30 | J14 |
| Borthwick Pl. | 19 | K16 |
| Borthwick's Cl.*=High St. | | |
| Boswall Av. | 11 | K19 |
| Boswall Cr. | 11 | K19 |
| Boswall Dr. | 10 | K19 |
| Boswall Gdns. | 11 | K19 |
| Boswall Gr. | 11 | L19 |
| Boswall Gro. | 11 | K19 |
| Boswall Ln. | 11 | K19 |
| Boswall Mews* =Boswall Loan | | |
| Boswall Parkway | 10 | K19 |
| Boswall Pl. | 11 | K19 |
| Boswall Qt. | 11 | K19 |
| Boswall Rd. | 11 | L19 |
| Boswall Sq. | 11 | K19 |
| Boswall Terr. | 11 | K19 |
| Bothwell St. | 21 | O17 |
| Boundary Rd. | 37 | D12 |
| Bowbridge | 41 | L10 |
| Bowhill Terr. | 11 | L18 |
| Bowie's Cl. | 12 | O19 |
| Bowling Gr., The | 12 | N19 |
| Bowmont Pl. | 7 | N15 |
| Boyd's Entry* =St. Mary's St. | | |
| Brae Pk. | 8 | E18 |
| Brae Park Rd. | 8 | D18 |
| Braefoot Terr. | 33 | O13 |
| Braehead Av. | 8 | E18 |
| Braehead Bk. | 8 | E18 |
| Braehead Cr. | 8 | E18 |
| Braehead Dr. | 8 | E18 |
| Braehead Gro. | 8 | E18 |
| Braehead Ln. | 8 | E18 |
| Braehead Pk. | 8 | E18 |
| Braehead Rd. | 8 | E18 |
| Braehead Row* =Braehead Av. | | |
| Braehead Vw. | 8 | E18 |
| Braeside Rd. | 48 | P8 |
| Braepark Rd. | 8 | E18 |
| Braid Av. | 31 | L13 |
| Braid Cr. | 31 | L13 |
| Braid Farm Rd. | 31 | L13 |
| Braid Hills | 42 | M12 |
| Braid Hills Approach | 31 | L12 |
| Braid Hills Av. | 31 | L13 |
| Braid Hills Cr. | 31 | L12 |
| Braid Hills Dr. | 32 | M13 |
| Braid Hills Golf Course | 41 | M12 |
| Braid Hills Rd. | 41 | L12 |
| Braid Mount | 41 | L12 |
| Braid Mt. Crest | 41 | L12 |
| Braid Mt. Rise | 41 | L12 |
| Braid Mt. Vw. | 41 | L12 |
| Braid Rd. | 31 | L12 |
| Braidburn Cr. | 31 | L13 |
| Braidburn Terr. | 31 | L13 |
| Braidburn Valley Pk. | 41 | L12 |
| Bramble Dr. | 16 | E17 |
| Bramdean Gro. | 41 | L12 |
| Bramdean Pl. | 41 | L12 |
| Bramdean Rise | 41 | L12 |
| Bramdean Vw. | 41 | L12 |
| Brampton Lodge | 26 | B13 |
| Brand Dr. | 23 | R15 |
| Brand Gdns. | 23 | S16 |
| Brand Pl.*=Abbeyhill | | |
| Brandfield St. | 6 | L15 |
| Brandon St. | 20 | M17 |
| Brandon Terr. | 20 | M17 |
| Brass Rubbing Centre | 7 | N16 |
| Bread St. | 6 | L16 |
| Bread St. La.*=Bread St. | | |
| Bread Terr. | 19 | L16 |
| Breadalbane St. | 12 | N19 |
| Breadalbane Terr. | 19 | L16 |
| Brewery La.* =Great Junction St. | | |
| Briarbank Terr. | 30 | K14 |
| Brickfield*=Pipe St. | | |
| Brickwork Cl.*=Giles St. | | |
| Bridge End | 33 | O14 |
| Bridge Pl. | 19 | L17 |
| Bridge Rd. | 39 | H11 |
| Bridge Rd. | 45 | C9 |
| Bridge St. | 22 | R17 |
| Bridge St. La. | 22 | R17 |
| Bridge St., Muss. | 25 | V15 |
| Briery Bauks | 7 | N15 |
| Bright Terr. | 19 | L16 |
| Brighton Pk | 22 | R16 |
| Brighton Pl. | 22 | R16 |
| Brighton St. | 7 | M16 |
| Bright's Cr. | 32 | N14 |
| Bristo Pl. | 7 | M16 |
| Bristo Port | 7 | M16 |
| Bristo Sq. | 7 | M16 |
| British Geological Survey | 32 | M14 |
| British Geological Survey | 32 | N13 |
| Britwell Cr. | 22 | P17 |
| Broad Wynd | 12 | O19 |
| Broombank Terr. | 29 | F14 |
| Broomburn Gro. | 29 | G15 |
| Broomfield Cr. | 29 | G14 |
| Broomhall Av. | 29 | F14 |
| Broomhall Bk. | 28 | F15 |
| Broomhall Cr. | 28 | F15 |
| Broomhall Dr. | 28 | F15 |
| Broomhall Gdns. | 28 | F15 |
| Broomhall Ln. | 28 | F15 |
| Broomhall Pk. | 28 | F15 |
| Broomhall Pl. | 28 | F15 |
| Broomhall Rd. | 28 | F15 |
| Broomhall Terr. | 28 | F15 |
| Broomhill Dr. | 49 | T9 |
| Broomhill Ho. | 49 | S9 |
| Broomhill Pk. | 49 | T9 |
| Broomhills | 42 | M10 |
| Broomhouse Av. | 29 | F14 |
| Broomhouse Bk. | 29 | G14 |
| Broomhouse Cotts. E. | 29 | G14 |
| Broomhouse Cotts. W. | 29 | F14 |
| Broomhouse Ct. | 29 | G14 |
| Broomhouse Cr. | 29 | G14 |
| Broomhouse Dr. | 29 | F14 |
| Broomhouse Gdns. | 29 | F14 |
| Broomhouse Gdns. E. | 29 | G14 |
| Broomhouse Gdns. W. | 29 | F14 |
| Broomhouse Gro. | 29 | G14 |
| Broomhouse Ln. | 29 | G14 |
| Broomhouse Market | 29 | G14 |
| Broomhouse Medway | 29 | G14 |
| Broomhouse Pk. | 29 | F14 |
| Broomhouse Path | 29 | F14 |
| Broomhouse Pl. N. | 29 | F14 |
| Broomhouse Pl. S. | 29 | G14 |
| Broomhouse Rd. | 28 | F14 |
| Broomhouse Row | 29 | G14 |
| Broomhouse Sch. | 29 | G14 |
| Broomhouse Sq. | 29 | G14 |
| Broomhouse St. N. | 29 | F14 |
| Broomhouse St. S. | 29 | G13 |
| Broomhouse Terr. | 29 | G14 |
| Broomhouse Walk | 29 | G14 |
| Broomhouse Way | 29 | G14 |
| Broomhouse Wynd | 29 | G14 |
| Broomieknowe | 49 | R8 |
| Broomieknowe Gdns. | 49 | R8 |
| Broomieknowe Golf Course | 49 | S9 |
| Broomieknowe Pk. | 49 | R8 |
| Broomlea Cr. | 29 | F15 |
| Broompark Rd. | 29 | F15 |
| Broomside Terr. | 29 | G15 |
| Broomview Ho. | 29 | F13 |
| Broomyknowe | 40 | H12 |
| Brougham Pl. | 6 | M15 |
| Brougham St. | 6 | L15 |
| Broughton Market | 7 | M17 |
| Broughton Pl. | 20 | M17 |
| Broughton Rd. | 12 | M18 |
| Broughton Sch. | 12 | M18 |
| Broughton Sch. (Sec.) | 19 | K17 |
| Broughton St. | 7 | M17 |
| Broughton St. La. | 7 | M17 |
| Brown St. | 7 | N22 |
| Brown's Cl.*=Canongate | | |
| Brown's Pl.*=Vennel | | |
| Bruce Gdns., Dalk. | 50 | U9 |
| Bruce St. | 31 | L13 |
| Brunstane Bk. | 23 | S15 |
| Brunstane Cr. | 23 | S15 |
| Brunstane Dr. | 23 | S15 |
| Brunstane Gdns. | 23 | S16 |
| Brunstane Gdns. Mews* =Brunstane Gdns. | | |
| Brunstane Mill | 24 | T16 |
| Brunstane Rd. | 23 | S16 |
| Brunstane Rd. N. | 23 | S16 |
| Brunstane Rd. S. | 23 | S15 |
| Brunstane Sch. | 23 | S15 |
| Brunstanegate | 23 | S15 |
| Brunswick Pl. | 20 | N17 |
| Brunswick Rd. | 20 | N17 |
| Brunswick St. | 20 | N17 |
| Brunswick St. La. | 20 | N17 |
| Brunton Gdns.* =Montgomery St. | | |
| Brunton Hall and Theatre, Muss. | 25 | V15 |
| Brunton Pl. | 20 | N17 |
| Brunton Terr. | 20 | N17 |
| Brunton's Cl.*=High St. | | |
| Bruntsfield Av. | 31 | L15 |
| Bruntsfield Cr. | 31 | L15 |
| Bruntsfield Gdns. | 31 | L15 |
| Bruntsfield Golf Course | 8 | F19 |
| Bruntsfield Health Centre | 31 | L15 |
| Bruntsfield Links | 32 | L15 |
| Bruntsfield Pl. | 31 | L15 |
| Bruntsfield Sch. | 31 | L15 |
| Bruntsfield Terr. | 31 | L15 |
| Bryce Av. | 22 | Q17 |
| Bryce Cr. | 38 | E11 |
| Bryce Gdns.*=Bryce Rd. | | |
| Bryce Gro. | 22 | Q17 |
| Bryce Pl. | 38 | E11 |
| Bryce Rd. | 38 | E11 |
| Bryson Rd. | 31 | K15 |
| Buccleuch Pl. | 7 | M15 |
| Buccleuch St. | 7 | N15 |
| Buccleuch St., Dalk. | 50 | U10 |
| Buccleuch Terr. | 20 | N15 |
| Buchanan St. | 12 | N18 |
| Buckingham Terr. | 19 | K17 |
| Buckstane Park | 41 | L12 |
| Buckstone Av. | 41 | L11 |
| Buckstone Bk. | 41 | L12 |
| Buckstone Circle | 41 | M11 |
| Buckstone Circle S. | 41 | M11 |
| Buckstone Cl. | 41 | M11 |
| Buckstone Ct. | 41 | L11 |
| Buckstone Cr. | 41 | L12 |
| Buckstone Crook | 41 | M11 |
| Buckstone Dell | 41 | L12 |
| Buckstone Dr. | 41 | L12 |
| Buckstone Gdns. | 41 | L11 |
| Buckstone Gate | 41 | M11 |
| Buckstone Gr. | 41 | L11 |

| | | |
|---|---|---|
| Buckstone Gro. | 41 | L12 |
| Buckstonehead | 41 | M11 |
| Buckstone Hill | 41 | L12 |
| Buckstone Howe | 41 | M11 |
| Buckstone Lea | 41 | M11 |
| Buckstone Ln. | 41 | L15 |
| Buckstone Ln. E. | 41 | M11 |
| Buckstone Neuk | 41 | M11 |
| Buckstone Pl. | 41 | L11 |
| Buckstone Rise | 41 | M11 |
| Buckstone Rd. | 41 | L11 |
| Buckstone Row | 41 | M12 |
| Buckstone Sch. | 41 | M11 |
| Buckstone Shaw | 41 | M11 |
| Buckstoneside* =Buckstone Circle | | |
| Buckstone Terr. | 41 | L11 |
| Buckstone Vw. | 41 | L12 |
| Buckstone Way | 41 | L12 |
| Buckstone Wood | 41 | L11 |
| Buckstone Wynd | 41 | M11 |
| Bughtlin Dr. | 16 | E17 |
| Bughtlin Gdns. | 16 | E16 |
| Bughtlin Gr. | 16 | E16 |
| Bughtlin Ln. | 16 | E16 |
| Bughtlin Market | 16 | E16 |
| Bughtlin Pk. | 16 | E16 |
| Bughtlin Pl. | 16 | E17 |
| Bull's Cl. | 7 | N16 |
| Burdiehouse Av. | 42 | O10 |
| Burdiehouse Burn Pk. | 43 | P10 |
| Burdiehouse Cr. | 43 | O10 |
| Burdiehouse Crossway | 42 | O10 |
| Burdiehouse Dr. | 42 | O10 |
| Burdiehouse Ln. | 42 | O10 |
| Burdiehouse Medway | 42 | O10 |
| Burdiehouse Pl. | 42 | O10 |
| Burdiehouse Rd. | 42 | O10 |
| Burdiehouse Sch. | 43 | O10 |
| Burdiehouse Sq. | 42 | O10 |
| Burdiehouse St. | 42 | O10 |
| Burdiehouse Terr. | 42 | O10 |
| Burgess St. | 12 | O19 |
| Burgess Terr. | 33 | O14 |
| Burghlee Cr. | 47 | P8 |
| Burghlee Terr. | 47 | P8 |
| Burghtoft | 43 | Q18 |
| Burlington St. | 12 | N19 |
| Burnbrae | 16 | E16 |
| Burndene Dr. | 47 | O9 |
| Burnhead Cr. | 42 | O11 |
| Burnhead Gro. | 42 | O11 |
| Burnhead Ln. | 42 | O11 |
| Burnhead Path E. | 42 | O11 |
| Burnhead Path W. | 42 | O11 |
| Burns St. | 12 | O18 |
| Burnside | 16 | E16 |
| Burnside Pk. | 44 | B9 |
| Bush St., Muss. | 24 | U16 |
| Bush Terr., Muss. | 24 | U15 |
| Bus Sta. | 7 | M17 |
| Cables Wynd | 12 | N19 |
| Cables Wynd Ho. | 12 | N19 |
| Caddell's Row | 8 | E19 |
| Cadiz St. | 12 | O19 |
| Cadogan Rd. | 42 | O12 |
| Cadzow Pl. | 21 | O17 |
| Caerketton Cotts. | 40 | K12 |
| Caerketton Ct. | 40 | K12 |
| Caerlaverock Ct.* =Craigievar Wynd | | |
| Cairds Row, Muss. | 24 | U16 |
| Cairns Dr. | 44 | B8 |
| Cairns Gdns. | 44 | B8 |
| Cairngorm Ho. | 12 | N19 |
| Cairnmuir Rd. | 17 | G16 |
| Cairnpark Sch. | 30 | H13 |
| Cairntows Close | 33 | P14 |
| Caithness Pl.*=Clark Rd. | | |
| Caithness Pl. | 11 | L19 |
| Caiy Stane | 41 | L11 |
| Caiyside | 41 | L10 |
| Caiystane Av. | 41 | L11 |
| Caiystane Cr. | 41 | L11 |
| Caiystane Dr. | 41 | K11 |
| Caiystane Gdns. | 41 | K11 |
| Caiystane Hill | 41 | L11 |
| Caiystane Terr. | 41 | K11 |
| Caiystane Vw. | 41 | L11 |
| Calder Ct. | 28 | F13 |
| Calder Cr. | 28 | E13 |
| Calder Dr. | 28 | F13 |
| Calder Gdns. | 28 | E13 |
| Calder Gro. | 28 | F13 |
| Calder Pk. | 28 | F13 |
| Calder Pl. | 28 | F13 |
| Calder Rd. | 36 | A12 |
| Calder Rd. Gdns. | 29 | H14 |
| Calder Vw. | 28 | E13 |
| Caledonian Cr. | 19 | K15 |
| Caledonian Pl. | 19 | K15 |
| Caledonian Rd. | 19 | L15 |
| Calton Hill | 7 | N17 |
| Calton Hill (Street) | 7 | N17 |
| Calton New Burial Ground | 7 | N17 |
| Calton Rd. | 7 | N16 |
| Cambridge Av. | 12 | N18 |
| Cambridge Gdns. | 12 | N18 |
| Cambridge St. | 6 | L16 |
| Cambridge St. La. | 6 | L16 |
| Cambusnethan St. | 21 | O17 |
| Cameo Cinema | 6 | L15 |
| Cameron Cr. | 33 | O14 |
| Cameron Ho. Av | 33 | O14 |
| Cameron March | 33 | O14 |
| Cameron Pk. | 33 | O14 |
| Cameron Smail Rd. | 37 | D12 |
| Cameron Terr. | 33 | O14 |
| Cameron Toll | 33 | O14 |
| Cameron Toll Gdns. | 33 | O14 |
| Cameron Toll Shopping Centre | 33 | O14 |
| Cammo Bk. | 16 | E17 |
| Cammo Brae | 16 | E17 |
| Cammo Cr. | 16 | E17 |
| Cammo Gdns. | 16 | E17 |
| Cammo Gro. | 16 | D17 |
| Cammo Hill | 16 | D17 |
| Cammo Home Farm | 15 | D17 |
| Cammo Parkway | 16 | E17 |
| Cammo Pl. | 16 | E17 |
| Cammo Rd. | 15 | C17 |
| Cammo Walk | 16 | D17 |
| Campbell Av. | 18 | J16 |
| Campbell Pk. | 39 | G11 |
| Campbell Park Cr. | 39 | G11 |
| Campbell Park Dr. | 39 | G11 |
| Campbell Rd. | 18 | J16 |
| Campbell's Cl.* =Calton Rd. | | |
| Campie Court* =Campie Gdns. | | |
| Campie Gdns., Muss. | 24 | U15 |
| Campie La., Muss. | 24 | U15 |
| Campie Rd., Muss. | 24 | U15 |
| Campie Sch., Muss. | 24 | U15 |
| Campview | 51 | R12 |
| Campview Av. | 51 | R12 |
| Campview Cr. | 51 | R12 |
| Campview Gdns. | 51 | R12 |
| Campview Gro. | 51 | S12 |
| Campview Rd. | 49 | R8 |
| Campview Terr. | 51 | R12 |
| Camus Av. | 41 | L11 |
| Camus Pk. | 41 | L11 |
| Camus Pl. E. | 41 | L11 |
| Camus Rd. E. | 41 | L11 |
| Camus Rd. W. | 41 | L11 |
| Canaan Home | 31 | L14 |
| Canaan La. | 31 | L14 |
| Canaan Lodge | 31 | L14 |
| Candlemaker Row | 7 | M16 |
| Candlemaker's Cr. | 43 | Q11 |
| Candlemaker's Pk. | 43 | Q11 |
| Canning St. | 6 | L16 |
| Canning St. La. | 6 | L16 |
| Cannon Film Centre | 6 | L16 |
| Cannon Wynd | 12 | N19 |
| Canon La. | 20 | M17 |
| Canon St. | 20 | M17 |
| Canongate | 7 | N16 |
| Canongate Tolbooth | 7 | N16 |
| Canonmills | 20 | M18 |
| Canonmills Sch. | 20 | M17 |
| Capelaw Ct. | 40 | K12 |
| Capelaw Rd. | 39 | H11 |
| Captain's Dr. | 42 | O11 |
| Captain's Ln. | 42 | O11 |
| Captain's Rd. | 42 | O11 |
| Captain's Row | 42 | O11 |
| Carberry Pl. | 18 | K16 |
| Carberry Rd., Muss. | 25 | V14 |
| Carfrae Gdns. | 17 | H17 |
| Carfrae Gro. | 17 | H17 |
| Carfrae Pk. | 17 | H17 |
| Carfrae Rd. | 18 | H17 |
| Cargil Ct. | 11 | L19 |
| Cargil Terr. | 11 | L19 |
| Cargilfield Sch. | 8 | E18 |
| Carlton Cricket Grd. | 32 | M14 |
| Carlton St. | 6 | L17 |
| Carlton Terr. | 7 | N17 |
| Carlton Terr. Brae | 7 | N17 |
| Carlton Terr. La. | 7 | N17 |
| Carlton Terr. Mews | 7 | N17 |
| Carlyle Pl. | 21 | O17 |
| Carlyle Pl., Muss. | 24 | V15 |
| Carnegie Ct. | 7 | N16 |
| Carnethy Av. | 39 | H11 |
| Caroline Gdns. | 17 | G16 |
| Caroline Pk. | 10 | J20 |
| Caroline Park Av. | 10 | J20 |
| Caroline Park Gro. | 10 | J19 |
| Caroline Pl. | 17 | G16 |
| Caroline Terr. | 16 | F16 |
| Carpet La.*=Bernard St. | | |
| Carrick Cr., Dalk. | 50 | V8 |
| Carrick Knowe Av. | 29 | G15 |
| Carrick Knowe Dr. | 29 | G15 |
| Carrick Knowe Gdns. | 29 | G15 |
| Carrick Knowe Golf Course | 29 | H15 |
| Carrick Knowe Gro. | 29 | G15 |
| Carrick Knowe Hill | 29 | G15 |
| Carrick Knowe Ln. | 29 | G15 |
| Carrick Knowe Parkway | 29 | G15 |
| Carrick Knowe Pl. | 29 | G15 |
| Carrick Knowe Rd. | 29 | G14 |
| Carrick Knowe Sch. | 29 | G15 |
| Carrick Knowe Terr. | 29 | G15 |
| Carrington Cr.* =Crewe Rd. | | |
| Carrington Rd. | 19 | K17 |
| Carron Pl. | 13 | O19 |
| Carrubber's Cl.*=High St. | | |
| Casselbank St. | 12 | N18 |
| Cassel's La. | 12 | N18 |
| Castle | 6 | M16 |
| Castle Av. | 29 | F15 |
| Castle Esplanade | 6 | M16 |
| Castle Gogar | 15 | C16 |
| Castle St. | 6 | L16 |
| Castle Terr. | 6 | L16 |
| Castle Wynd N. | 20 | M16 |
| Castle Wynd S. | 20 | M16 |
| Castlebrae Sch. | 34 | Q14 |
| Castlebrae Sch. Annexe | 34 | Q14 |
| Castlehill | 6 | M16 |
| Castlelaw Rd. | 39 | H11 |
| Castleview Ho. | 33 | P12 |
| Cat & Dog Home | 13 | Q18 |
| Cathcart Pl. | 19 | K15 |
| Cathedral La. | 7 | M17 |
| Catherine Pl. | 11 | M18 |
| Catherine Pl.* =Canonmills | | |
| Cattle Rd. | 30 | H14 |
| Cauldcoats | 35 | R13 |
| Causeway, The | 21 | P15 |
| Causewayside | 32 | N15 |
| Cavalry Park Dr. | 22 | P15 |
| Cedars, The | 39 | H12 |
| Central Library | 7 | M16 |
| Chalmers Bdgs.* =Fountainbridge | | |
| Chalmers Cl.*=High St. | | |
| Chalmers Cr. | 32 | M15 |
| Chalmers Hosp. | 6 | M16 |

Chalmers St. 20 M15
Chamberlain Rd. 31 L14
Chambers St. 7 M16
Champigny Ct., Muss. 25 W15
Chancelot Cr. 12 M19
Chancelot Gro. 11 M19
Chancelot Mills 12 N20
Chancelot Terr. 12 M19
Chapel Ct. 34 Q14
Chapel La.*=Maritime St.
Chapel St. 7 N15
Chapel Wynd*=West Port
Charlesfield*=Bristo Sq.
Charles St. 7 M16
Charles St. La. 7 M23
Charlotte La. 6 L16
Charlotte Sq. 6 L16
Charterhall Gro. 32 M14
Charterhall Rd. 32 M13
Chatterrig 40 V12
Cherry Tree Av. 45 C10
Cherry Tree Cr. 45 D10
Cherry Tree Gdns. 45 C10
Cherry Tree Gro. 45 C10
Cherry Tree Ln. 45 D10
Cherry Tree Pk. 45 C10
Cherry Tree Vw. 45 D10
Chessels Ct. 20 N16
Chesser Av. 30 H14
Chesser Cotts.*
=Gorgie Rd.
Chesser Cr. 30 J14
Chesser Gdns. 30 H14
Chesser Gro. 30 H14
Chesser Ho. 30 H14
Chesser Ln. 30 H14
Chester St. 19 L16
Chestnut St. 10 K20
Cheyne St. 19 L17
Christian Cr. 23 R16
Christian Gro. 23 R16
Christian Path 22 R16
Christiemiller Av. 22 Q17
Christiemiller Gro. 22 Q17
Christiemiller Pl. 22 Q17
Church Hill 31 L14
Church Hill Pl. 31 L14
Church Hill Theatre 31 L14
Church Hill Dr. 31 L14
Church La., Muss. 24 V15
Church Rd. 48 Q9
Church St. 47 P8
Church St. 25 V15
Circle, The 51 R12
Circus Gdns. 6 L17
Circus La. 6 L17
Citadel Ct. 12 N19
Citadel St. 12 N19
Citadel Pl.*
=Commercial St.
City Art Centre 7 M16
City Chambers 7 M16
City Hosp. 30 K12
City Observatory 7 N17
City of Edinburgh Bypass 27 D14
Civil Service Sports Grd. 9 H19
Clackmae Gro. 42 N12
Clackmae Rd. 42 N12
Clapper La. 33 O13
Clapperton Pl.*
=Lower London Rd.
Clarebank Cr. 13 O18
Claremont Bk. 12 M17
Claremont Ct. 12 M18
Claremont Cr. 12 M29
Claremont Gdns. 13 O18
Claremont Gro. 12 M18
Claremont Pk. 13 O18
Claremont Rd. 13 O18
Clarence St. 19 L17
Clarendon Cr. 19 L17
Clarinda Gdns., Dalk. 50 V9
Clarinda Terr. 33 O13
Clark Av. 11 M19
Clark Pl. 11 L19
Clark Rd. 11 L19
Claverhouse Dr. 33 O12
Clayhills Gro. 44 B9
Clayhills Pk. 44 B9
Clayknowes Dr., Muss. 24 T15
Clayknowes Pl., Muss. 24 U15
Clayknowes Rd., Muss. 24 U15
Clayknowes Wy., Muss. 24 U15
Clearburn Cr. 33 O14
Clearburn Gdns. 33 O14
Clearburn Rd. 33 O14
Cleekim Dr. 34 R14
Cleekim Rd. 34 R14
Cleikiminfield 35 R14
Cleikiminrig 35 R14
Clerk St. 20 N15
Clerk St. 47 P8
Clermiston Av. 16 F17
Clermiston Cr. 17 F17
Clermiston Dr. 16 F17
Clermiston Gdns. 17 F17
Clermiston Gr. 16 F17
Clermiston Gro. 17 F17
Clermiston Hill 17 F17
Clermiston Ln. 16 F17
Clermiston Medway 17 F17
Clermiston Pk. (st.) 17 F17
Clermiston Pk. 16 F17
Clermiston Pl. 17 F17
Clermiston Rd. 17 G16
Clermiston Rd. N. 17 G17
Clermiston Sch. 16 F17
Clermiston Terr. 17 G16
Clermiston Vw. 17 G17
Clerwood Bk. 16 F16
Clerwood Gdns. 16 F16
Clerwood Gro. 17 G16
Clerwood Ln. 16 F16
Clerwood Pk. 17 F16
Clerwood Pl. 17 G16
Clerwood Row 16 F16
Clerwood Terr. 17 G16
Clerwood Vw. 17 G16
Clerwood Way 16 F16
Clifton Sq.*
=Baileyfield Rd.
Clifton Terr. 19 L16
Clinton Rd. 31 L14
Clockmill La. 21 O17
Clovenstone Dr. 39 G12
Clovenstone Gdns. 39 G12
Clovenstone Pk. 39 G12
Clovenstone Rd. 39 G12
Clovenstone Sch. 39 G12
Cluny Av. 31 L13
Cluny Dr. 31 L13
Cluny Gdns. 31 L13
Cluny Pl. 31 M14
Cluny Terr. 31 L13
Clyde St. 7 M17
Coalhill 12 N19
Coates Cr. 6 L16
Coates Gdns. 19 K16
Coates Pl. 19 L16
Coatfield La. 12 O19
Cobbinshaw Ho. 28 F13
Cobden Cr. 32 N14
Cobden Rd. 32 N14
Cobden Terr. 19 L16
Coburg St. 12 N19
Cochran Pl.*
=East London St.
Cochran Terr. 20 M17
Cochrane Pl. 13 O18
Cockburn 44 A8
Cockburn Cr. 44 C8
Cockburn St. 7 M16
Cockburnhill Rd. 44 B8
Cockit Hat Plantation 40 K11
Cocklaw 37 C11
Cockmylane 41 K11
Coffin La. 19 K15
Coillesdene Av. 23 S16
Coillesdene Cr. 23 S16
Coillesdene Dr. 23 S16
Coillesdene Gdns. 23 S16
Coillesdene Gro. 23 S16
Coillesdene Ho. 23 S16
Coillesdene Ln. 23 T16
Coillesdene Terr. 23 S16
Colinton Castle 39 H12
Colinton Dell 39 H12
Colinton Gro. 30 J13
Colinton Grove W. 30 J13
Colinton Mains Cr. 40 K11
Colinton Mains Dr. 40 J12
Colinton Mains Gdns. 40 J12
Colinton Mains Gr. 40 J12
Colinton Mains Gro. 40 K12
Colinton Mains Ln. 40 J12
Colinton Mains Pk. 40 K12
Colinton Mains Pl. 40 K12
Colinton Mains Rd. 40 J12
Colinton Mains Terr. 40 K12
Colinton Rd. 30 J13
Colinton Sch. (Primary) 40 J12
College St. S. 7 M16
College St. W. 7 M16
College Wynd*=Cowgate
Collins Pl. 19 L17
Colmestone Gate 41 L11
Coltbridge Av. 18 J16
Coltbridge Gdns. 18 K16
Coltbridge Terr. 18 J16
Coltbridge Vale 18 K16
Columba Av. 18 H17
Columba Rd. 18 H17
Colville Pl. 19 L17
Comely Bk. 19 K17
Comely Bank Av. 19 L17
Comely Bank Cem. 18 K17
Comely Bank Gro. 19 K17
Comely Bank Pl. 19 L17
Comely Bk. Pl. Mews 19 L17
Comely Bank Rd. 19 K17
Comely Bank Row 19 L17
Comely Bank St. 19 K17
Comely Bank Terr. 19 L17
Comely Gr. Cr. 21 O17
Comely Gr. Pl. 21 O17
Comiston Dr. 31 K13
Comiston Gdns. 31 L13
Comiston Gro. 41 L12
Comiston Pl. 31 L13
Comiston Rise 41 L12
Comiston Rd. 41 L12
Comiston Sch. 40 K11
Comiston Springs Av. 41 L12
Comiston Terr. 31 L13
Comiston Vw. 41 L12
Commercial St. 12 N19
Connaught Pl. 12 M19
Considine Gdns. 21 P17
Considine Terr. 21 P17
Constitution Pl. 12 O19
Constitution St. 12 O19
Convening Ct.*
=Dean Path
Corbiehill Av. 9 H18
Corbiehill Cr. 9 G18
Corbiehill Gdns. 9 H18
Corbiehill Gro. 9 H18
Corbiehill Pk. 9 H18
Corbiehill Pl. 9 G18
Corbiehill Rd. 9 G18
Corbiehill Terr. 9 G18
Corbieshot 35 R15
Corn Exchange 30 J14
Cornhill Terr. 13 O29
Cornwall St. 6 L16
Cornwallis Pl. 12 M17
Coronation Walk 19 M15
Corporation Bdgs.*
=Sheriff Brae
Corrennie Dr. 31 L13
Corrennie Gdns. 31 L13
Corslet Cr. 38 E11
Corslet Pl. 38 E11
Corslet Rd. 38 E11
Corstorphine Bank Av. 16 F16
Corstorphine Bank Dr. 16 F16
Corstorphine Bank Terr. 16 F16
Corstorphine High St. 16 F15
Corstorphine Hill 17 G17
Corstorphine Hill Av. 17 G16

| | | |
|---|---|---|
| Corstorphine Hill Cem. | 16 | F16 |
| Corstorphine Hill Cr. | 17 | G16 |
| Corstorphine Hill Gdns. | 17 | G16 |
| Corstorphine Hill Rd. | 17 | G16 |
| Corstorphine Hosp. | 17 | G15 |
| Corstorphine Ho. Av. | 17 | G15 |
| Corstorphine Ho. Terr. | 17 | G15 |
| Corstorphine Park | 17 | G15 |
| Corstorphine Park Gdns. | 17 | G15 |
| Corstorphine Rd. | 17 | G15 |
| Corstorphine Sch. | 16 | F15 |
| Cortleferry Dr. | 49 | T9 |
| Cortleferry Gro. | 49 | T8 |
| Cortleferry Pk. | 49 | T9 |
| Cortleferry Terr. | 49 | T9 |
| Corunna Pl. | 12 | N19 |
| Cottage Gr. | 8 | E18 |
| Cottage Homes | 40 | H11 |
| Cottage La., Muss. | 25 | W15 |
| Cottage Pk. | 17 | H17 |
| County Hall | 7 | M16 |
| Couper St. | 12 | N19 |
| Cowan Rd. | 30 | K14 |
| Cowan's Cl. | 7 | N15 |
| Cowden Cr., Dalk. | 50 | V10 |
| Cowden Gr., Dalk. | 50 | V10 |
| Cowden La., Dalk. | 50 | V10 |
| Cowden Pk., Dalk. | 50 | V10 |
| Cowden Terr., Dalk. | 50 | V10 |
| Cowden Vw., Dalk. | 50 | V10 |
| Cowgate | 7 | M16 |
| Cowgatehead | 20 | M16 |
| Cowpits Rd. | 25 | W13 |
| Coxfield | 30 | J14 |
| Craighall Terr., Muss. | 25 | W15 |
| Craig Ho.* =Thomas Clouston Clinic | | |
| Craig Pk. | 35 | S14 |
| Craigcrook Av. | 17 | G17 |
| Craigcrook Gdns. | 18 | H17 |
| Craigcrook Gro. | 18 | H17 |
| Craigcrook Pk. | 17 | H17 |
| Craigcrook Pl. | 18 | H17 |
| Craigcrook Rd. | 17 | G17 |
| Craigcrook Sq. | 17 | H17 |
| Craigcrook Terr. | 18 | H17 |
| Craigentinny Av. | 22 | Q17 |
| Craigentinny Av. N. | 13 | P18 |
| Craigentinny Cr. | 22 | Q17 |
| Craigentinny Golf Course | 13 | P18 |
| Craigentinny Gro. | 22 | Q17 |
| Craigentinny Pl. | 22 | Q17 |
| Craigentinny Rd. | 22 | P17 |
| Craigentinny Sch. | 22 | P17 |
| Craighall Av. | 11 | M19 |
| Craighall Bk. | 11 | M19 |
| Craighall Cr. | 11 | M19 |
| Craighall Gdns. | 11 | M19 |
| Craighall Rd. | 11 | M19 |
| Craighall Terr. | 11 | M19 |
| Craighill Gdns. | 31 | K13 |
| Craighouse Av. | 31 | K13 |
| Craighouse Gdns. | 31 | K13 |
| Craighouse Pk. | 31 | K13 |
| Craighouse Rd. | 31 | K13 |
| Craighouse Terr. | 31 | K13 |
| Craigievar Ct.* =Craigievar Wynd | | |
| Craigievar Sq. | 16 | E16 |
| Craigievar Wynd | 16 | E16 |
| Craigilfield Sch. | 8 | E18 |
| Craiglea Dr. | 31 | K13 |
| Craiglea Pl. | 31 | K13 |
| Craigleith Av. N. | 18 | J16 |
| Craigleith Av. S. | 18 | J16 |
| Craigleith Bk. | 18 | J17 |
| Craigleith Cr. | 18 | J17 |
| Craigleith Dr. | 18 | J17 |
| Craigleith Gdns. | 18 | J17 |
| Craigleith Gro. | 18 | J17 |
| Craigleith Hill | 18 | J17 |
| Craigleith Hill Av. | 18 | J17 |
| Craigleith Hill Cr. | 18 | J17 |
| Craigleith Hill Gdns. | 18 | J17 |
| Craigleith Hill Gr. | 18 | J17 |

| | | |
|---|---|---|
| Craigleith Hill Gro. | 18 | J17 |
| Craigleith Hill Ln. | 18 | J17 |
| Craigleith Hill Pk. | 18 | J17 |
| Craigleith Hill Row | 18 | J17 |
| Craigleith Rise | 18 | J16 |
| Craigleith Rd. | 18 | J17 |
| Craigleith Vw. | 18 | J16 |
| Craiglockhart Av. | 30 | J13 |
| Craiglockhart Bk. | 30 | J13 |
| Craiglockhart Cr. | 30 | J13 |
| Craiglockhart Dell | 30 | J13 |
| Craiglockhart Dell Rd. | 30 | J13 |
| Craiglockhart Dr. N. | 30 | J13 |
| Craiglockhart Dr. S. | 30 | J13 |
| Craiglockhart Gdns. | 30 | J13 |
| Craiglockhart Golf Course | 30 | K13 |
| Craiglockhart Gro. | 30 | J12 |
| Craiglockhart Ln. | 30 | J13 |
| Craiglockhart Pk. | 30 | J13 |
| Craiglockhart Pl. | 30 | J13 |
| Craiglockhart Qt. | 30 | J13 |
| Craiglockhart Rd. | 30 | J12 |
| Craiglockhart Rd. N. | 30 | J13 |
| Craiglockhart Sch. | 31 | K14 |
| Craiglockhart Sports Centre | 30 | J13 |
| Craiglockhart Terr. | 30 | K14 |
| Craiglockhart Vw. | 30 | J13 |
| Craigmillar Castle | 34 | P13 |
| Craigmillar Castle Av. | 34 | P14 |
| Craigmillar Castle Gdns. | 34 | P14 |
| Craigmillar Castle Gro. | 34 | P14 |
| Craigmillar Castle Ln. | 34 | Q14 |
| Craigmillar Castle Rd. | 34 | P14 |
| Craigmillar Castle | 34 | P14 |
| Craigmillar Ct. | 33 | P14 |
| Craigmillar Pk. (street) | 33 | N14 |
| Craigmillar Pk. | 34 | P14 |
| Craigmillar Park Golf Course | 32 | N13 |
| Craigmillar Sch. | 34 | Q14 |
| Craigmount Appr. | 16 | F16 |
| Craigmount Av. | 16 | F16 |
| Craigmount Av. N. | 16 | E17 |
| Craigmount Bk. | 16 | E17 |
| Craigmount Bank W. | 16 | E17 |
| Craigmount Brae | 16 | E17 |
| Craigmount Cr. | 16 | E16 |
| Craigmount Ct. | 16 | E17 |
| Craigmount Dr. | 16 | E16 |
| Craigmount Gdns. | 16 | E16 |
| Craigmount Gro. | 16 | E16 |
| Craigmount Gro. N. | 16 | E16 |
| Craigmount Hill | 16 | E17 |
| Craigmount Ln. | 16 | E16 |
| Craigmount Pk. | 16 | E16 |
| Craigmount Pl. | 16 | E16 |
| Craigmount Sch. | 16 | E16 |
| Craigmount Terr. | 16 | E16 |
| Craigmount Vw. | 16 | E16 |
| Craigmount Way | 16 | F17 |
| Craigmuir Sch. | 10 | J19 |
| Craigour Av. | 43 | Q12 |
| Craigour Cr. | 43 | Q12 |
| Craigour Dr. | 43 | Q12 |
| Craigour Gdns. | 43 | Q12 |
| Craigour Gr. | 43 | P12 |
| Craigour Gro. | 43 | Q12 |
| Craigour Ln. | 43 | Q12 |
| Craigour Pl. | 43 | P12 |
| Craigour Terr. | 43 | Q12 |
| Craigroyston Sch. | 10 | J18 |
| Craigs Av. | 16 | E15 |
| Craigs Bk. | 16 | E16 |
| Craigs Cr. | 16 | E16 |
| Craigs Dr. | 16 | E16 |
| Craigs Gdns. | 16 | E16 |
| Craigs Gro. | 16 | F15 |
| Craigs Ln. | 16 | F16 |
| Craigs Pk. | 16 | E16 |
| Craigs Rd. | 16 | E16 |
| Crame Terr. | 49 | T9 |
| Cramond Av. | 8 | E19 |
| Cramond Bk. | 8 | E19 |
| Cramond Brig Toll | 8 | D18 |
| Cramond Cr. | 8 | E19 |

| | | |
|---|---|---|
| Cramond Gdns. | 8 | E19 |
| Cramond Glebe Gdns. | 8 | F19 |
| Cramond Glebe Rd. | 8 | E19 |
| Cramond Glebe Terr. | 8 | E19 |
| Cramond Gr. | 8 | E19 |
| Cramond Gro. | 8 | E19 |
| Cramond Pk. | 8 | E19 |
| Cramond Pl. | 8 | F19 |
| Cramond Regis | 8 | E18 |
| Cramond Rd. N. | 8 | F19 |
| Cramond Rd. S. | 9 | F19 |
| Cramond Sch. | 8 | E19 |
| Cramond Sch. Annexe | 8 | E19 |
| Cramond Terr. | 8 | E19 |
| Cramond Tower | 8 | F19 |
| Cramond Vale | 8 | E19 |
| Cranston St. | 7 | N16 |
| Crarae Av. | 18 | J16 |
| Craufordland | 8 | E18 |
| Crawford Bridge | 21 | O17 |
| Crawfurd Rd. | 33 | O14 |
| Crescent, The | 31 | L13 |
| Crescent, The* =Gorgie Rd. | | |
| Crewe Bank | 10 | K19 |
| Crewe Cr. | 10 | J19 |
| Crewe Gro. | 10 | K19 |
| Crewe Ln. | 10 | J19 |
| Crewe Path | 10 | J19 |
| Crewe Pl. | 10 | J19 |
| Crewe Rd. Gdns. | 10 | J19 |
| Crewe Rd. N. | 10 | J19 |
| Crewe Rd. S. | 10 | K18 |
| Crewe Rd. W. | 10 | J19 |
| Crewe Terr. | 10 | J19 |
| Crewe Toll | 10 | J18 |
| Crichton St. | 7 | M23 |
| Crighton Pl. | 12 | N18 |
| Croall Pl. | 20 | N17 |
| Croft-an-righ | 21 | N17 |
| Croft St., Dalk. | 50 | U10 |
| Cromwell Pl. | 12 | N19 |
| Crown Office Bldgs. | 7 | N17 |
| Crookston Rd., Muss. | 24 | W14 |
| Cross Rd. | 47 | O8 |
| Crosswood Av. | 44 | B8 |
| Crosswood Cr. | 44 | B8 |
| Crosswood Rd. | 44 | B8 |
| Crown Pl. | 12 | N18 |
| Crown St. | 12 | N18 |
| Cuddy La. | 31 | L14 |
| Cultins Rd. | 28 | E14 |
| Cumberland St. | 19 | M17 |
| Cumberland St. La., N.E. | 19 | M17 |
| Cumberland St. La., N.W. | 19 | M17 |
| Cumberland St. La., S.E. | 19 | M17 |
| Cumberland St. La., S.W. | 19 | M17 |
| Cumin Pl. | 32 | N15 |
| Cumlodden Av. | 18 | J16 |
| Cumnor Cr. | 33 | O13 |
| Cunningham Pl. | 12 | N18 |
| Currie High Sch. | 37 | D10 |
| Curriehill Castle Dr. | 45 | C10 |
| Curriehill Rd. | 37 | C12 |
| Curriehill Sch. | 38 | E10 |
| Curriehill Sta. | 37 | D11 |
| Currievale | 37 | D11 |
| Currievale Dr. | 37 | D10 |
| Currievale Pk. | 37 | D10 |
| Currievale Park Gr. | 37 | D10 |
| Custom Ho. | 12 | O19 |
| Daiches Braes | 23 | S15 |
| Dairsie Pl.*=Stanley Pl. | | |
| Daisy Terr.* =Merchiston Gro. | | |
| Dalgety Av. | 21 | O17 |
| Dalgety Rd. | 21 | O17 |
| Dalgety St. | 21 | O17 |
| Dalhousie Rd. | 50 | T9 |
| Dalhousie Terr. | 31 | L13 |
| Dalkeith Rd. | 32 | N15 |
| Dalkeith Sch., Dalk. | 50 | U10 |
| Dalkeith St. | 23 | S16 |

| | | |
|---|---|---|
| Dalkeith Western Bypass | 49 | S10 |
| Dalmahoy Country Club | 36 | A11 |
| Dalmahoy Cr. | 44 | C10 |
| Dalmahoy Golf Course | 36 | A11 |
| Dalmahoy Mains | 36 | A10 |
| Dalmahoy Rd. | 26 | A13 |
| Dalmeny Pk. | 12 | N18 |
| Dalmeny Rd. | 12 | M19 |
| Dalmeny St. | 12 | N18 |
| Dalry Cem. | 19 | K15 |
| Dalry Pl. | 19 | L16 |
| Dalry Rd. | 19 | K15 |
| Dalry Rd. La.*=Dalry Rd. | | |
| Dalry Sch. | 19 | K15 |
| Dalrymple Cr. | 32 | N14 |
| Dalrymple Cr., Muss. | 24 | U15 |
| Dalrymple Ln., Muss. | 25 | V15 |
| Dalum Ct. | 47 | O8 |
| Dalum Dr. | 47 | O8 |
| Dalum Gr. | 47 | O8 |
| Dalum Ln. | 47 | O8 |
| Dalziel Pl.*=London Rd. | | |
| Damhead | 46 | M8 |
| Damside | 19 | L16 |
| Danderhall Community Leisure Centre | 51 | S12 |
| Danderhall Cr. | 51 | R12 |
| Danderhall Sch. | 51 | R12 |
| Danube St. | 19 | L17 |
| Darling's Bdgs.* =Saunder's St. | | |
| Darnaway St. | 6 | L17 |
| Darnell Rd. | 11 | L19 |
| David Hume Tower | 7 | M15 |
| Davidson Gdns. | 9 | H18 |
| Davidson Pk. | 10 | K18 |
| Davidson Rd. | 10 | J18 |
| Davidson's Mains Pk. | 9 | G18 |
| Davidson's Mains Sch. | 9 | G18 |
| Davie St. | 20 | N16 |
| Dean Bank La. | 19 | L17 |
| Dean Bridge | 6 | L17 |
| Dean Cem. | 19 | K17 |
| Dean Centre | 19 | K16 |
| Dean Park Cr. | 19 | L17 |
| Dean Park Mews | 19 | L17 |
| Dean Park Sch. | 44 | C8 |
| Dean Park School Annexe | 44 | C9 |
| Dean Park St. | 19 | L17 |
| Dean Path | 19 | K17 |
| Dean Path Bdgs.* =Dean Path | | |
| Dean St. | 19 | L17 |
| Dean Terr. | 19 | L17 |
| Deanery Cl. | 21 | P17 |
| Deanhaugh St. | 19 | L17 |
| Deanpark Av. | 44 | C9 |
| Deanpark Bk. | 45 | C9 |
| Deanpark Brae | 45 | C9 |
| Deanpark Ct. | 44 | B9 |
| Deanpark Cr. | 45 | C9 |
| Deanpark Gdns. | 45 | C9 |
| Deanpark Gro. | 45 | C9 |
| Deanpark Pl. | 44 | C9 |
| Deanpark Sq. | 44 | C9 |
| Dechmont Rd. | 16 | E16 |
| Delhaig | 30 | J14 |
| Dell Rd. | 39 | H12 |
| Delta Pl., Muss. | 25 | V14 |
| Denham Green Av. | 11 | L19 |
| Denham Green Pl. | 11 | L30 |
| Denham Green Terr. | 11 | L19 |
| Derby St. | 11 | M19 |
| Devon Pl. | 19 | K16 |
| Dewar Pl. | 6 | L16 |
| Dewar Pl. La. | 6 | L16 |
| Dick Pl. | 32 | M14 |
| Dickson St. | 12 | N18 |
| Dickson's Cl.*=High St. | | |
| Dickson's Ct.*=Bristo St. | | |
| Dinmont Dr. | 33 | O13 |
| Distillery La.*=Dalry Rd. | | |
| Dobbie's Rd. | 49 | R8 |
| Dochart Dr. | 16 | F17 |
| Dock Pl. | 12 | N19 |
| Dock St. | 12 | N19 |
| Dolphin Av. | 37 | D10 |
| Dolphin Gdns. E. | 37 | D10 |
| Dolphin Gdns. W. | 37 | D10 |
| Dolphin Rd. | 37 | D10 |
| Dominion Cinema | 31 | L14 |
| Donaldson's Sch. (for the deaf) | 19 | K16 |
| Dorset Pl. | 19 | L15 |
| Double Dykes, Muss. | 25 | V14 |
| Double Hedges Pk. | 33 | O13 |
| Double Hedges Rd. | 33 | O13 |
| Douglas Cr. | 49 | R8 |
| Douglas Cr. | 19 | K16 |
| Douglas Gdns. | 19 | K16 |
| Douglas Gdns. Mews | 19 | K16 |
| Douglas Terr. | 19 | L16 |
| Doune Terr. | 6 | L17 |
| Dovecot Gro. | 29 | H13 |
| Dovecot Ln. | 29 | H13 |
| Dovecot Pk. (st.) | 29 | H13 |
| Dovecot Pk. | 29 | H13 |
| Dovecot Rd. | 29 | F15 |
| Dowie's Mill La. | 8 | D18 |
| Downfield Pl. | 19 | K15 |
| Downie Gro. | 17 | G15 |
| Downie Pl., Muss. | 25 | V15 |
| Downie Terr. | 17 | G15 |
| Dreghorn Av. | 40 | K11 |
| Dreghorn Dr. | 40 | K11 |
| Dreghorn Gdns. | 40 | K11 |
| Dreghorn Gro. | 40 | K11 |
| Dreghorn Link | 40 | K11 |
| Dreghorn Ln. | 39 | H11 |
| Dreghorn Pk. | 40 | J11 |
| Dreghorn Pl. | 40 | K11 |
| Drum Av. | 43 | Q11 |
| Drum Brae Av. | 16 | F16 |
| Drum Brae Cr. | 16 | F17 |
| Drum Brae Dr. | 16 | F17 |
| Drum Brae Gdns. | 16 | F16 |
| Drum Brae Gro. | 16 | F17 |
| Drum Brae Neuk | 16 | F16 |
| Drum Brae N. | 16 | E17 |
| Drum Brae Pk. (st.) | 16 | F16 |
| Drum Brae Pk. | 16 | F17 |
| Drum Brae Park Appr.* =Drum Brae Pk. | | |
| Drum Brae Pl. | 16 | F16 |
| Drum Brae S. | 16 | F16 |
| Drum Brae Terr. | 16 | F17 |
| Drum Brae Walk | 16 | F17 |
| Drum Cotts. | 43 | Q11 |
| Drum Cr. | 43 | Q11 |
| Drum Farm | 51 | R11 |
| Drum Park Yard* =Albion Rd. | | |
| Drum Pl. | 43 | Q11 |
| Drum St. | 43 | Q11 |
| Drum Terr. | 21 | O17 |
| Drum View Av. | 51 | R12 |
| Drumbrae Sch. | 16 | F16 |
| Drumdryan St. | 6 | M15 |
| Drummond Pl. | 6 | M17 |
| Drummond Sch. | 20 | M17 |
| Drummond St. | 7 | N16 |
| Drumsheugh Gdns. | 6 | L16 |
| Drumsheugh Pl* =Queensferry St. | | |
| Dryden Av. | 47 | O8 |
| Dryden Cr. | 47 | O8 |
| Dryden Gdns. | 12 | N18 |
| Dryden Pl. | 32 | N15 |
| Dryden St. | 12 | N18 |
| Dryden Terr. | 12 | N18 |
| Dryden Terr. | 47 | O8 |
| Dryden Vw. | 47 | O8 |
| Drylaw Av. | 18 | J17 |
| Drylaw Cr. | 18 | H17 |
| Drylaw Gdns. | 18 | H18 |
| Drylaw Gr. | 18 | H17 |
| Drylaw Gro. | 18 | H17 |
| Drylaw Ho. | 10 | H18 |
| Drylaw Ho. Gdns. | 10 | H18 |
| Drylaw Ho. Padd. | 10 | H18 |
| Drylaw Sch. | 10 | J18 |
| Duart Cr. | 16 | F17 |
| Dublin Meuse | 6 | M17 |
| Dublin St. | 7 | M17 |
| Dublin St. La. | 7 | M17 |
| Duddingston Av. | 22 | Q15 |
| Duddingston Cr. | 22 | R15 |
| Duddingston Gdns. N. | 22 | Q16 |
| Duddingston Gdns. S. | 22 | Q15 |
| Duddingston Golf Course | 22 | Q15 |
| Duddingston Gro. E. | 22 | Q16 |
| Duddingston Gro. W. | 22 | Q15 |
| Duddingston Ln. | 22 | Q15 |
| Duddingston Mains Cotts.*=Milton Rd. | | |
| Duddingston Mills Cotts. | 22 | Q16 |
| Duddingston Pk. | 22 | R16 |
| Duddingston Park S. | 34 | R15 |
| Duddingston Rise | 22 | Q15 |
| Duddingston Rd. | 22 | Q16 |
| Duddingston Rd. W. | 22 | P15 |
| Duddingston Row | 22 | Q15 |
| Duddingston Sch. | 22 | Q16 |
| Duddingston Sq. E. | 22 | Q16 |
| Duddingston Sq. W. | 22 | Q16 |
| Duddingston Vw. | 22 | Q15 |
| Duddingston Village | 21 | P15 |
| Duddingston Yards* =Duddingston Pk. S. | | |
| Dudley Av. | 12 | M19 |
| Dudley Av. S. | 12 | N19 |
| Dudley Bk. | 12 | M19 |
| Dudley Cr. | 12 | M19 |
| Dudley Gdns. | 12 | M19 |
| Dudley Gro. | 12 | M19 |
| Dudley Terr. | 12 | M19 |
| Duff St. | 19 | K15 |
| Duff St. La. | 19 | K15 |
| Duke Pl. | 12 | O18 |
| Duke St. | 12 | O18 |
| Duke St., Dalk. | 50 | U10 |
| Duke's Walk | 21 | O17 |
| Dumbiedykes Rd. | 7 | N16 |
| Dumbryden Dr. | 29 | G13 |
| Dumbryden Gdns. | 29 | G13 |
| Dumbryden Gro. | 29 | G13 |
| Dumbryden Rd. | 29 | G13 |
| Dumbryden Sch. | 29 | G13 |
| Dun-Ard Gdns. | 32 | M14 |
| Dunbar St. | 6 | L15 |
| Duncan Pl. | 12 | O18 |
| Duncan St. | 32 | N14 |
| Duncans Gait | 29 | H13 |
| Dundas Cr. | 50 | T9 |
| Dundas Gro., Dalk. | 50 | T9 |
| Dundas Pk. | 49 | S8 |
| Dundas Rd. | 50 | T9 |
| Dundas St. | 49 | R8 |
| Dundas St. | 20 | M17 |
| Dundee St. | 19 | K15 |
| Dundee Terr. | 19 | K15 |
| Dundonald St. | 20 | M17 |
| Dundrennan Cotts. | 33 | P13 |
| Dunedin Sch. | 33 | O13 |
| Dunedin St. | 12 | M18 |
| Dunlop's Ct.* =Grassmarket | | |
| Dunollie Ct.* =Craigievar Wynd | | |
| Dunrobin Pl. | 19 | L17 |
| Dunsmuir Ct. | 16 | F15 |
| Dunsyre Ho. | 28 | F13 |
| Dunvegan Ct. | 8 | E18 |
| Durar Dr. | 16 | F17 |
| Durham Av. | 22 | Q16 |
| Durham Dr. | 22 | R15 |
| Durham Gdns. N. | 22 | R16 |
| Durham Gdns. S. | 22 | R15 |
| Durham Gro. | 22 | R16 |
| Durham Pl.*=Dundas St. | | |
| Durham Pl. E. | 22 | R16 |
| Durham Pl. W. | 22 | Q16 |
| Durham Pl. La. | 22 | R16 |
| Durham Rd. | 22 | R16 |
| Durham Rd. S. | 22 | R15 |
| Durham Sq. | 22 | R16 |
| Durham Terr. | 22 | Q16 |
| Durward Gro. | 33 | O13 |

| | | |
|---|---|---|
| Earl Grey St. | 6 | L16 |
| Earl Haig Gdns. | 11 | L19 |
| Earl Haig Homes | 29 | H14 |
| Earlston Pl. | 21 | O17 |
| East Adam St. | 7 | N16 |
| East Barnton Av. | 9 | G18 |
| East Barnton Gdns. | 9 | G18 |
| East Brighton Cr. | 22 | R16 |
| East Broughton Pl.* =Broughton Pl. | | |
| East Caiystane Pl. | 41 | L11 |
| East Caiystane Rd. | 41 | L11 |
| East Castle Rd. | 31 | L15 |
| East Champanyie | 32 | N14 |
| East Chatterrig | 40 | V12 |
| East Clapperfield | 33 | O13 |
| East Claremont St. | 12 | M17 |
| East Ct. | 18 | J17 |
| East Comiston | 41 | L11 |
| East Craigie | 8 | D19 |
| East Craigs | 16 | E16 |
| East Craigs Fm. | 16 | E16 |
| East Craigs Sch. | 16 | E16 |
| East Croft | 26 | A13 |
| East Cromwell St. | 12 | N19 |
| East Crosscauseway | 7 | N15 |
| East Farm of Gilmerton | 43 | Q11 |
| East Fettes Av. | 11 | K18 |
| East Fountainbridge | 6 | L16 |
| East Hannahfield | 44 | B9 |
| East Hatton Mains | 36 | A12 |
| East Hermiston | 28 | E13 |
| East Hermitage Pl. | 13 | O18 |
| East Lillypot | 11 | L19 |
| East London St. | 20 | M17 |
| East Market St. | 7 | N16 |
| East Mayfield | 32 | N14 |
| East Newington Pl. | 32 | N15 |
| East Norton Pl. | 21 | N17 |
| East Parkside | 20 | N15 |
| East Pilton Pk. | 10 | K19 |
| East Preston St. | 20 | N15 |
| East Preston St. La.* =East Preston St. | | |
| East Princes St. Gdns. | 7 | M16 |
| East Restalrig Terr. | 13 | O18 |
| East Savile Rd. | 32 | N14 |
| East Sciennes St. | 20 | N15 |
| East Silvermills La. | 20 | L17 |
| East Suffolk Rd. | 33 | O14 |
| East Telferton | 22 | Q17 |
| East Trinity Rd. | 11 | L19 |
| East Way, The | 22 | Q16 |
| East Werberside | 10 | K18 |
| Easter Belmont Rd. | 18 | H16 |
| Easter Craiglockhart Hill | 30 | K13 |
| Easter Currie Ct. | 38 | E10 |
| Easter Currie Cr. | 38 | E11 |
| Easter Currie Pl. | 38 | E11 |
| Easter Currie Terr. | 38 | E10 |
| Easter Drylaw Av. | 10 | J18 |
| Easter Drylaw Bk. | 10 | J18 |
| Easter Drylaw Dr. | 10 | J18 |
| Easter Drylaw Gdns. | 10 | J18 |
| Easter Drylaw Gro. | 10 | J18 |
| Easter Drylaw Ln. | 10 | J18 |
| Easter Drylaw Pl. | 10 | J18 |
| Easter Drylaw Vw. | 10 | J18 |
| Easter Drylaw Way | 10 | J18 |
| Easter Haugh | 40 | K12 |
| Easter Norton | 26 | B15 |
| Easter Park Dr. | 9 | G18 |
| Easter Rd. | 21 | N17 |
| Eastern Cem. | 12 | O18 |
| Eastern General Hosp. | 13 | P18 |
| Easter Steil | 31 | K13 |
| Easter Warriston | 11 | M18 |
| Eastfield | 23 | T16 |
| Eastfield Gdns. | 23 | T16 |
| Eastfield Rd. | 14 | B15 |
| Eastfield Pl. | 24 | E16 |
| Easthouses Rd., Dalk. | 50 | V9 |
| Eden La. | 31 | L14 |
| Eden Terr.* =Newbattle Terr. | | |
| Edenhall Bk., Muss. | 25 | W15 |
| Edenhall Cr., Muss. | 25 | W15 |
| Edenhall Hospital, Muss. | 25 | W14 |
| Edenhall Rd., Muss. | 25 | W15 |
| Edgefield | 48 | P9 |
| Edgefield Industrial Estate | 47 | P9 |
| Edgefield Pl. | 47 | P8 |
| Edgefield Rd. | 47 | P9 |
| Edgefield Toll | 48 | P9 |
| Edina Pl. | 21 | O17 |
| Edina St. | 20 | N17 |
| Edinburgh Acad. | 19 | L17 |
| Edinburgh Acad. New Field | 11 | K18 |
| Edinburgh Acad. (Primary) | 11 | L18 |
| Edinburgh Acad. Sports Ground | 19 | L17 |
| Edinburgh Airport | 14 | A16 |
| Edinburgh Butterfly and Insect World | 51 | S10 |
| Edinburgh Coll. of Art | 6 | M16 |
| Edinburgh Dental Hosp. & Sch. | 7 | M16 |
| Edinburgh Dungeon | 6 | L16 |
| Edinburgh Exhibition and Trade Centre | 14 | A16 |
| Edinburgh Experience | 7 | N17 |
| Edinburgh Rd., Dalk. | 50 | U10 |
| Edinburgh Rd., Eskbank | 50 | T9 |
| Edinburgh Rd., Muss. | 24 | T16 |
| Edinburgh Southern Harriers | 43 | Q12 |
| Edinburgh University Sports Grd. | 33 | P14 |
| Edinburgh University Theatre | 33 | M15 |
| Edmonstone Av. | 51 | R12 |
| Edmonstone Dr. | 51 | R12 |
| Edmonstone Rd. | 51 | R12 |
| Edmonstone Terr. | 51 | R12 |
| Education Committee Athletic Grd. | 30 | J14 |
| Eglinton Cr. | 19 | K16 |
| Eglinton St. | 19 | K16 |
| Egypt Mews | 31 | M14 |
| Eildon St. | 11 | M18 |
| Eildon Terr. | 11 | L18 |
| Elbe St. | 12 | O19 |
| Elcho Terr. | 23 | S16 |
| Elder St. | 7 | M17 |
| Elder St. E. | 7 | M17 |
| Eldindean Pl. | 49 | R8 |
| Eldindean Rd. | 49 | R8 |
| Eldindean Terr. | 49 | R8 |
| Electra Pl. | 22 | R17 |
| Elgin Pl. | 19 | K16 |
| Elgin Terr. | 20 | N17 |
| Elizafield | 12 | N18 |
| Elizafield* =Newhaven Rd. | | |
| Ellangowan Terr. | 33 | P13 |
| Ellen's Glen | 43 | P12 |
| Ellen's Glen Rd. | 43 | P12 |
| Ellersly Rd. | 18 | J16 |
| Elliot Gdns. | 40 | J12 |
| Elliot Pk. | 40 | J12 |
| Elliot Pl. | 40 | J12 |
| Elliot Rd. | 40 | J12 |
| Elliot St. | 12 | N17 |
| Elm Pl. | 13 | O18 |
| Elm Row | 20 | N17 |
| Elm Row | 49 | R9 |
| Elmfield Ct., Dalk. | 50 | U10 |
| Elmfield Pk., Dalk. | 50 | U10 |
| Elmfield Rd., Dalk. | 50 | U10 |
| Elmwood Terr. | 13 | O18 |
| Eltringham Gdns. | 30 | J14 |
| Eltringham Gro. | 30 | J14 |
| Eltringham Terr. | 30 | J14 |
| Engine Rd. | 47 | P8 |
| Episcopal Theological Coll. | 19 | K16 |
| Erskine Pl.* =Shandwick Pl. | | |
| Esdaile | 32 | M14 |
| Esk Pl., Dalk. | 50 | T10 |
| Eskbank Rd. | 49 | S8 |
| Eskbank Rd., Dalk. | 50 | T9 |
| Eskbank Terr., Dalk. | 50 | T9 |
| Eskdaill Ct., Dalk.* =South St. | | |
| Eskdaill St., Dalk. | 50 | U10 |
| Eskdale Ct. | 49 | R8 |
| Eskdale Dr. | 48 | R8 |
| Eskdale Mews, Muss. | 24 | V15 |
| Eskdale Terr. | 49 | R8 |
| Eskgrove | 48 | Q8 |
| Eskmill Villas, Muss. | 24 | U15 |
| Eskside Court* =Ironmills Road | | |
| Eskside E., Muss. | 25 | V15 |
| Eskside W., Muss. | 24 | V15 |
| Eskview Av., Muss. | 24 | U15 |
| Eskview Cr., Muss. | 24 | U15 |
| Eskview Gr., Dalk. | 50 | T10 |
| Eskview Gr., Muss. | 24 | U15 |
| Eskview Pl. | 50 | T10 |
| Eskview Rd., Muss. | 24 | U15 |
| Eskview Terr., Muss. | 24 | U15 |
| Eskview Villas, Muss. | 50 | T9 |
| Esplanade | 8 | F20 |
| Esplanade Terr. | 23 | S16 |
| Essendean Pl. | 16 | F17 |
| Essendean Terr. | 16 | F17 |
| Essex Brae | 8 | E18 |
| Essex Pk. | 8 | E18 |
| Essex Rd. | 8 | E18 |
| Esslemont Rd. | 32 | N13 |
| Ethel Terr. | 31 | L13 |
| Eton Terr. | 6 | L17 |
| Ettrick Gro. | 31 | L15 |
| Ettrick Rd. | 31 | K14 |
| Ettrickdale Pl. | 19 | L17 |
| Eva Pl. | 32 | N13 |
| Evans Gdns. | 49 | S8 |
| Ewerland | 8 | E18 |
| Eyre Cr. | 19 | M17 |
| Eyre Pl. | 19 | M17 |
| Eyre Terr. | 19 | M17 |
| Fair-a-Far | 8 | E19 |
| Fair-a-Far Cotts. | 8 | E19 |
| Fairford Gdns. | 33 | O13 |
| Fairhaven Villas, Dalk. | 50 | T9 |
| Fairmile Av. | 41 | L11 |
| Fairmile Marie Curie Home | 41 | M11 |
| Fairmilehead | 41 | L11 |
| Fairmilehead Pk. | 41 | L11 |
| Fairview Rd. | 14 | A16 |
| Fairways | 24 | U14 |
| Fairways, Muss. | 24 | U15 |
| Fala Ct. | 43 | O11 |
| Falcon Av. | 31 | L14 |
| Falcon Ct. | 31 | L14 |
| Falcon Gdns. | 31 | L14 |
| Falcon Rd. | 31 | L14 |
| Falcon Rd. W. | 31 | L14 |
| Falkland Gdns. | 17 | G17 |
| Farrer Gro. | 22 | Q17 |
| Farrer Terr. | 22 | Q17 |
| Fauldburn | 16 | E17 |
| Fauldburn Pk. | 16 | E17 |
| Featherhall Av. | 16 | F15 |
| Featherhall Cr. N. | 16 | F15 |
| Featherhall Cr. S. | 16 | F15 |
| Featherhall Gro. | 16 | F15 |
| Featherhall Pl. | 16 | F15 |
| Featherhall Rd. | 16 | F15 |
| Featherhall Terr. | 16 | F15 |
| Ferguson Ct., Muss. | 24 | V14 |
| Ferguson Dr., Muss. | 24 | U14 |
| Ferguson Gdns, Muss.* =Ferguson Dr. | | |
| Ferguson Gr., Muss. | 24 | U14 |
| Ferguson Vw., Muss. | 24 | U14 |
| Ferniehill Av. | 43 | Q11 |
| Ferniehill Dr. | 43 | Q11 |
| Ferniehill Gdns. | 43 | Q12 |
| Ferniehill Gro. | 43 | Q12 |

| | | |
|---|---|---|
| Ferniehill Pl. | 43 | Q11 |
| Ferniehill Rd. | 43 | Q11 |
| Ferniehill Sq. | 43 | Q11 |
| Ferniehill St. | 43 | Q12 |
| Ferniehill Terr. | 43 | Q11 |
| Ferniehill Way | 43 | Q12 |
| Fernielaw, Muss. | 25 | V13 |
| Fernielaw Av. | 39 | H11 |
| Fernieside Av. | 43 | Q12 |
| Fernieside Cr. | 43 | Q12 |
| Fernieside Dr. | 43 | Q12 |
| Fernieside Gdns. | 43 | Q12 |
| Fernieside Gro. | 43 | Q12 |
| Fernieside Sch. | 43 | Q12 |
| Ferry Rd. | 10 | H18 |
| Ferry Rd. Av. | 10 | J18 |
| Ferry Rd. Dr. | 10 | J19 |
| Ferry Rd. Gdns. | 10 | J18 |
| Ferry Rd. Gro. | 10 | J18 |
| Ferry Rd. Pl. | 10 | J18 |
| Ferryfield | 11 | K19 |
| Ferryhill Sch. | 10 | J18 |
| Festival Fringe Office | 7 | M16 |
| Festival Office | 7 | M16 |
| Festival Sq. | 6 | L16 |
| Fettes Av. | 19 | K17 |
| Fettes Coll. | 10 | K18 |
| Fettes Rise | 11 | K18 |
| Fettes Row | 20 | M28 |
| Fettes Sch. | 10 | K18 |
| Fidra Ct. | 9 | H19 |
| Figgate Bk. | 23 | R17 |
| Figgate Burn Pk. | 22 | Q16 |
| Figgate La. | 22 | R17 |
| Figgate St. | 22 | R17 |
| Fillyside Av. | 22 | Q17 |
| Fillyside Rd. | 13 | Q18 |
| Fillyside Terr. | 22 | Q18 |
| Filmhouse | 6 | L16 |
| Findhorn Pl. | 32 | N14 |
| Findlay Av. | 13 | P18 |
| Findlay Cotts. | 13 | P18 |
| Findlay Gdns. | 13 | P18 |
| Findlay Gro. | 13 | P18 |
| Findlay Medway | 13 | P18 |
| Fingal Pl. | 32 | M15 |
| Fingzies Pl. | 13 | O18 |
| Finlaggan Ct.* =Craigievar Wynd | | |
| Firrhill Cr. | 40 | K12 |
| Firrhill Dr. | 40 | K12 |
| Firrhill Ln. | 40 | K12 |
| Firrhill Sch. | 40 | J12 |
| First Gait | 37 | D12 |
| Fish Market | 12 | M20 |
| Fisherrow Harbour, Muss. | 24 | U16 |
| Fisherrow Links, Muss. | 25 | V16 |
| Fisherrow Sands, Muss. | 25 | V16 |
| Fishers Wynd, Muss. | 24 | U15 |
| Fishmarket Sq. | 12 | M20 |
| Fishwives' Causeway | 22 | Q17 |
| Fleshmarket Cl.* =High St. | | |
| Flora Stevenson Sch. | 19 | K17 |
| Forbes Rd. | 31 | L15 |
| Forbes St. | 7 | N15 |
| Fords Rd. | 30 | H14 |
| Forestry Commission | 17 | G15 |
| Forres St. | 6 | L17 |
| Forrest Hill | 7 | M16 |
| Forrest Rd. | 7 | M16 |
| Forrester Park Av. | 29 | F14 |
| Forrester Park Dr. | 29 | F14 |
| Forrester Park Gdns. | 28 | F14 |
| Forrester Park Gr. | 29 | G14 |
| Forrester Park Gro. | 29 | F14 |
| Forrester Park Ln. | 29 | F14 |
| Forrester Rd. | 16 | F16 |
| Forrester Sch. | 28 | F14 |
| Fort Ho. | 12 | N19 |
| Fort Sch. | 12 | N19 |
| Forteviot Ho. | 43 | P12 |
| Forteviot Sch. | 32 | M14 |
| Forth St. | 7 | M17 |
| Forth View Av. | 38 | D10 |
| Forth View Cr. (Currie) | 37 | D10 |
| Forth View Cr. (Danderhall) | 51 | R12 |
| Forth View Rd. | 38 | D10 |
| Forthview Rd. | 18 | J17 |
| Forthview Terr. | 18 | H17 |
| Foulis Cr. | 39 | F11 |
| Foundry La. | 48 | P9 |
| Fountainbridge | 6 | L15 |
| Fountain Pl. | 47 | P8 |
| Fountainhall Rd. | 32 | N14 |
| Fourth Gait | 37 | D12 |
| Fowler Sq. | 48 | P8 |
| Fowler Terr. | 31 | K15 |
| Fox Covert Av. | 17 | G17 |
| Fox Covert Gro. | 17 | G17 |
| Fox Covert Sch. | 17 | G16 |
| Fox Spring Cr. | 41 | L12 |
| Fox Spring Rise | 41 | L12 |
| Fraser Av. | 11 | L19 |
| Fraser Cr. | 11 | L19 |
| Fraser Gdns. | 11 | L19 |
| Fraser Gro. | 11 | L19 |
| Fraser Homes* =Spylaw Bank Rd. | | |
| Frederick St. | 6 | M17 |
| Free Church Coll. | 20 | M16 |
| Freemasons' Hall | 6 | M16 |
| Frogston Av. | 41 | L11 |
| Frogston Gdns. | 41 | L11 |
| Frogston Gro. | 41 | M11 |
| Frogston Rd. E. | 42 | N10 |
| Frogston Rd. W. | 41 | L11 |
| Frogston Terr. | 41 | M11 |
| Fruit Market | 30 | J14 |
| Fruit Market Gall. | 7 | M16 |
| Gabriel's Rd.* =West Register St. | | |
| Galachlaw Shot | 41 | M11 |
| Galachlawside | 41 | M11 |
| Gallolee, The | 40 | J11 |
| Galt Av., Muss. | 25 | X15 |
| Galt Cr., Muss. | 25 | X15 |
| Gamekeeper's Ln. | 8 | E19 |
| Gamekeeper's Pk. | 8 | E18 |
| Gamekeeper's Rd. | 8 | E19 |
| Garden Terr. | 9 | G18 |
| Gardiner Gro. | 17 | H17 |
| Gardiner Rd. | 17 | H17 |
| Gardiner Terr. | 17 | H17 |
| Gardner St.* =Lower London Rd. | | |
| Gardner's Cr. | 6 | L16 |
| Garscube Terr. | 18 | J16 |
| Garvald Ct. | 42 | O11 |
| Gayfield Pl. | 20 | N17 |
| Gayfield Pl. La. | 20 | N17 |
| Gayfield Sq. | 20 | N17 |
| Gayfield St. | 20 | N17 |
| Gaynor Av. | 47 | O8 |
| General Post Office | 7 | M16 |
| General's Entry* =Bristo St. | | |
| George Av. | 47 | O8 |
| George Cr. | 47 | P9 |
| George Dr. | 47 | O8 |
| George IV Bridge | 7 | M16 |
| George Heriot's Sch. | 7 | M16 |
| George Heriot's Sports Grd. | 11 | L18 |
| George Sq. | 7 | M15 |
| George Sq. La. | 7 | M15 |
| George St. | 6 | L16 |
| George Terr. | 47 | O8 |
| George Watson's Coll. | 31 | L14 |
| George Watson's Coll. Recreation Grd. | 31 | K14 |
| Gibb's Entry* =Simon Sq. | | |
| Gibraltar Ct., Dalk. | 50 | U10 |
| Gibraltar Gdns., Dalk. | 50 | U10 |
| Gibraltar Rd., Dalk. | 50 | U10 |
| Gibraltar Terr., Dalk. | 50 | U10 |
| Gibson Dr., Dalk. | 50 | V10 |
| Gibson St. | 12 | N18 |
| Gibson Terr. | 19 | L15 |
| Gifford Pk. | 7 | N15 |
| Gilbertstoun | 23 | S15 |
| Gilbertstoun Pl. | 23 | S15 |
| Gilchrist's Entry* =Leith St. | | |
| Gilchrist's La.* =Greenside Row | | |
| Giles St. | 12 | N19 |
| Gillespie Cr. | 19 | L15 |
| Gillespie Pl. | 19 | L15 |
| Gillespie Rd. | 39 | G11 |
| Gillespie St. | 19 | L15 |
| Gillsland Pk. | 31 | K14 |
| Gillsland Rd. | 31 | K14 |
| Gilmerton Dykes Av. | 43 | P11 |
| Gilmerton Dykes Cr. | 43 | P11 |
| Gilmerton Dykes Dr. | 43 | P11 |
| Gilmerton Dykes Gdns. | 43 | P11 |
| Gilmerton Dykes Gro. | 43 | P11 |
| Gilmerton Dykes Ln. | 43 | P11 |
| Gilmerton Dykes Pl. | 43 | P11 |
| Gilmerton Dykes Rd. | 43 | P10 |
| Gilmerton Dykes St. | 43 | P11 |
| Gilmerton Dykes Terr. | 43 | P11 |
| Gilmerton Dykes Vw. | 43 | P11 |
| Gilmerton Pk. | 43 | Q12 |
| Gilmerton Pl. | 43 | P11 |
| Gilmerton Rd. | 33 | O13 |
| Gilmerton Rd. | 50 | T9 |
| Gilmerton Sch. | 43 | P11 |
| Gilmerton Station Rd. | 43 | Q10 |
| Gilmore Pk. | 19 | L15 |
| Gilmore Pl. | 19 | L15 |
| Gilmore Pl. La. | 19 | L15 |
| Gilmour's Entry* =Gilmour St. | | |
| Gilmour Rd. | 32 | N14 |
| Gilmour St. | 7 | N16 |
| Gladstone Pl. | 13 | O18 |
| Gladstone Terr. | 20 | N15 |
| Glanville Pl.*=Kerr St. | | |
| Glasgow Rd. | 14 | A15 |
| Glebe Gdns. | 17 | G15 |
| Glebe Gro. | 17 | F15 |
| Glebe Pl.*=High St. | | |
| Glebe Pl. | 48 | Q9 |
| Glebe Rd. | 17 | F15 |
| Glebe St., Dalk. | 50 | U10 |
| Glebe Terr. | 17 | F15 |
| Glebe, The | 8 | E19 |
| Glen St. | 6 | M15 |
| Glenallan Dr. | 33 | O13 |
| Glenallan Ln. | 33 | O13 |
| Glenalmond Ct. | 29 | F13 |
| Glencairn Cr. | 19 | K16 |
| Glenbrook | 44 | A8 |
| Glenbrook Ho. | 44 | A8 |
| Glenbrook Rd. | 44 | A8 |
| Glendevon Av. | 18 | H15 |
| Glendevon Gdns. | 18 | H15 |
| Glendevon Gro. | 18 | H15 |
| Glendevon Park | 18 | H15 |
| Glendevon Pl. | 18 | H15 |
| Glendevon Rd. | 18 | H15 |
| Glendevon Terr. | 18 | H15 |
| Glendinning Cr. | 42 | O12 |
| Glenesk Cr., Dalk. | 50 | T9 |
| Glenfinlas St. | 6 | L16 |
| Glengyle Terr. | 19 | L15 |
| Glenisla Gdns. | 32 | M14 |
| Glenisla Gdns. La.* =Glenisla Gdns. | | |
| Glenlea Cotts. | 30 | J14 |
| Glenlee Av. | 21 | P16 |
| Glenlee Gdns. | 21 | P16 |
| Glenlockhart Bk. | 30 | J13 |
| Glenlockhart Rd. | 30 | J13 |
| Glenlockhart Valley | 30 | J13 |
| Glenogle Ho. | 19 | L17 |
| Glenogle Pl. | 19 | L17 |
| Glenogle Rd. | 19 | L17 |
| Glenogle Terr. | 19 | L18 |
| Glenorchy Pl.* =Greenside Row | | |
| Glenorchy Terr. | 32 | N14 |
| Glenpark | 44 | A9 |
| Glenure Loan | 16 | F17 |

| | | |
|---|---|---|
| Glenvarloch Cr. | 33 | O12 |
| Gloucester La. | 6 | L17 |
| Gloucester Pl. | 6 | L17 |
| Gloucester Sq.* =Gloucester La. | | |
| Gloucester St. | 6 | L17 |
| Goff Av. | 22 | Q17 |
| Gogar Mains | 14 | C16 |
| Gogar Mains Farm Rd. | 15 | C16 |
| Gogar Mount | 26 | B15 |
| Gogar Park Curling Club | 27 | C15 |
| Gogar Park House | 21 | D15 |
| Gogar Station Rd. | 27 | D13 |
| Gogarbank | 27 | D14 |
| Gogarburn Fm. | 27 | D14 |
| Gogarburn Golf Course | 27 | C15 |
| Gogarburn Hosp. | 27 | C15 |
| Gogarburn Hospital Sch. | 27 | C15 |
| Gogarloch Rd. | 28 | E15 |
| Gogarside Roundabout | 15 | D15 |
| Goldenacre Terr. | 11 | L18 |
| Goldie Terr. | 47 | O8 |
| Golf Course Rd. | 49 | R8 |
| Golf Driving Range, Liberton | 42 | N12 |
| Gordon Ln. | 17 | G16 |
| Gordon Rd. | 17 | G16 |
| Gordon St. | 12 | O18 |
| Gordon Terr. | 33 | O13 |
| Gorgie Cotts.* =Gorgie Rd. | | |
| Gorgie Rd. | 30 | H14 |
| Gosford Pl. | 12 | M19 |
| Goodtrees | 44 | B8 |
| Goose Green Av., Muss. | 25 | V16 |
| Goose Green Cr., Muss. | 25 | V16 |
| Goose Green Pl., Muss. | 25 | V16 |
| Goose Green Rd., Muss. | 25 | V16 |
| Gowanhill | 36 | C11 |
| Gowanhill Rd. | 36 | C11 |
| G.P.O. Sorting Office | 20 | N17 |
| Gracefield Ct.* =Fishers Wynd | | |
| Gracemount Av. | 42 | O12 |
| Gracemount Dr. | 42 | O11 |
| Gracemount Pk. | 43 | P11 |
| Gracemount Pl. | 42 | O11 |
| Gracemount Rd. | 42 | O11 |
| Gracemount Sch. | 43 | O11 |
| Gracemount Sch. (Secondary) | 43 | P11 |
| Gracemount Sq. | 42 | O12 |
| Graham St. | 12 | N19 |
| Grampian Ho. | 12 | N19 |
| Granby Rd. | 32 | N14 |
| Grandfield | 11 | M19 |
| Grandville | 11 | M19 |
| Grange Cem. | 32 | M14 |
| Grange Ct.* =Causewayside | | |
| Grange Cr. | 32 | M14 |
| Grange Cricket Grd. | 19 | L17 |
| Grange Ln. | 32 | M14 |
| Grange Loan Gdns. | 32 | M14 |
| Grange Rd. | 32 | M15 |
| Grange Terr. | 32 | M14 |
| Grant Av. | 39 | H11 |
| Granton Cr. | 10 | K19 |
| Granton Cr. Pk. | 11 | K19 |
| Granton Gdns. | 11 | K19 |
| Granton Gro. | 11 | K19 |
| Granton Medway | 10 | K19 |
| Granton Park Av. | 10 | K20 |
| Granton Pl. | 11 | K19 |
| Granton Rd. | 11 | L19 |
| Granton Sch. | 10 | K19 |
| Granton Sq. | 11 | K20 |
| Granton Terr. | 11 | K19 |
| Granton Vw. | 11 | K19 |
| Grantully Pl. | 32 | N14 |
| Granville Terr. | 31 | L15 |
| Grassmarket | 6 | M16 |
| Gray's Loan | 31 | K14 |
| Graysmill Sch. | 30 | H13 |
| Great Cannon Bk. | 22 | R17 |
| Great Junction St. | 12 | N19 |
| Great King St. | 6 | M17 |
| Great Michael Rise | 12 | M19 |
| Great Michael Sq.* =Main St. | | |
| Great Stuart St. | 6 | L16 |
| Green St. | 20 | M17 |
| Green, The | 9 | G18 |
| Green, The | 45 | C8 |
| Green Way, The | 39 | G12 |
| Greenbank Av. | 31 | L13 |
| Greenbank Cr. | 31 | K12 |
| Greenbank Dr. | 31 | K13 |
| Greenbank Gdns. | 31 | K12 |
| Greenbank Gro. | 41 | K12 |
| Greenbank La. | 31 | K13 |
| Greenbank Ln. | 31 | K12 |
| Greenbank Pk. | 31 | K12 |
| Greenbank Pl. | 31 | L13 |
| Greenbank Rise | 41 | K12 |
| Greenbank Rd. | 31 | K12 |
| Greenbank Row | 41 | K12 |
| Greenbank Terr. | 31 | L13 |
| Greendykes Av. | 34 | Q14 |
| Greendykes Dr. | 34 | Q14 |
| Greendykes Gdns. | 34 | Q14 |
| Greendykes Ho. | 34 | Q14 |
| Greendykes Ln. | 34 | Q14 |
| Greendykes Rd. | 34 | Q14 |
| Greendykes Sch. | 34 | Q14 |
| Greendykes Terr. | 34 | Q14 |
| Greenend Dr. | 43 | P12 |
| Greenend Gdns. | 43 | P12 |
| Greenend Gro. | 43 | P12 |
| Greenfield Cr. | 45 | C8 |
| Greenfield Rd. | 45 | C8 |
| Greenhill Gdns. | 31 | L15 |
| Greenhill Pk. | 31 | L14 |
| Greenhill Pl. | 31 | L14 |
| Greenhill Terr. | 31 | L15 |
| Greenlaw Hedge | 40 | K12 |
| Greenlaw Rig | 40 | K12 |
| Greenmantle Ln. | 33 | O12 |
| Greenside Ct.* =Greenside Row | | |
| Greenside La. | 7 | N17 |
| Greenside Pl. | 7 | N17 |
| Greenwood | 18 | J16 |
| Greenside Row | 7 | N17 |
| Greyfriars Kirk | 7 | M16 |
| Greyfriars Pl.* =Candlemaker Row | | |
| Grierson Av. | 11 | L19 |
| Grierson Cr. | 11 | L19 |
| Grierson Gdns. | 11 | L19 |
| Grierson Rd. | 11 | K19 |
| Grierson Sq. | 11 | L19 |
| Grierson Villas | 11 | L19 |
| Grigor Av. | 10 | J18 |
| Grigor Dr. | 10 | J18 |
| Grigor Gdns. | 10 | J19 |
| Grigor Terr. | 10 | J18 |
| Grindlay St. | 6 | L16 |
| Grindlay St. Ct. | 6 | L16 |
| Groathill Av. | 18 | J17 |
| Groathill Gdns. E. | 18 | J17 |
| Groathill Gdns. W. | 18 | J17 |
| Groathill Rd. N. | 10 | J18 |
| Groathill Rd. S. | 18 | J17 |
| Grosvenor Cr. | 19 | K16 |
| Grosvenor Gdns. | 19 | K16 |
| Grosvenor St. | 19 | L16 |
| Grove End | 49 | R8 |
| Grove Pl. | 38 | F11 |
| Grove St. | 6 | L16 |
| Grove St., Muss. | 25 | V15 |
| Grove, The, Muss. | 25 | W15 |
| Grove Terr.*=Grove St. | | |
| Guardianswood | 18 | J16 |
| Gullan's Cl. | 7 | N16 |
| Gunnet Ct. | 9 | H19 |
| Guthrie St. | 7 | M16 |
| Gyle Park, The | 16 | E15 |
| Gyle Park Gdns. | 16 | E15 |
| Gylemuir Rd. | 16 | F15 |
| Gylemuir Sch. | 16 | F15 |
| Gypsy Brae | 10 | J19 |
| Haddington Pl. | 20 | N17 |
| Haddington's Entry* =Reid's Cl. | | |
| Haddon Ct.*=Howden St. | | |
| Hailes Appr. | 39 | H12 |
| Hailes Av. | 39 | H12 |
| Hailes Bk. | 39 | H12 |
| Hailes Cr. | 39 | H12 |
| Hailes Gdns. | 39 | G12 |
| Hailes Gro. | 39 | H12 |
| Hailes Pk. (street) | 39 | G12 |
| Hailes Pk. | 29 | G13 |
| Hailes Quarry Cott.* =Murrayburn Rd. | | |
| Hailes St. | 19 | L15 |
| Hailes Terr. | 39 | H12 |
| Hailesland Gdns. | 29 | G13 |
| Hailesland Gro. | 29 | G13 |
| Hailesland Pk. | 29 | G13 |
| Hailesland Pl. | 29 | G13 |
| Hailesland Rd. | 29 | G13 |
| Hailesland Sch. | 39 | G12 |
| Hainburn Pk. | 40 | K11 |
| Hall Terr. | 17 | G15 |
| Hallhead Rd | 33 | N13 |
| Halmyre St. | 12 | N18 |
| Hamburgh Pl.* =Lindsay Rd. | | |
| Hamilton Dr. | 22 | Q16 |
| Hamilton Dr. W. | 22 | Q16 |
| Hamilton Gdns. | 22 | Q16 |
| Hamilton Gro. | 22 | Q16 |
| Hamilton Park | 22 | Q16 |
| Hamilton Pl. | 19 | L17 |
| Hamilton Terr. | 22 | R16 |
| Hamilton Wynd | 12 | N19 |
| Hampton Pl.* =West Catherine Pl. | | |
| Hampton Terr. | 18 | K16 |
| Hanover St. | 6 | M17 |
| Harbour Pl. | 22 | R17 |
| Harbour Rd., Muss. | 24 | U15 |
| Harbour Rd. | 22 | R17 |
| Harden Pl. | 31 | K15 |
| Hardengreen Ind. Est. | 50 | T9 |
| Hardwell Cl. | 20 | N15 |
| Harelaw Rd. | 39 | H11 |
| Harewood Cr. | 34 | Q14 |
| Harewood Dr. | 34 | Q14 |
| Harewood Rd. | 34 | Q14 |
| Harlaw | 45 | D8 |
| Harlaw March | 45 | C8 |
| Harlaw Rd. | 45 | C8 |
| Harmeny | 45 | C8 |
| Harmeny Sch. | 45 | C8 |
| Harrison Gdns. | 30 | K14 |
| Harrison La. | 31 | K15 |
| Harrison Pk. | 31 | K15 |
| Harrison Pl. | 30 | K14 |
| Harrison Rd. | 31 | K15 |
| Hart St. | 7 | M17 |
| Hart St. La.*=Hart St. | | |
| Hartington Gdns. | 31 | L15 |
| Hartington Pl. | 31 | L15 |
| Hatton Pl. | 32 | M15 |
| Haugh Pk., Muss. | 24 | U15 |
| Haugh St. | 19 | L17 |
| Hawkhead Cr. | 42 | O12 |
| Hawkhead Gro. | 42 | O12 |
| Hawkhill Av. | 12 | O18 |
| Hawkhill Ct. | 13 | O18 |
| Hawkhill Villas* =Lochend Rd. | | |
| Hawthorn Bdgs.* =Belford Rd. | | |
| Hawthorn Gdns. | 47 | O9 |
| Hawthorn Terr.* =Hawthornbank La. | | |
| Hawthornbank La. | 19 | L16 |
| Hawthornbank Pl. | 12 | N19 |
| Hawthornbank Terr. | 12 | N19 |
| Hawthornden Av. | 49 | R8 |
| Hawthornden Gdns. | 49 | R8 |
| Hawthornden Pl. | 12 | N18 |
| Hawthorne Pl. | 43 | Q11 |
| Hawthornvale | 12 | M19 |
| Hay Av. | 34 | Q14 |

| | | |
|---|---|---|
| Hay Dr. | 34 | R14 |
| Hay Pl. | 34 | Q14 |
| Hay Rd. | 34 | Q14 |
| Hay Terr. | 34 | Q14 |
| Hayfield | 16 | E16 |
| Haymarket | 19 | L16 |
| Haymarket Sta. | 19 | L16 |
| Haymarket Terr. | 19 | K16 |
| Hazelbank Terr. | 30 | K14 |
| Hazeldean Terr. | 33 | O13 |
| Hazelwood Gro. | 33 | P13 |
| Headrigg Row | 33 | O13 |
| Heart of Midlothian Stadium | 30 | K15 |
| Henderland Rd. | 18 | J16 |
| Henderson Gdns. | 12 | N19 |
| Henderson Pl. | 19 | M17 |
| Henderson Pl. La. | 19 | M17 |
| Henderson Row. | 19 | L17 |
| Henderson St. | 12 | N19 |
| Henderson Terr. | 19 | K15 |
| Henry Pl. | 20 | N15 |
| Henry St. | 20 | N15 |
| Hepburn Dr., Dalk. | 50 | V9 |
| Hercus Ln., Muss. | 24 | U15 |
| Herd Terr. | 47 | O8 |
| Heriot Bridge | 6 | M16 |
| Heriot Cross* =Heriot Bridge | | |
| Heriot Hill Terr. | 12 | M18 |
| Heriot Pl. | 20 | M16 |
| Heriot Row | 6 | L17 |
| Heriot-Watt University | 37 | D12 |
| Heriot-Watt University | 20 | M16 |
| Hermand Cr. | 30 | K14 |
| Hermand St. | 30 | J14 |
| Hermand Terr. | 30 | J14 |
| Hermiston Ho. | 27 | D13 |
| Hermiston Ho. Rd. | 27 | D13 |
| Hermiston Ct. | 28 | F13 |
| Hermitage Dr. | 31 | L13 |
| Hermitage Gdns. | 31 | L13 |
| Hermitage of Braid | 31 | L13 |
| Hermitage Pk. | 13 | O18 |
| Hermitage Pk. Gr. | 13 | O18 |
| Hermitage Park Sch. | 13 | O18 |
| Hermitage Park S. | 13 | O18 |
| Hermitage Pl. | 12 | O18 |
| Hermitage Terr. | 31 | L13 |
| Hibernian Stadium | 12 | O17 |
| High Buckstone | 41 | M11 |
| High Buckstone | 41 | M11 |
| High Riggs | 6 | L16 |
| High School Yards | 20 | N16 |
| High St. | 7 | M16 |
| High St., Bonnyrigg | 49 | R8 |
| High St., Lasswade | 49 | R9 |
| High St., Loanhead | 48 | P8 |
| High St., Dalk. | 50 | U10 |
| High St., Muss. | 25 | V15 |
| Highlea Circle | 44 | B8 |
| Highlea Gro. | 44 | B8 |
| Highway, The | 22 | Q16 |
| Hill Pl. | 7 | N16 |
| Hill Sq. | 7 | N16 |
| Hill St. | 6 | L17 |
| Hill St. La. N. | 6 | L17 |
| Hill St. La. S. | 6 | M17 |
| Hillcoat Ln. | 22 | R17 |
| Hillcoat Pl. | 22 | R17 |
| Hillend Country Pk. | 46 | L9 |
| Hillend Pl.*=London Rd. | | |
| Hillend Ski Slope | 46 | L9 |
| Hillhead | 49 | R8 |
| Hillhouse Rd. | 9 | G18 |
| Hillpark Av. | 17 | G18 |
| Hillpark Brae | 17 | G17 |
| Hillpark Ct. | 17 | G18 |
| Hillpark Cr. | 17 | G17 |
| Hillpark Dr. | 17 | G18 |
| Hillpark Gdns. | 17 | G17 |
| Hillpark Gr. | 17 | G17 |
| Hillpark Ln. | 17 | H17 |
| Hillpark Rd. | 17 | G17 |
| Hillpark Terr. | 17 | G17 |
| Hillpark Way | 17 | H17 |
| Hillpark Wood | 17 | H17 |
| Hillside Cr. | 20 | N17 |
| Hillside St. | 20 | N17 |
| Hilltown Terr. | 35 | S13 |
| Hillview | 18 | H17 |
| Hillview Cr. | 16 | F16 |
| Hillview Dr. | 16 | F16 |
| Hillview Rd. | 16 | F16 |
| Hillview Terr. | 16 | F16 |
| Hollybank Terr. | 30 | K14 |
| Holy Cross Sch. | 11 | M19 |
| Holy Rood Sch. | 22 | P15 |
| Holyrood Ct. | 20 | N16 |
| Holyrood Pk. | 21 | O16 |
| Holyrood Park Rd. | 20 | N15 |
| Holyrood Rd. | 7 | N16 |
| Holyroodhouse, Palace of | 7 | N16 |
| Home St. | 19 | L15 |
| Hope La. | 23 | R16 |
| Hope Park Cr. | 20 | N15 |
| Hope Park Sq.* =Meadow La. | | |
| Hope Park Terr. | 20 | N15 |
| Hope Pl., Muss. | 25 | W16 |
| Hope St. | 6 | L16 |
| Hope St. La. | 19 | L16 |
| Hope Terr. | 31 | M14 |
| Hopefield Terr. | 12 | N19 |
| Hopetoun Cr. | 20 | N17 |
| Hopetoun Cr. La. | 20 | N17 |
| Hopetoun St. | 12 | N18 |
| Horne Terr. | 19 | L15 |
| Horsburgh Bk. | 45 | C10 |
| Horsburgh Gdns. | 45 | C10 |
| Horsburgh Gr. | 45 | C10 |
| Horse Wynd | 20 | N16 |
| Hoseason Gdns. | 16 | F17 |
| Hosie Rigg | 35 | R15 |
| House of Cockburn | 44 | A8 |
| House o' Hill Av. | 9 | H18 |
| House o' Hill Brae | 9 | H18 |
| House o' Hill Cr. | 9 | H18 |
| House o' Hill Gdns. | 9 | H18 |
| House o' Hill Gr. | 9 | H18 |
| House o' Hill Gro. | 9 | H18 |
| House o' Hill Pl. | 9 | H18 |
| House o' Hill Rd. | 9 | H18 |
| House o' Hill Row | 9 | H18 |
| House o' Hill Terr. | 18 | H17 |
| Howard Pl. | 11 | M18 |
| Howard St | 11 | M18 |
| Howden Hall Ct. | 42 | N11 |
| Howden Hall Cr. | 42 | N11 |
| Howden Hall Dr. | 42 | N11 |
| Howden Hall Gdns. | 42 | O11 |
| Howden Hall Ln. | 42 | N11 |
| Howden Hall Pk. | 42 | N11 |
| Howden Hall Rd. | 42 | O11 |
| Howden Hall Way | 42 | O11 |
| Howden Pk. | 42 | N11 |
| Howden St. | 7 | N15 |
| Howe Dean | 32 | N12 |
| Howe Pk. | 40 | K11 |
| Howe St. | 6 | M17 |
| Hugh Miller Pl. | 19 | L17 |
| Hunt Cl., Dalk. | 50 | U10 |
| Hunter Av. | 48 | P8 |
| Hunter Ct. | 48 | P8 |
| Hunter Sq. | 7 | M16 |
| Hunter Terr. | 49 | R8 |
| Hunter Terr. | 48 | P8 |
| Hunter's Tryst | 40 | K11 |
| Hunter's Tryst Sch. | 40 | K12 |
| Huntly Ho. Mus. | 7 | N16 |
| Huntly St. | 11 | M18 |
| Hutchison Av. | 30 | J14 |
| Hutchison Cotts. | 30 | J14 |
| Hutchison Crossway | 30 | J14 |
| Hutchison Gdns. | 30 | J14 |
| Hutchison Gro. | 30 | J14 |
| Hutchison Ho. | 30 | J14 |
| Hutchison Ln. | 30 | J14 |
| Hutchison Medway | 30 | J14 |
| Hutchison Pk. | 30 | J14 |
| Hutchison Pl. | 30 | J14 |
| Hutchison Rd. | 30 | J14 |
| Hutchison Terr. | 30 | J14 |
| Hutchison Vw. | 30 | J14 |
| Hyvot Av. | 43 | P11 |
| Hyvot Ct. | 43 | P11 |
| Hyvot Gdns. | 43 | P11 |
| Hyvot Gr. | 43 | P11 |
| Hyvot Gro. | 43 | P11 |
| Hyvot Ln. | 43 | P11 |
| Hyvot Pk. | 43 | P11 |
| Hyvot Terr. | 43 | P11 |
| Hyvot Vw. | 43 | P11 |
| Hyvot's Bank Av. | 43 | Q11 |
| Hyvot's Bank Valley Pk. | 43 | P11 |
| Ice Rink, Murrayfield | 18 | J15 |
| Inch Nurseries | 33 | O13 |
| Inch Park, The | 33 | O13 |
| Inchcolm Ct. | 10 | J19 |
| Inchgarvie Ct. | 10 | J19 |
| Inchkeith Ct. | 12 | N18 |
| Inchmickery Ct. | 9 | H19 |
| Inchview Sch. | 10 | J18 |
| Inchview Terr. | 22 | Q17 |
| India Bdgs.*=Victoria St. | | |
| India Pl. | 6 | L17 |
| India St. | 6 | L17 |
| Industrial Rd. | 13 | O18 |
| Industry Home* =Industry La. | | |
| Industry La. | 12 | N19 |
| Infirmary St. | 7 | N16 |
| Inglewood Pl. | 42 | O12 |
| Inglis Ct.*=West Port | | |
| Inglis Green Rd. | 30 | H13 |
| Ingliston | 14 | A16 |
| Ingliston Rd. | 14 | A15 |
| Innocent Railway (walkway), The | 33 | O15 |
| Inveralmond Dr. | 8 | E19 |
| Inveralmond Gdns. | 8 | E19 |
| Inveralmond Gr. | 8 | E19 |
| Inveravon Rd. | 47 | O9 |
| Inveravon Terr., Muss. | 24 | V15 |
| Inveresk Brae, Muss. | 25 | V15 |
| Inveresk Cemetery, Muss. | 25 | V15 |
| Inveresk Ho., Muss. | 25 | V15 |
| Inveresk Ind. Estate, Muss. | 25 | V15 |
| Inveresk Mills Ind. Estate, Muss. | 24 | U15 |
| Inveresk Rd., Muss. | 25 | V15 |
| Inveresk Village Rd., Muss. | 25 | V15 |
| Inverleith Av. | 11 | L18 |
| Inverleith Av. S. | 11 | L18 |
| Inverleith Gdns. | 11 | L18 |
| Inverleith Gro. | 11 | K18 |
| Inverleith Ho. | 11 | L18 |
| Inverleith Pk. | 11 | L18 |
| Inverleith Pl. | 11 | L18 |
| Inverleith Place La. | 11 | L18 |
| Inverleith Row | 11 | L18 |
| Inverleith Terr. | 11 | L18 |
| Inverleith Terr. La. | 11 | L18 |
| Ironmill's Rd., Dalk. | 50 | T10 |
| Iona St. | 12 | N18 |
| Ivanhoe Cr. | 33 | O13 |
| Ivy Terr. | 30 | K15 |
| Jack Kane Centre | 34 | R14 |
| Jamaica St. | 6 | L17 |
| Jamaica St. N. La. | 6 | L17 |
| Jamaica St. S. La. | 6 | L17 |
| James' Ct.*=Lawnmarket | | |
| James Craig Walk* =Leith St. | | |
| James Gillespie's Sch. | 32 | M15 |
| James Gillespie's Sch. Annexe | 19 | L15 |
| James Lean Av., Dalk. | 50 | U10 |
| James Leary Way | 49 | S8 |
| James St. | 23 | S16 |
| James St. La. | 23 | S16 |
| James St., Muss. | 25 | V15 |
| Jameson Pl. | 12 | N18 |

Jane St. 12 N18
Jane Terr.*
=Comely Green Cr.
Janefield 42 O10
Jarnac Ct., Dalk. 50 U10
Jawbone Walk 7 M15
Jean Armour Av. 33 O13
Jean Armour Dr., Dalk. 50 V9
Jeffrey Av. 18 H17
Jeffrey St. 7 N16
Jessfield Terr. 12 M19
Jewel and Esk Valley College, The 23 S15
Jewel and Esk Valley Coll., The, Dalk. 50 T9
Jewel Pk. 34 R15
Jewel, The 34 R15
Jock's Lodge 21 P17
John Knox's Ho. 7 N16
John St. 23 S16
John St. La. 23 S16
John St. La. W. 23 S16
John's La. 12 O19
John's Pl. 12 O19
Johnsburn Gr. 44 B9
Johnsburn Haugh 44 B9
Johnsburn Pk. 44 B9
Johnsburn Rd. 44 B9
Johnston Terr. 6 M16
Joppa Gdns. 23 S16
Joppa Gro. 23 S16
Joppa Pk. 23 S16
Joppa Quarry Pk. 23 S16
Joppa Rd. 23 S16
Joppa Terr. 23 S16
Jordan La. 31 L14
Jubilee Rd. 14 A16
Junction Pl. 12 N19
Juniper Av. 38 F11
Juniper Gdns. 38 F11
Juniper Green Sch. 38 F11
Juniper Green Sch. Annexe 38 F11
Juniper Gro. 38 F11
Juniper La. 38 F11
Juniperlee*
=Lanark Rd.
Juniperlee 38 F11
Juniper Park Rd. 38 F11
Juniper Terr. 38 F11

Kaimes Rd. 17 G16
Kaimes Sch. 43 P11
Kaimes Vw. 51 R12
Katesmill Rd. 39 H12
Keddie Gdns. 12 N19
Kedslie Pl. 42 N12
Kedslie Rd. 42 N12
Keir St. 6 M16
Keith Cr. 17 H17
Keith Row 18 J17
Keith Terr. 17 H17
Kekewich Av. 22 Q17
Kellarstane 27 C14
Kemp Pl. 19 L17
Kenilworth Dr. 42 O12
Kenmure Av. 21 P16
Kennington Av. 47 O8
Kennington Terr. 47 O8
Kerr Av. 50 T9
Kerr St. 6 L17
Kerr's Wynd, Muss. 25 V15
Kevock Rd. 48 Q8
Kew Terr. 18 K16
Kilchurn Ct.*
=Craigievar Wynd
Kilgraston Ct. 32 M14
Kilgraston Rd. 32 M14
Kilmaurs Rd. 33 O14
Kilmaurs Terr. 33 O14
Kilncroftside 30 H13
Kilwinning Pl., Muss. 25 V15
Kilwinning St., Muss. 25 V15
Kilwinning Terr., Muss. 25 V15
Kinellan Gdns. 18 J16
Kinellan Rd. 18 J16
King George V Pk. 20 M17
King George V Park, Bonnyrigg 49 R8
King George's Field 47 O8
King St. 12 N19
King St., Muss. 25 V15
Kinghorn Pl. 12 M19
King's Bridge 6 M16
King's Bdgs., The 32 N13
King's Crammond 8 E18
King's Haugh 33 P14
King's Park Sch., Dalk. 50 U9
King's Pk., Dalk. 50 U9
King's Pl. 22 R17
King's Rd. 22 R17
King's Stables Rd. 6 L16
King's Stables La. 6 M16
King's Terr. 22 Q17
King's Theatre 6 L15
Kingsburgh Rd. 18 J16
Kingsinch Sch. 33 O13
Kingsknowe Av. 29 H13
Kingsknowe Cr. 29 H13
Kingsknowe Ct. 29 G13
Kingsknowe Dr. 29 H13
Kingsknowe Gdns. 39 H12
Kingsknowe Golf Course 39 G12
Kingsknowe Gro. 39 H12
Kingsknowe Pk. 39 H12
Kingsknowe Pl. 29 G13
Kingsknowe Rd. N. 29 H13
Kingsknowe Rd. S. 29 H13
Kingsknowe Sta. 29 H13
Kingsknowe Terr. 29 H13
Kingston Av. 33 P13
Kinnaird Pk. 35 S14
Kinnear Rd. 11 K18
Kippielaw Dr., Dalk. 50 V9
Kippielaw Gdns., Dalk. 50 V9
Kippielaw Medway, Dalk. 50 V9
Kippielaw Pk., Dalk. 50 V9
Kippielaw Rd., Dalk. 50 V9
Kippielaw Wk., Dalk. 50 V9
Kirkbrae 33 O13
Kirk Cramond 8 E19
Kirk Ln. 17 G15
Kirk Pk. 42 O12
Kirk St. 12 N18
Kirkgate, Leith*
=Leith Walk
Kirkgate, Liberton 42 O12
Kirkgate Ho. 12 O19
Kirkhill Dr. 33 O14
Kirkhill Gdns. 33 O15
Kirkhill Rd. 33 O15
Kirkhill Terr. 33 O15
Kirklands*=Ladywell Av.
Kirkwood Pl.*
=London Rd.
Kisimul Ct.*
=Craigievar Wynd
Kittle Yards 32 N14
Klondyke St. 35 T14
Klondyke Way 35 T14
Komarom Pl., Dalk. 50 V10
Kyle Pl.*=Montrose Terr.

Labourfield 28 F13
Lade, The 45 C8
Ladehead 12 M18
Ladiemeadow*
=Roull Rd.
Ladie Meadow 29 G15
Lady Ct. 45 C9
Ladyfield Pl.*
=Morrison St.
Ladyfield Pl. 6 L16
Lady Lawson St. 6 M16
Lady Menzies Pl. 21 O17
Lady Nairne Cr. 22 P16
Lady Nairne Gro. 22 P16
Lady Nairne Ln. 22 P16
Lady Nairne Pl. 22 P16
Lady Rd. 33 O14
Lady Stair's Clo.*
=North Bank St.
Lady Wynd 6 M16
Ladysmith Rd. 32 N13
Ladywell, Muss. 25 V15
Ladywell Av. 28 F15
Ladywell Gdns. 16 F15
Ladywell Ho. 16 F15
Ladywell Rd. 16 F15
Ladywell Way, Muss.*
=North High St.
Laichfield 30 H14
Laichpark Pl. 30 J14
Laichpark Rd. 30 H14
Laing Terr. 23 S16
Lamb's Cl.*
=East Crosscauseway
Lamermoor Terr. 33 P13
Lampacre Rd. 29 G15
Lanark Rd. 39 G11
Lanark Rd. W. 44 A9
Lang Ln. 47 O9
Lang Linn Path 32 M13
Langloan Rd. 47 O9
Langton Rd. 32 N14
Lansbury Ct., Dalk.*
=Wheatsheaf La.
Lansdowne Cr. 19 K16
Lapicide Pl. 12 N19
Larch Gr. 44 B9
Larchfield 44 C9
Larchfield Neuk 44 C9
Largo Pl. 12 N19
Larkfield 49 S9
Larkfield Dr. 49 S9
Larkfield Rd. 49 T9
Lasswade Bk. 43 P11
Lasswade Gro. 43 P11
Lasswade Rd. 50 T9
Lasswade Rd. 42 O12
Lasswade Rd., Lasswade 48 Q9
Lasswade Rd., Loanhead 48 P8
Lasswade Sch. 49 S8
Lasswade Sch. 48 R8
Lauder Ln. 32 N14
Lauder Rd. 32 M15
Lauder Rd., Dalk. 50 U9
Lauderdale St. 32 M15
Laurel Bk., Dalk. 50 V9
Laurel Terr. 31 K15
Laurie St. 12 O18
Lauriston Castle 9 G19
Lauriston Dental Centre 32 N14
Lauriston Farm Rd. 9 G18
Lauriston Gdns. 20 M15
Lauriston Pk. 20 M15
Lauriston Pl. 6 M16
Lauriston St. 6 M16
Lauriston Terr. 6 M16
Laverockbank Av. 11 M19
Laverockbank Cr. 11 M19
Laverockbank Gdns. 11 M19
Laverockbank Gro. 11 M19
Laverockbank Rd. 11 M19
Laverockbank Terr. 11 M19
Laverockdale Cr. 39 H11
Laverockdale Ln. 39 H11
Laverockdale Pk. 39 H11
Law Courts 7 M16
Law Pl.*=Pipe St.
Lawnmarket 7 M16
Lawrie Terr. 47 O8
Leadervale Rd. 42 N12
Leadervale Terr. 42 N12
Leamington Pl.*
=Leamington Terr.
Leamington Rd. 19 L15
Leamington Terr. 31 L15
Learmonth Av. 19 K17
Learmonth Cr. 19 K17
Learmonth Ct. 19 K17

| | | |
|---|---|---|
| Learmonth Gdns. | 19 | K17 |
| Learmonth Gdns. La. | 19 | K17 |
| Learmonth Gdns. Mews | 19 | L17 |
| Learmonth Gro. | 19 | K17 |
| Learmonth Pk. | 19 | K17 |
| Learmonth Pl. | 19 | K17 |
| Learmonth Terr. | 19 | K17 |
| Learmonth Terr. La. | 19 | K17 |
| Learmonth Vw.* =Learmonth Terr. | | |
| Lecture Theatre | 7 | M16 |
| Lee Cr. | 22 | R16 |
| Leith | 12 | N19 |
| Leith Acad. | 12 | O18 |
| Leith Hosp. | 12 | N19 |
| Leith Links | 12 | O18 |
| Leith Sch. (Primary) | 12 | O18 |
| Leith St. | 20 | M17 |
| Leith St. Terr.*=Leith St. | | |
| Leith Walk | 20 | N17 |
| Leith Walk Sch. | 20 | N17 |
| Lennel Av. | 18 | J16 |
| Lennie Cotts. | 15 | C16 |
| Lennie Mains | 15 | C17 |
| Lennie Pk. | 15 | C16 |
| Lennox Row | 11 | L19 |
| Lennox St. | 19 | L17 |
| Lennox St. La. | 19 | L17 |
| Lennymuir | 14 | B17 |
| Leopold Pl. | 20 | N17 |
| Leslie Pl. | 19 | L17 |
| Leven Cl.*=Leven St. | | |
| Leven St. | 19 | L15 |
| Leven Terr. | 20 | M15 |
| Lewis Terr. | 19 | L16 |
| Lewisvale Av. | 25 | W15 |
| Lewisvale Ct., Muss. | 25 | W15 |
| Lewisvale Pk., Muss. | 25 | V15 |
| Leyden Pk. | 49 | R8 |
| Leyden Pl. | 49 | R8 |
| Liberton Brae | 33 | O13 |
| Liberton Cem. | 42 | O12 |
| Liberton Dr. | 42 | N12 |
| Liberton Gdns. | 42 | O11 |
| Liberton Golf Course | 33 | P13 |
| Liberton Hosp. | 43 | O11 |
| Liberton Pk. | 42 | O12 |
| Liberton Rd. | 33 | O13 |
| Liberton Sch. | 43 | P12 |
| Liberton Sch. Annexe | 33 | P13 |
| Liberton Sch. (Primary) | 33 | O13 |
| Liberton Tower | 42 | N12 |
| Liddesdale Pl. | 19 | L17 |
| Lily Terr.*=Shandon Pl. | | |
| Lilyhill Terr. | 21 | P17 |
| Limes, The | 31 | L14 |
| Lindean Pl. | 13 | O18 |
| Linden Pl. | 48 | P8 |
| Lindsay Pl.* =Chambers St. | | |
| Lindsay Pl. | 12 | N19 |
| Lindsay Rd. | 12 | N19 |
| Lindsay St. | 12 | N19 |
| Linkfield Ct. | 25 | W15 |
| Linkfield Rd., Muss. | 25 | V15 |
| Links Av., Muss. | 24 | U16 |
| Links Gdns. | 13 | O19 |
| Links Gdns. La. | 13 | O19 |
| Links La. | 12 | O19 |
| Links Pl. | 12 | O19 |
| Links St., Muss. | 25 | V15 |
| Links Vw., Muss. | 25 | U16 |
| Linksview Ho. | 12 | O19 |
| Lismore Av. | 21 | P17 |
| Lismore Cr. | 21 | P17 |
| Lismore Sch. | 22 | Q15 |
| Little Acre, Dalk. | 50 | V8 |
| Little France Ho. | 43 | P12 |
| Little France Mills | 34 | P13 |
| Little France Mills* =Dalkeith Rd. | | |
| Little King St. | 7 | M17 |
| Little Lyceum | 6 | L16 |
| Little Rd. | 42 | O12 |
| Livingstone Pl. | 32 | M15 |
| Lixmount Av. | 11 | M19 |
| Lixmount Gdns. | 11 | M19 |

| | | |
|---|---|---|
| Loan, The | 47 | O8 |
| Loanhead Cr. | 48 | P8 |
| Loanhead Hosp. | 48 | P8 |
| Loanhead Memorial Pk. | 47 | O8 |
| Loanhead Rd. | 47 | O9 |
| Loanhead Sch. | 48 | P8 |
| Loaning Cres. | 21 | P17 |
| Loaning Rd. | 21 | P17 |
| Loch Rd. | 17 | H17 |
| Lochend Av. | 13 | O18 |
| Lochend Castle Barns | 21 | O28 |
| Lochend Cl.*=Canongate | | |
| Lochend Cr. | 21 | P17 |
| Lochend Dr. | 21 | O17 |
| Lochend Gdns. | 21 | O17 |
| Lochend Gro. | 21 | P17 |
| Lochend Ho. | 21 | P17 |
| Lochend Pk. (street) | 21 | O17 |
| Lochend Pk. | 21 | O17 |
| Lochend Qt. | 21 | P17 |
| Lochend Rd. | 12 | O18 |
| Lochend Rd. S. | 21 | O17 |
| Lochend Rd. N., Muss. | 24 | U15 |
| Lochend Rd. S., Muss. | 24 | U15 |
| Lochend Sq. | 21 | O17 |
| Lochrin Bdgs. | 19 | L15 |
| Lochrin Pl. | 19 | L15 |
| Lochrin Terr.* =Thornybauk | | |
| Lochview Ct. | 20 | N16 |
| Lockerby Cotts. | 43 | P11 |
| Lockerby Cr. | 43 | P11 |
| Lockerby Gro. | 43 | P11 |
| Lockharton Av. | 30 | J13 |
| Lockharton Cr. | 30 | K13 |
| Lockharton Gdns. | 30 | K14 |
| Logan St. | 19 | M17 |
| Loganlea Av. | 21 | P17 |
| Loganlea Dr. | 21 | P17 |
| Loganlea Gdns. | 21 | P17 |
| Loganlea Loan | 21 | P17 |
| Loganlea Pl. | 21 | P17 |
| Loganlea Rd. | 21 | P17 |
| Loganlea Terr. | 21 | P17 |
| Logie Green Gdns. | 11 | M18 |
| Logie Green Loan | 11 | M18 |
| Logie Green Rd. | 11 | M18 |
| Logie Mill | 11 | M18 |
| Lomond Rd. | 11 | L19 |
| London Rd. | 7 | N17 |
| London Rd., Dalk. | 50 | U10 |
| London St. | 20 | M17 |
| London St. Sch. | 20 | M17 |
| Longformacus Rd. | 42 | O12 |
| Long Hermiston | 28 | D13 |
| Longmore Hosp. | 32 | N15 |
| Longstone Av. | 29 | H13 |
| Longstone Cotts.* =Longstone Rd. | | |
| Longstone Cr. | 29 | H14 |
| Longstone Gdns. | 29 | G14 |
| Longstone Gro. | 29 | H13 |
| Longstone Pk. | 29 | H13 |
| Longstone Rd. | 29 | G13 |
| Longstone Sch. | 29 | H13 |
| Longstone St. | 29 | H13 |
| Longstone Terr. | 29 | G14 |
| Longstone Vw. | 29 | G14 |
| Lonsdale Terr. | 20 | M15 |
| Loretto Ct., Muss. | 24 | U14 |
| Loretto Playing Fields, Muss. | 25 | V16 |
| Loretto Primary Sch. | 25 | V15 |
| Loretto Sch., Muss. | 25 | V15 |
| Lord Russell Pl.* =Causewayside | | |
| Lorne Gro. | 47 | O9 |
| Lorne Pl. | 12 | N18 |
| Lorne Sch. | 12 | N18 |
| Lorne Sq. | 12 | N18 |
| Lorne St. | 12 | N18 |
| Lothian Bk., Dalk. | 50 | T9 |
| Lothian Dr., Dalk. | 50 | V8 |
| Lothian Ho. | 6 | L16 |
| Lothian Region Health Board | 20 | N16 |
| Lothian Rd. | 6 | L16 |

| | | |
|---|---|---|
| Lothian Rd., Dalk. | 50 | U10 |
| Lothian St. | 7 | M16 |
| Lothian St. | 49 | S8 |
| Lothian St., Dalk. | 50 | U10 |
| Lothianburn Golf Course | 46 | L10 |
| Lovedale Av. | 44 | B9 |
| Lovedale Cr. | 44 | B9 |
| Lovedale Gdns. | 44 | B9 |
| Lovedale Gro. | 44 | B9 |
| Lovedale Rd. | 44 | C9 |
| Lovers' Ln. | 32 | M15 |
| Lower Broomieknowe | 49 | R8 |
| Lower Gilmore Pl. | 19 | L15 |
| Lower Granton Rd. | 11 | K20 |
| Lower Joppa | 23 | S16 |
| Lower London Rd. | 21 | O17 |
| Lufra Bk. | 11 | L19 |
| Lugton Brae, Dalk. | 50 | T10 |
| Lussielaw Rd. | 32 | N13 |
| Lutton Pl. | 20 | N15 |
| Lyceum Theatre | 19 | L16 |
| Lygon Rd. | 32 | N13 |
| Lyne St. | 21 | O17 |
| Lynedoch Pl. | 19 | L16 |
| Lynedoch Pl. La. | 19 | L16 |
| Lymphoy | 50 | D10 |
| Macbeth Moir Rd., Muss. | 25 | X15 |
| McDonald Pl. | 12 | M18 |
| McDonald Rd. | 12 | M18 |
| McDonald St. | 12 | N18 |
| McDowall Rd. | 32 | N14 |
| McEwan Hall | 7 | M16 |
| McKelvie Parade | 11 | L20 |
| McLaren Rd. | 33 | O14 |
| McLaren Terr. | 19 | L16 |
| McLeod St. | 18 | K15 |
| McLeod St. Sports Centre | 18 | K15 |
| Mackenzie Pl. | 6 | L17 |
| Mckinlay Terr. | 47 | O8 |
| McNeill Av. | 47 | O8 |
| McNeill Pl. | 47 | O8 |
| McNeill St. | 19 | L15 |
| McNeill Terr. | 47 | O8 |
| McQuade St. | 49 | S8 |
| Madeira Pl. | 12 | N19 |
| Madeira St. | 12 | N19 |
| Magdala Cr. | 19 | K16 |
| Magdala Mews | 19 | K16 |
| Magdalene Av. | 23 | R15 |
| Magdalene Ct. | 22 | R15 |
| Magdalene Dr. | 23 | R15 |
| Magdalene Gdns. | 23 | R15 |
| Magdalene Ln. | 23 | R15 |
| Magdalene Medway | 22 | R15 |
| Magdalene Pl. | 23 | R15 |
| Maidencraig Ct. | 18 | J17 |
| Maidencraig Cr. | 18 | J17 |
| Maidencraig Gro. | 18 | J17 |
| Main Point | 20 | M16 |
| Main St. | 9 | G18 |
| Main St., Balerno | 45 | C9 |
| Mains of Craigimillar | 34 | P13 |
| Maitland Av., Muss. | 24 | U15 |
| Maitland Park Rd., Muss. | 24 | U15 |
| Maitland St., Muss. | 24 | U15 |
| Malcolmstone | 37 | D11 |
| Mall Av., Muss. | 25 | V15 |
| Malleny Av. | 45 | C8 |
| Malleny Ho. | 45 | C9 |
| Malleny Millgate | 45 | C8 |
| Malleny Pk. (Currie R.F.C.) | 45 | C9 |
| Malta Gr.* =St. Bernard's Row | | |
| Malta Terr. | 19 | L17 |
| Mandela Theatre | 21 | N17 |
| Manderston St. | 12 | N18 |
| Mannering Pl. | 42 | O12 |
| Manor Pl. | 19 | L16 |
| Manse Rd. | 17 | F15 |
| Manse St. | 16 | F15 |
| Mansfield Av., Muss. | 25 | V15 |
| Mansfield Ct., Dalk. | 25 | V15 |

| | | |
|---|---|---|
| Mansfield Pl. | 20 | M17 |
| Mansfield Pl., Muss. | 25 | V15 |
| Mansfield Rd., Muss. | 25 | V15 |
| Mansfield Rd. | 45 | C8 |
| Mansionhouse Rd. | 32 | M15 |
| March Gro. | 17 | G17 |
| March Pines | 17 | G17 |
| March Rd. | 17 | G17 |
| Marchbank Dr. | 45 | C8 |
| Marchbank Gdns. | 45 | C8 |
| Marchbank Gr. | 45 | C8 |
| Marchbank Pl. | 45 | C8 |
| Marchbank Wy. | 45 | C9 |
| Marchfield Gdns.* =Hillhouse Rd. | | |
| Marchfield Gro. | 9 | H29 |
| Marchfield Pk. | 9 | G18 |
| Marchfield Pk. La. | 9 | G18 |
| Marchfield Terr. | 9 | H17 |
| Marchhall Cr. | 33 | O15 |
| Marchhall Pl. | 33 | O15 |
| Marchhall Rd. | 33 | O15 |
| Marchmont Cr. | 32 | M15 |
| Marchmont Rd. | 32 | M15 |
| Marchmont St. | 32 | M15 |
| Mardale Cr. | 31 | L14 |
| Marine Dr. | 9 | G19 |
| Marine Esplanade | 13 | P19 |
| Marine Gardens Ind. Site | 22 | Q17 |
| Marionville Av. | 21 | O17 |
| Marionville Cr. | 21 | P17 |
| Marionville Dr. | 21 | P17 |
| Marionville Gro. | 21 | P17 |
| Marionville Medwy. | 21 | P17 |
| Marionville Pk. | 21 | O17 |
| Marionville Rd. | 21 | O17 |
| Marischal Pl.* =Queensferry Rd. | | |
| Maritime La. | 12 | O19 |
| Maritime St. | 12 | O19 |
| Market St. | 7 | M16 |
| Market St., Muss. | 24 | U15 |
| Markfield Park La. | 9 | G18 |
| Marlborough St. | 23 | R16 |
| Marmion Cr. | 33 | O13 |
| Marshall Pl.* =Kirkwood Pl. | | |
| Marshall St. | 7 | M16 |
| Marshall's Ct. | 7 | N17 |
| Martello Ct. | 9 | H19 |
| Martin's Ct.*=Bernard St. | | |
| Martin Gro. | 49 | S8 |
| Martin Pl., Dalk. | 49 | T9 |
| Maryburn Rd., Dalk. | 50 | V8 |
| Mary Erskine Sch., The | 18 | H16 |
| Maryfield, Abbeyhill | 21 | N17 |
| Maryfield, Portobello | 22 | R17 |
| Maryfield Pl. | 21 | O17 |
| Maryfield Pl. | 49 | S8 |
| Mary's Pl.*=Raeburn Pl. | | |
| Marytree Ho. | 43 | P12 |
| Masson Hall | 32 | N14 |
| Maulsford Av. | 51 | R12 |
| Maurice Pl. | 32 | M13 |
| Mavis Bk. | 48 | P8 |
| Maxton Ct., Dalk. | 50 | U10 |
| Maxwell St. | 31 | L14 |
| May Ct. | 9 | H19 |
| May Pk., Muss. | 24 | U15 |
| Maybank Villas* =St. John's Rd. | | |
| Mayburn Av. | 47 | O8 |
| Mayburn Av. | 47 | O9 |
| Mayburn Bk. | 47 | O8 |
| Mayburn Cr. | 47 | O9 |
| Mayburn Ct. | 47 | O8 |
| Mayburn Dr. | 47 | O9 |
| Mayburn Gro. | 47 | O8 |
| Mayburn Hill | 47 | O8 |
| Mayburn Ln. | 47 | O9 |
| Mayburn Terr. | 47 | O9 |
| Mayburn Vale | 47 | O8 |
| Mayburn Walk | 47 | O8 |
| Maybury Dr. | 16 | E16 |
| Maybury Gdns. | 47 | O8 |
| Maybury Rd. | 16 | E17 |
| Mayfield Av., Muss. | 24 | U14 |
| Mayfield Cr. | 48 | P8 |
| Mayfield Cr. | 24 | U14 |
| Mayfield Ct.* =High St.,Loanhead | | |
| Mayfield Gdns. | 32 | N14 |
| Mayfield Gdns. La. | 32 | N14 |
| Mayfield Gdns. La.* =East Mayfield | | |
| Mayfield Pk., Muss.* =Mayfield Av. | | |
| Mayfield Pl. | 16 | F15 |
| Mayfield Pl., Muss. | 24 | U14 |
| Mayfield Rd. | 32 | N14 |
| Mayfield Terr. | 32 | N14 |
| Mayshade Rd. | 47 | O9 |
| Mayville Gdns. E. | 11 | M19 |
| Meadow La. | 20 | M15 |
| Meadow Pl.* =Roseneath Terr. | | |
| Meadow Pl. La. | 32 | M15 |
| Meadow Pl. Rd. | 28 | F15 |
| Meadowbank Av. | 21 | O17 |
| Meadowbank Cr. | 21 | O17 |
| Meadowbank Pl.* =London Rd. | | |
| Meadowbank Sports Centre | 21 | O17 |
| Meadowbank Terr. | 21 | O17 |
| Meadowfield | 15 | D16 |
| Meadowfield Av. | 22 | P16 |
| Meadowfield Ct. | 9 | P16 |
| Meadowfield Dr. | 21 | P16 |
| Meadowfield Gdns. | 21 | P15 |
| Meadowfield Terr. | 21 | P15 |
| Meadowhead | 42 | N12 |
| Meadowfield Pk. | 21 | P16 |
| Meadowhouse Rd. | 17 | G15 |
| Meadow Rd. | 37 | D12 |
| Meadows, The | 20 | M15 |
| Mearnside | 16 | E16 |
| Medical Sch. | 7 | M16 |
| Medwin Ho. | 28 | F13 |
| Meggetland Athletic Grd. | 30 | J14 |
| Meggetland Gate | 30 | J14 |
| Meggetland Terr. | 30 | K14 |
| Melbourne Pl.* =George IV Bridge | | |
| Melgund Terr. | 20 | M17 |
| Melville Cr. | 6 | L16 |
| Melville Dr. | 20 | M15 |
| Melville Dykes | 49 | S9 |
| Melville Gate Rd. | 49 | S10 |
| Melville Grange | 51 | R10 |
| Melville Mains | 48 | R9 |
| Melville Nurseries | 51 | S10 |
| Melville Pl.* =Queensferry St. | | |
| Melville St. | 19 | L16 |
| Melville St. La. | 19 | L16 |
| Melville Terr. | 32 | M15 |
| Melville terr., Dalk. | 50 | T9 |
| Melville Vw. | 49 | R8 |
| Mentone Av. | 22 | R17 |
| Mentone Gdns. | 32 | N14 |
| Mentone Terr. | 32 | N14 |
| Merchant St.* =Candlemaker Row | | |
| Merchiston Av. | 31 | L15 |
| Merchiston Bank Av. | 31 | L14 |
| Merchiston Bk. Gdns. | 31 | L14 |
| Merchiston Castle Sch. | 39 | H12 |
| Merchiston Cr. | 31 | L14 |
| Merchiston Gdns. | 31 | K14 |
| Merchiston Gro. | 30 | K14 |
| Merchiston Mews | 31 | L15 |
| Merchiston Pk. | 31 | L15 |
| Merchiston Pl. | 31 | L15 |
| Mertoun Pl. | 31 | K15 |
| Meuse La. | 7 | M16 |
| Mid Gillsland Rd. | 31 | K14 |
| Mid Hermiston | 27 | D13 |
| Mid Liberton | 33 | O13 |
| Mid Lothian District Council H.Q., Dalk. | 50 | U10 |
| Mid New Cultins | 28 | E13 |
| Mid Steil | 31 | K13 |
| Mid Straiton Cotts. | 47 | O9 |
| Middle Meadow Walk | 20 | M15 |
| Middle Norton | 26 | A15 |
| Middle Pier | 11 | K20 |
| Middleby St. | 32 | N14 |
| Middlefield | 12 | N18 |
| Midmar Av. | 31 | M13 |
| Midmar Dr. | 31 | M13 |
| Midmar Gdns. | 31 | L13 |
| Mill La. | 12 | N19 |
| Millar Cr. | 31 | L14 |
| Millar Pl. | 31 | L14 |
| Millar Pl. La. | 31 | L14 |
| Miller Row | 19 | L16 |
| Millerfield Pl. | 32 | M15 |
| Millerhill Rd. | 35 | R13 |
| Millhill, Muss. | 25 | V15 |
| Millhill La., Muss. | 25 | V15 |
| Milnacre | 12 | M19 |
| Milton Cr. | 22 | R15 |
| Milton Dr. | 23 | S16 |
| Milton Gdns. N. | 22 | R15 |
| Milton Gdns. S. | 22 | R15 |
| Milton Gro. | 23 | T16 |
| Milton Link | 23 | S15 |
| Milton Rd. | 22 | R15 |
| Milton Rd. E. | 23 | S15 |
| Milton Rd. W. | 22 | Q15 |
| Milton St. | 21 | O17 |
| Milton Terr. | 23 | T16 |
| Minto St. | 32 | N15 |
| Mitchell St. | 12 | O19 |
| Mitchell St., Dalk. | 50 | T10 |
| Moat Dr. | 30 | J14 |
| Moat Ho. | 30 | J14 |
| Moat Pl. | 30 | J14 |
| Moat St. | 30 | J14 |
| Moat Terr. | 30 | J14 |
| Moira Pk. | 22 | Q17 |
| Moira Terr. | 22 | Q17 |
| Moncreiff Terr. | 32 | N15 |
| Moncreiffe Ho. | 43 | P12 |
| Monkbarns Gdns. | 42 | O12 |
| Monkton Hall, Muss. | 24 | U14 |
| Monktonhall Golf Course | 25 | V14 |
| Monktonhall Hall Pl., Muss. | 24 | V14 |
| Monktonhall Ho., Muss. | 24 | U14 |
| Monktonhall Pl., Muss. | 24 | U15 |
| Monktonhall Terr., Muss. | 24 | U14 |
| Monkwood Ct. | 32 | M14 |
| Monmouth Terr. | 11 | L18 |
| Montague St. | 7 | N15 |
| Montagu Terr. | 11 | L18 |
| Montgomery Pl. E. | 20 | N17 |
| Montgomery Pl. W. | 20 | N17 |
| Montgomery St. | 20 | N17 |
| Montgomery St. La. | 20 | N17 |
| Montpelier | 31 | L15 |
| Montpelier Pk. | 31 | L15 |
| Montpelier Terr. | 31 | L15 |
| Montrose Terr. | 20 | N17 |
| Moorfield Cotts. | 35 | S12 |
| Moray House Coll. of Education | 7 | N16 |
| Moray House Coll. of Physical Education | 8 | F19 |
| Moray Pl. | 6 | L17 |
| Moredun Dykes Rd. | 43 | P11 |
| Moredun Ho. | 43 | P12 |
| Moredun Institute (Animal Diseases) | 43 | P12 |
| Moredun Park Ct. | 43 | P12 |
| Moredun Park Dr. | 43 | P12 |
| Moredun Park Gdns. | 43 | P12 |
| Moredun Park Gr. | 43 | Q12 |
| Moredun Park Gro. | 43 | Q12 |
| Moredun Park Ln. | 43 | P12 |
| Moredun Park Rd. | 43 | P12 |
| Moredun Park St. | 43 | P12 |
| Moredun Park Vw. | 43 | Q12 |
| Moredun Park Walk | 43 | Q12 |
| Moredun Park Way | 43 | P12 |
| Moredun Sch. | 43 | P12 |
| Moredunvale Bk. | 43 | P12 |

| | | |
|---|---|---|
| Moredunvale Gr. | 43 | P12 |
| Moredunvale Gro. | 43 | P12 |
| Moredunvale Ln. | 43 | P12 |
| Moredunvale Pk. | 43 | P12 |
| Moredunvale Pl. | 43 | P12 |
| Moredunvale Rd. | 43 | P12 |
| Moredunvale Vw. | 43 | P12 |
| Moredunvale Way | 43 | P12 |
| Morgan Athletic Grd. | 33 | O14 |
| Morningside Cem. | 31 | L13 |
| Morningside Ct. | 31 | L13 |
| Morningside Dr. | 31 | K13 |
| Morningside Gdns. | 31 | K13 |
| Morningside Gro. | 31 | K13 |
| Morningside Pk. (street) | 31 | L14 |
| Morningside Pk. | 31 | L13 |
| Morningside Pl. | 31 | L14 |
| Morningside Rd. | 31 | L14 |
| Morningside Terr. | 31 | L14 |
| Morrison Link | 19 | L16 |
| Morrison St. | 6 | L16 |
| Morrison St. Link | 19 | L16 |
| Morton Mains | 41 | M10 |
| Morton St. | 23 | S16 |
| Mortonhall Crem. | 42 | N11 |
| Mortonhall Garden Centre | 42 | N11 |
| Mortonhall Gate | 42 | N11 |
| Mortonhall Golf Course | 41 | M12 |
| Mortonhall Park Av. | 42 | N11 |
| Mortonhall Park Bk. | 42 | O11 |
| Mortonhall Park Cr. | 42 | O11 |
| Mortonhall Park Dr. | 42 | O11 |
| Mortonhall Park Gdns. | 42 | N11 |
| Mortonhall Park Gr. | 42 | N11 |
| Mortonhall Park Gro. | 42 | N11 |
| Mortonhall Park Ln. | 42 | N11 |
| Mortonhall Park Pl. | 42 | O11 |
| Mortonhall Pk. Terr.* =Mortonhall Pk. Dr. | | |
| Mortonhall Park Vw. | 42 | N11 |
| Mortonhall Park Way | 42 | N11 |
| Mortonhall Rd. | 32 | M14 |
| Morven St. | 16 | F17 |
| Mossgiel Walk* =Cumnor Cr. | | |
| Moston Terr. | 32 | N14 |
| Mound Pl. | 6 | M16 |
| Mound, The | 6 | M16 |
| Mount Alvernia Convent | 43 | O12 |
| Mount Grange | 32 | M14 |
| Mount Lodge Pl. | 23 | R16 |
| Mount Vernon Cem. | 43 | O12 |
| Mount Vernon Rd. | 42 | O12 |
| Mountbatten Bdg. | 6 | M16 |
| Mountcastle Bk. | 22 | Q16 |
| Mountcastle Cr. | 22 | Q16 |
| Mountcastle Dr. N. | 22 | Q16 |
| Mountcastle Dr. S. | 22 | Q16 |
| Mountcastle Gdns. | 22 | Q16 |
| Mountcastle Gr. | 22 | Q17 |
| Mountcastle Gro. | 22 | Q16 |
| Mountcastle Ln. | 22 | Q16 |
| Mountcastle Pk.* =Mountcastle Cr. | | |
| Mountcastle Pl. | 22 | Q17 |
| Mountcastle Terr. | 22 | Q16 |
| Mounthooly Ln. | 41 | M11 |
| Mountjoy Terr., Muss. | 25 | V16 |
| Mucklets Av., Muss. | 24 | U14 |
| Mucklets Cr., Muss. | 24 | U14 |
| Mucklets Ct., Muss. | 24 | U14 |
| Mucklets Dr. | 24 | U14 |
| Mucklets Pl., Muss. | 24 | U14 |
| Muir Wood Cr. | 38 | E11 |
| Muir Wood Dr. | 38 | E11 |
| Muir Wood Gro. | 38 | E11 |
| Muir Wood Pl. | 38 | E11 |
| Muir Wood Rd. | 38 | E11 |
| Muirdale Terr. | 18 | H17 |
| Muirend Av. | 39 | G12 |
| Muirfield Gdns. | 47 | P8 |
| Muirhouse Av. | 10 | H18 |
| Muirhouse Bk. | 9 | H18 |
| Muirhouse Cr. | 10 | H19 |
| Muirhouse Dr. | 9 | H19 |
| Muirhouse Gdns. | 9 | H19 |

| | | |
|---|---|---|
| Muirhouse Gr. | 9 | H18 |
| Muirhouse Gro. | 9 | H19 |
| Muirhouse Ln. | 9 | H19 |
| Muirhouse Medway | 9 | H18 |
| Muirhouse Pk. (street) | 9 | H18 |
| Muirhouse Pk. | 9 | H18 |
| Muirhouse Parkway | 9 | H19 |
| Muirhouse Pl. E. | 10 | H18 |
| Muirhouse Pl. W. | 10 | H18 |
| Muirhouse Sch. | 10 | H18 |
| Muirhouse Terr. | 9 | H18 |
| Muirhouse Vw. | 9 | H19 |
| Muirhouse Way | 10 | H18 |
| Muirpark | 50 | T9 |
| Muirside | 40 | K11 |
| Mulberry Pl.* =Newhaven Rd. | | |
| Munro Dr. | 39 | H11 |
| Munro Pl.*=Canonmills | | |
| Murano Pl. | 20 | N17 |
| Murchison Ho. | 32 | N13 |
| Murdoch Terr. | 19 | L15 |
| Murieston Cr. | 19 | K15 |
| Murieston Cr. La. | 19 | K15 |
| Murieston La. | 19 | K15 |
| Murieston Pl. | 19 | K15 |
| Murieston Rd. | 19 | K15 |
| Murieston Terr. | 19 | K15 |
| Murray Cotts. | 16 | F15 |
| Murray Gr. | 16 | F15 |
| Murray Home | 43 | P12 |
| Murrayburn Appr. | 28 | F13 |
| Murrayburn Dr. | 28 | F13 |
| Murrayburn Gate | 28 | F13 |
| Murrayburn Gdns. | 29 | G13 |
| Murrayburn Gr. | 29 | G13 |
| Murrayburn Gro. | 29 | G13 |
| Murrayburn Pk. | 28 | F13 |
| Murrayburn Pl. | 29 | F13 |
| Murrayburn Rd. | 29 | F13 |
| Murrayburn Sch. | 29 | G13 |
| Murrayfield Av. | 18 | J16 |
| Murrayfield Dr. | 18 | J16 |
| Murrayfield Gdns. | 18 | J16 |
| Murrayfield Golf Course | 18 | H16 |
| Murrayfield Hosp. | 17 | H16 |
| Murrayfield Ho. | 18 | J16 |
| Murrayfield Pl. | 18 | J16 |
| Murrayfield Rd. | 18 | J16 |
| Murrayfield (S.R.U. Grd.) | 18 | J15 |
| Murrayfield Stadium | 18 | J15 |
| Murrays, The | 43 | P10 |
| Murrays Brae, The | 43 | P10 |
| Museum of Childhood* =High St. | | |
| Music Hall | 6 | M16 |
| Musselburgh Burgh Sch., Muss. | 24 | V15 |
| Musselburgh Links, Muss. | 25 | V16 |
| Musselburgh Links Golf Course | 25 | W16 |
| Musselburgh Links Race Course | 25 | W16 |
| Musselburgh Loretto Sch., Muss. | 25 | V15 |
| Musselburgh Rd. | 23 | S16 |
| Musselburgh Rd., Dalk. | 50 | U10 |
| Musselburgh R.C. School | 25 | V15 |
| Musselburgh Sch., Muss. | 25 | V15 |
| Myreside Ct. | 31 | K13 |
| Myreside Rd. | 31 | K14 |
| Myrtle Terr. | 30 | K15 |
| Nantwich Dr. | 13 | Q18 |
| Napier Rd. | 31 | K14 |
| Napier University (Sighthill Campus) | 28 | F13 |
| Napier University (Craiglockhart Campus) | 30 | J13 |
| Napier University (Merchiston Campus) | 31 | L14 |
| Napier University (Spylaw Road) | 31 | K14 |

| | | |
|---|---|---|
| Napier University (Bryson Road) | 31 | K15 |
| Napier University (Marchmont) | 32 | M15 |
| National Gallery | 6 | M16 |
| National Library of Scotland | 7 | M16 |
| National Library of Scotland-Scottish Science Library | 32 | N15 |
| Nazareth Ho. | 49 | R9 |
| Neidpath Ct.* =Craigievar Wynd | | |
| Nellfield | 43 | O12 |
| Nelson Pl.* =Dublin Meuse | | |
| Nelson St. | 6 | M17 |
| Nether Craigour | 34 | P13 |
| Nether Craigwell | 7 | N16 |
| Nether Currie Cr. | 38 | E11 |
| Nether Currie Pl. | 38 | E11 |
| Nether Currie Rd. | 38 | E11 |
| Nether Currie Sch. | 38 | E11 |
| Nether Lennie | 15 | C18 |
| Netherbow Arts Centre | 7 | N16 |
| Netherby Rd. | 11 | L19 |
| New Arthur Pl. | 7 | N15 |
| New Belfield | 22 | Q16 |
| New Bells Ct. | 12 | O19 |
| New Broompark | 10 | K20 |
| New Broughton | 7 | M17 |
| New Coll. | 20 | M16 |
| New John's Pl. | 7 | N15 |
| New La. | 12 | M19 |
| New Market Rd. | 30 | J14 |
| New Markets | 30 | J14 |
| New Mart Rd. | 30 | H14 |
| New Meadowspott, Dalk. | 50 | T9 |
| New Orchardfield | 12 | N18 |
| New St. Andrews Ho. | 7 | M17 |
| New St. | 20 | N16 |
| New St. | 43 | P11 |
| New St., Muss. | 24 | U15 |
| New Swanston | 40 | K11 |
| Newbattle Abbey Cres., Dalk. | 50 | T9 |
| Newbattle Abbey Hostel, Dalk. | 50 | U9 |
| Newbattle Golf Course, Dalk. | 50 | U9 |
| Newbattle Rd. | 50 | T9 |
| Newbattle Terr. | 31 | L14 |
| Newbigging, Muss. | 25 | V15 |
| Newcraighall Dr. | 35 | S14 |
| Newcraighall Ind. Estate | 35 | R14 |
| Newcraighall Pk. | 35 | T14 |
| Newcraighall Rd. | 35 | R14 |
| Newcraighall Sch. | 35 | T14 |
| Newhaven Main St. | 11 | M20 |
| Newhaven Pl. | 12 | M20 |
| Newhaven Rd. | 12 | M19 |
| Newhailes, Muss. | 24 | T15 |
| Newhailes Av., Muss. | 24 | U15 |
| Newhailes Cr., Muss. | 24 | U15 |
| Newhailes Rd., Muss. | 24 | U15 |
| Newhouse | 36 | B10 |
| Newington Cem. | 33 | O14 |
| Newington Rd. | 32 | N15 |
| Newkirkgate | 12 | N18 |
| Newlands Pk.* =Mayfield Gdns. | | |
| Newmills Av. | 45 | C10 |
| Newmills Cr. | 45 | C10 |
| Newmills Gro. | 45 | C10 |
| Newmills Rd., Dalk. | 50 | U10 |
| Newmills Terr.* =James Lean Av. | | |
| Newmills Rd. | 45 | C10 |
| Newport St. | 6 | L16 |
| Newtoft St. | 43 | Q11 |
| Newton Church Rd. | 51 | S12 |
| Newton St. | 30 | K15 |
| Newton St., Dalk. | 50 | V8 |
| Newton Village | 51 | S12 |
| Nicolson Sq. | 7 | N16 |
| Nicolson St. | 7 | N16 |
| Niddrie Cotts. | 35 | S14 |

| | | |
|---|---|---|
| Niddrie Farm Gro. | 34 | Q14 |
| Niddrie House Av. | 34 | R14 |
| Niddrie House Dr. | 34 | R14 |
| Niddrie House Gdns. | 34 | R14 |
| Niddrie House Gro. | 42 | R14 |
| Niddrie House Pk. | 34 | Q14 |
| Niddrie House Sq. | 34 | Q14 |
| Niddrie Mains Ct. | 34 | R14 |
| Niddrie Mains Dr. | 34 | Q14 |
| Niddrie Mains Rd. | 34 | P14 |
| Niddrie Mains Terr. | 34 | Q14 |
| Niddrie Marischal Cr. | 34 | Q14 |
| Niddrie Marischal Dr. | 34 | Q14 |
| Niddrie Marischal Gdns. | 34 | Q14 |
| Niddrie Marischal Gr. | 34 | Q14 |
| Niddrie Marischal Gro. | 34 | R14 |
| Niddrie Marischal Ln. | 34 | Q14 |
| Niddrie Marischal Pl. | 34 | Q14 |
| Niddrie Marischal Rd. | 34 | R14 |
| Niddrie Marischal St. | 34 | Q14 |
| Niddrie Mill Av. | 34 | R14 |
| Niddrie Mill Cr. | 34 | R15 |
| Niddrie Mill Dr. | 34 | R14 |
| Niddrie Mill Gro. | 34 | R14 |
| Niddrie Mill Pl. | 34 | R14 |
| Niddrie Mill Terr. | 34 | R14 |
| Niddrie Policies | 34 | R14 |
| Niddrie Sch. | 34 | R14 |
| Niddry St. | 7 | M16 |
| Niddry St. S.*=Cowgate | | |
| Nigel Ln. | 42 | O12 |
| Nile Gro. | 31 | L14 |
| Niven's Knowe Rd. | 47 | N8 |
| Nivensknowe Caravan Park | 47 | N8 |
| Nisbet Ct. | 13 | O18 |
| Noble Pl. | 13 | O18 |
| North Bank St. | 6 | M16 |
| North Bridge | 7 | M16 |
| North Bughtlin Bk. | 16 | E17 |
| North Bughtlin Brae | 16 | E17 |
| North Bughtlin Gate | 16 | E17 |
| North Bughtlin Neuk | 16 | E17 |
| North Bughtlin Pl. | 16 | E17 |
| North Bughtlin Rd. | 16 | E17 |
| North Bughtlinfield | 16 | E17 |
| North Bughtlinrig | 16 | E17 |
| North Bughtlinside | 16 | E17 |
| North Cairntow | 33 | P15 |
| North Castle St. | 6 | L17 |
| North Charlotte St. | 6 | L16 |
| North Clyde St. La. | 7 | M17 |
| North East Circus Pl. | 6 | L17 |
| North Fort St. | 12 | N19 |
| North Greens | 34 | R15 |
| North Gyle Av. | 16 | E15 |
| North Gyle Dr. | 16 | E16 |
| North Gyle Farm Ct. | 16 | E15 |
| North Gyle Farm La. | 16 | E15 |
| North Gyle Gro. | 16 | E16 |
| North Gyle Ln. | 16 | E16 |
| North Gyle Pk. | 16 | E16 |
| North Gyle Rd. | 16 | E16 |
| North Gyle Terr. | 16 | E15 |
| North High St., Muss. | 24 | U15 |
| North High St., Muss. | 24 | V15 |
| North Hillhousefield | 12 | N19 |
| North Junction St. | 12 | N19 |
| North Leigh Mill | 12 | N19 |
| North Leith Sands | 12 | N19 |
| North Meadow Walk | 20 | M15 |
| North Meggetland | 16 | K14 |
| North Merchiston Cem. | 30 | K15 |
| North Park Terr. | 19 | L17 |
| North Peffer Pl. | 33 | P14 |
| North Richmond St.* =West Adam St. | | |
| North St. Andrew La.* =N. St. Andrew St. | | |
| North St. Andrew St. | 7 | M17 |
| North St. David St. | 20 | M17 |
| North Walk, The | 31 | L13 |
| North Way, The | 21 | P16 |
| North West Circus Pl. | 6 | L17 |
| North Werber Pk. | 10 | K18 |
| North Werber Pl. | 10 | K18 |
| North Werber Rd. | 10 | K18 |
| North Wynd, Dalk. | 50 | U10 |
| Northcote St. | 19 | K22 |
| Northern General Hosp. | 10 | K18 |
| Northfield Av. | 21 | P16 |
| Northfield Bdwy. | 22 | P17 |
| Northfield Circus | 22 | P16 |
| Northfield Cr. | 22 | P16 |
| Northfield Dr. | 22 | Q16 |
| Northfield Farm Av. | 22 | Q16 |
| Northfield Farm Rd. | 22 | Q16 |
| Northfield Gdns. | 22 | Q16 |
| Northfield Gro. | 22 | Q16 |
| Northfield Pk. | 22 | Q16 |
| Northfield Park Gro. | 22 | Q16 |
| Northfield Rd. | 22 | P16 |
| Northfield Sq. | 22 | Q16 |
| Northfield Terr.* =Willowbrae Rd. | | |
| Northlawn Terr. | 9 | G18 |
| Northumberland Pl.* =Northumberland St. | | |
| Northumberland Pl. La. | 6 | M17 |
| Northumberland St. | 6 | M17 |
| Northumberland St. La., N.E. | 6 | M17 |
| Northumberland St. La., N.W. | 6 | M17 |
| Northumberland St. La., S.E. | 6 | M17 |
| Northumberland St. La., S.W. | 6 | M17 |
| Northview Ct. | 10 | H19 |
| Norton Pk. | 21 | O17 |
| Norton Mains | 26 | A15 |
| Norton Rd. | 26 | B14 |
| Oak La. | 17 | G17 |
| Oakfield Pl. | 7 | N15 |
| Oaklands Sch. | 29 | G14 |
| Oakville Terr. | 13 | O18 |
| Observatory Gr. | 32 | N13 |
| Observatory Rd. | 32 | N13 |
| Ochiltree Gdns. | 33 | P13 |
| Odeon Cinema | 7 | N15 |
| Ogilvie Terr. | 31 | K14 |
| Old Assembly Cl.* =High St. | | |
| Old Broughton | 7 | M17 |
| Old Burdiehouse Rd. | 42 | O10 |
| Old Church La. | 21 | P15 |
| Old Dalkeith Rd. | 33 | O14 |
| Old Dalkeith Rd., Dalk. | 50 | T10 |
| Old Edinburgh Rd., Dalk. | 50 | T10 |
| Old Farm Av. | 40 | J12 |
| Old Farm Pl. | 40 | H12 |
| Old Fishmarket Cl. | 7 | M16 |
| Old Kirk Rd. | 17 | G16 |
| Old Mill La. | 33 | O13 |
| Old Newmills Rd. | 45 | C10 |
| Old Pentland | 47 | N9 |
| Old Quadrangle* =South Bridge | | |
| Old Tolbooth Wynd | 7 | N16 |
| Olive Bank Pk., Muss. | 24 | U15 |
| Olivebank Rd., Muss. | 24 | U15 |
| Orchard Bk. | 18 | K17 |
| Orchard Brae | 19 | K17 |
| Orchard Brae Av. | 19 | K17 |
| Orchard Brae Gdns. | 19 | K17 |
| Orchard Brae Gdns. W. | 18 | K17 |
| Orchard Brae Ho. | 19 | K17 |
| Orchard Brae West* =Orchard Brae | | |
| Orchard Cr. | 18 | J17 |
| Orchard Dr. | 18 | J17 |
| Orchard Gdns. | 18 | J17 |
| Orchard Gro. | 19 | K17 |
| Orchard Pl. | 19 | K17 |
| Orchard Rd. | 18 | K17 |
| Orchard Rd. S. | 18 | J17 |
| Orchard Terr. | 18 | K17 |
| Orchard Toll | 18 | K17 |
| Orchard Vw. | 49 | T9 |
| Orchardfield Av. | 17 | F15 |
| Orchardfield La. | 12 | N18 |
| Orchardhead Ln. | 42 | O12 |
| Orchardhead Rd. | 42 | O12 |
| Ormelie Terr. | 23 | S16 |
| Ormidale Terr. | 18 | J16 |
| Ormiston Terr. | 17 | F15 |
| Orrok Pk. | 33 | O13 |
| Orwell Pl. | 19 | K15 |
| Orwell Sch. | 19 | K15 |
| Orwell Terr. | 19 | K15 |
| Osborne Terr. | 19 | K16 |
| Oswald Ct. | 32 | M14 |
| Oswald Rd. | 32 | M14 |
| Oswald Terr. | 16 | F15 |
| Otterburn Pk. | 30 | J12 |
| Outlook Tower and Camera Obscura | 6 | M16 |
| Over Gogar | 27 | C13 |
| Oxcars Ct. | 9 | H19 |
| Oxcraig St. | 11 | K20 |
| Oxford St. | 20 | N15 |
| Oxford Terr. | 19 | L17 |
| Oxgangs Av. | 40 | K11 |
| Oxgangs Bk. | 40 | K11 |
| Oxgangs Brae | 40 | K11 |
| Oxgangs Bdwy. | 40 | K11 |
| Oxgangs Cr. | 40 | K12 |
| Oxgangs Dr. | 40 | K12 |
| Oxgangs Farm Av. | 40 | K11 |
| Oxgangs Farm Dr. | 40 | K11 |
| Oxgangs Farm Gdns. | 40 | K11 |
| Oxgangs Farm Gro. | 40 | K11 |
| Oxgangs Farm Ln. | 40 | K11 |
| Oxgangs Farm Terr. | 40 | K11 |
| Oxgangs Gdns. | 40 | K12 |
| Oxgangs Gr. | 40 | K12 |
| Oxgangs Gro. | 40 | K12 |
| Oxgangs Hill | 41 | K12 |
| Oxgangs Ho. | 40 | K12 |
| Oxgangs Library | 40 | K11 |
| Oxgangs Ln. | 41 | K12 |
| Oxgangs Medway | 40 | K11 |
| Oxgangs Pk. | 40 | K11 |
| Oxgangs Path | 40 | K11 |
| Oxgangs Path E. | 40 | K11 |
| Oxgangs Pl. | 40 | K12 |
| Oxgangs Rise | 40 | K12 |
| Oxgangs Rd. | 40 | K11 |
| Oxgangs Rd. N. | 40 | J12 |
| Oxgangs Row | 40 | K11 |
| Oxgangs Sch. | 40 | J12 |
| Oxgangs St. | 40 | K11 |
| Oxgangs Terr. | 40 | K11 |
| Oxgangs Vw. | 40 | K11 |
| Paddock, The, Muss.* =Balcarres Rd. | | |
| Paddockholm | 17 | G15 |
| Paisley Av. | 21 | P16 |
| Paisley Cr. | 21 | P16 |
| Paisley Dr. | 21 | P16 |
| Paisley Gdns. | 21 | P16 |
| Paisley Gro. | 21 | P16 |
| Paisley Terr. | 21 | P16 |
| Palmer Pl. | 38 | D10 |
| Palmer Rd. | 38 | D11 |
| Palmerston Pl. | 19 | L16 |
| Palmerston Pl. La.* =Palmerston Pl. | | |
| Palmerston Rd. | 32 | M15 |
| Pankhurst Ln. | 50 | V10 |
| Panmure Pl. | 6 | M15 |
| Pape's Cotts. | 18 | J16 |
| Paradykes Av. | 47 | O8 |
| Paradykes Sch. | 47 | O8 |
| Park Av. | 22 | R16 |
| Park Av. | 47 | O8 |
| Park Av., Muss. | 25 | W15 |
| Park Cr. | 49 | R8 |
| Park Cr. | 47 | O8 |
| Park Cr. | 42 | O12 |
| Park Ct., Muss. | 25 | W15 |
| Park Gdns. | 42 | O12 |
| Park Gr. | 42 | O12 |
| Park Grove Pl. | 25 | W15 |
| Park Grove Terr., Muss. | 25 | W15 |
| Park House Day Hospital | 25 | W15 |
| Park La., Muss. | 25 | W15 |

| | | |
|---|---|---|
| Park Pl. | 11 | M19 |
| Park Rd. | 11 | M19 |
| Park Rd. | 49 | R8 |
| Park Rd., Dalk. | 50 | T9 |
| Park Terr. | 35 | T14 |
| Park Vw. | 35 | S14 |
| Park Vw. | 47 | O8 |
| Park Vw., Muss. | 25 | W15 |
| Parker Av. | 22 | Q17 |
| Parker Rd. | 22 | Q17 |
| Parker Terr. | 22 | Q17 |
| Parkgrove Av. | 16 | F17 |
| Parkgrove Bk. | 16 | F17 |
| Parkgrove Cr. | 16 | F17 |
| Parkgrove Dr. | 16 | F17 |
| Parkgrove Gdns. | 16 | F17 |
| Parkgrove Gr. | 16 | F17 |
| Parkgrove Ln. | 16 | F17 |
| Parkgrove Neuk | 16 | F17 |
| Parkgrove Path* =Parkgrove Terr. | | |
| Parkgrove Pl. | 16 | F17 |
| Parkgrove Rd. | 16 | F17 |
| Parkgrove Row | 16 | F17 |
| Parkgrove St | 16 | F17 |
| Parkgrove Terr. | 16 | F17 |
| Parkgrove Vw. | 16 | F17 |
| Parkhead Av. | 29 | G13 |
| Parkhead Cr. | 29 | G13 |
| Parkhead Dr. | 29 | G13 |
| Parkhead Gdns. | 29 | G13 |
| Parkhead Gro. | 29 | G13 |
| Parkhead Ln. | 29 | G13 |
| Parkhead Pl. | 29 | G13 |
| Parkhead St. | 29 | G13 |
| Parkhead Terr. | 29 | G13 |
| Parkhead Vw. | 29 | G13 |
| Parkside Pl., Dalk. | 50 | U10 |
| Parkside St. | 7 | N15 |
| Parkside Terr. | 20 | N15 |
| Parsonage, Muss. | 25 | V15 |
| Parkvale Pl. | 13 | O18 |
| Parliament Ho. | 7 | M16 |
| Parliament Pl.* =Parliament St. | | |
| Parliament Sq.* =Newhaven Pl. | | |
| Parliament Sq. | 7 | M16 |
| Parliament St. | 12 | N19 |
| Parrotshot | 34 | R15 |
| Parsons Green Sch. | 21 | P16 |
| Parsons Green Terr. | 21 | P17 |
| Patie's Rd. | 40 | J12 |
| Patie's Rd. Recreation Grd. | 39 | H12 |
| Patriothall*=Hamilton Pl. | | |
| Pattison St. | 13 | O19 |
| Peacock Ct.* =Newhaven Pl. | | |
| Peacocktail Cl. | 35 | R14 |
| Pearce Av. | 16 | F16 |
| Pearce Gro. | 16 | F23 |
| Pearce Rd. | 16 | F16 |
| Peatville Gdns. | 29 | H13 |
| Peatville Terr. | 29 | H13 |
| Peel Terr. | 32 | N14 |
| Peffer Bk. | 33 | P14 |
| Peffer Pl. | 33 | P14 |
| Peffer St. | 33 | P14 |
| Peffermill Ct. | 33 | P14 |
| Peffermill Ho. | 33 | P14 |
| Peffermill Rd. | 33 | O14 |
| Peffermill Sch. | 34 | P14 |
| Peggy's Mill Rd. | 8 | E18 |
| Pembroke Pl. | 19 | K16 |
| Pendreich Av. | 49 | S8 |
| Pendreich Dr. | 49 | S8 |
| Pendreich Gr. | 49 | S8 |
| Pendreich Terr. | 49 | S8 |
| Pendreich Vw. | 49 | S8 |
| Pennywell Cotts. | 10 | H19 |
| Pennywell Ct. | 10 | H19 |
| Pennywell Gdns. | 9 | H19 |
| Pennywell Gro. | 9 | H19 |
| Pennywell Medway | 9 | H19 |
| Pennywell Pl. | 9 | H19 |
| Pennywell Rd. | 10 | H19 |
| Pennywell Villas | 10 | H19 |
| Pentland Av. | 37 | D10 |
| Pentland Av. | 39 | H12 |
| Pentland Ho. | 30 | H12 |
| Pentland Caravan Park | 47 | N8 |
| Pentland Cr. | 41 | L12 |
| Pentland Dr. | 41 | K11 |
| Pentland Gdn. Ctre. | 47 | N8 |
| Pentland Gdns. | 41 | L12 |
| Pentland Gro. | 41 | L12 |
| Pentland Hills | 39 | F10 |
| Pentland Ho. | 30 | J14 |
| Pentland Industrial Estate | 47 | N8 |
| Pentland Mains | 47 | N8 |
| Pentland Pl. | 38 | D10 |
| Pentland Rd. | 39 | H12 |
| Pentland Rd. | 48 | R8 |
| Pentland Rd. | 46 | M9 |
| Pentland Terr. | 41 | L12 |
| Pentland Vw., Comiston | 41 | L11 |
| Pentland Vw., Dalk. | 50 | V9 |
| Pentland Vw., Currie | 38 | D10 |
| Pentland View Ct. | 38 | D10 |
| People's Story | 7 | N16 |
| Persevere Ct. | 12 | N19 |
| Perth St. | 20 | L17 |
| Pettigrew's Cl., Dalk. | 50 | U10 |
| Peveril Terr. | 42 | O12 |
| Picardy Pl. | 7 | M17 |
| Pier Pl. | 11 | M20 |
| Piersfield Gro. | 21 | P17 |
| Piersfield Pl. | 21 | P17 |
| Piersfield Terr. | 21 | P17 |
| Piershill Cem. | 22 | Q17 |
| Piershill La. | 21 | P17 |
| Piershill Pl. | 21 | P17 |
| Piershill Sch. | 21 | P16 |
| Piershill Sq. E. | 21 | P17 |
| Piershill Sq. W. | 21 | P17 |
| Piershill Terr. | 21 | P17 |
| Pillars, The | 43 | P12 |
| Pilrig Cotts. | 12 | N18 |
| Pilrig Gdns. | 12 | N18 |
| Pilrig Ho. Cl. | 12 | N18 |
| Pilrig Pk. | 12 | N18 |
| Pilrig Park Sch. | 12 | N18 |
| Pilrig Pl. | 12 | N18 |
| Pilrig St. | 12 | N18 |
| Pilton Av. | 10 | K19 |
| Pilton Cr. | 10 | K19 |
| Pilton Dr. | 10 | K19 |
| Pilton Dr. N. | 10 | K19 |
| Pilton Gdns. | 10 | K19 |
| Pilton Ln. | 10 | K19 |
| Pilton Pk. | 10 | K19 |
| Pilton Pl. | 10 | K19 |
| Pinkhill | 17 | G15 |
| Pinkie Av., Muss. | 25 | W15 |
| Pinkie Dr., Muss. | 25 | W15 |
| Pinkie Hill Cr., Muss. | 25 | W15 |
| Pinkie Ho. | 25 | V15 |
| Pinkie Mains, Muss. | 25 | W15 |
| Pinkie Pl., Muss. | 25 | W15 |
| Pinkie Rd., Muss. | 25 | V15 |
| Pinkie Terr., Muss. | 25 | W15 |
| Pinkie St. Peter's Sch., Muss. | 25 | W15 |
| Pipe La. | 22 | R17 |
| Pipe St. | 22 | R17 |
| Pirniefield Bk. | 13 | P18 |
| Pirniefield Gdns. | 13 | P18 |
| Pirniefield Gro. | 13 | P18 |
| Pirniefield Pl. | 13 | P18 |
| Pirniefield Terr. | 13 | P18 |
| Pirniehall Sch. | 10 | J19 |
| Pirrie St. | 12 | N18 |
| Pitlochry Pl. | 21 | O17 |
| Pitsligo Rd. | 31 | L14 |
| Pitt St. | 12 | N19 |
| Pittencrieff Ct.* =Craighall Terr. | | |
| Pittville St. | 23 | R16 |
| Pittville St. La. | 23 | R16 |
| Place Charente, Dalk. | 50 | V10 |
| Playfair Steps* =N. Bank St. | | |
| Playhouse | 7 | N17 |
| Pleasance | 7 | N16 |
| Pleasance Sports Ctre. (Edinburgh University) | 7 | N16 |
| Pleasance Theatre | 7 | N16 |
| Plewlands Av. | 31 | K13 |
| Plewlands Gdns. | 31 | K13 |
| Plewlands Terr. | 31 | K13 |
| Pleydell Pl. | 42 | O12 |
| Pollock Halls | 33 | O15 |
| Polton Ct. | | R8 |
| Polton Gdns. | 48 | R8 |
| Polton Ho. | 48 | Q8 |
| Polton Pl. | | R8 |
| Polton Rd. | 48 | R8 |
| Polton Rd., Lasswade | 48 | R8 |
| Polton St. | 49 | R8 |
| Polwarth Cr. | 31 | L15 |
| Polwarth Gdns. | 31 | K15 |
| Polwarth Gro. | 31 | K15 |
| Polwarth Pk. | 31 | K15 |
| Polwarth Pl. | 31 | K14 |
| Polwarth Terr. | 31 | K13 |
| Ponton St. | 6 | L15 |
| Poplar La. | 13 | O19 |
| Port Royal Golf Range | 14 | A16 |
| Porterfield Rd. | 10 | K18 |
| Portgower Pl. | 19 | L17 |
| Portland Pl.* =North Junction St. | | |
| Portland Terr.* =North Junction St. | | |
| Portland St. | 12 | N19 |
| Portobello Cem. | 23 | S15 |
| Portobello Golf Course | 22 | R16 |
| Portobello High St. | 22 | R17 |
| Portobello Rd. | 22 | P17 |
| Portobello Sch. | 22 | Q16 |
| Portobello Sch. Annexe | 22 | R16 |
| Portsburgh Sq.* =West Port | | |
| Potterrow | 7 | M16 |
| Pottery, The*=Pipe La. | | |
| Powderhall Stadium | 12 | M18 |
| Preston St. Sch. | 32 | N15 |
| Prestonfield Av. | 33 | O14 |
| Prestonfield Bk. | 33 | O14 |
| Prestonfield Cr. | 33 | O14 |
| Prestonfield Gdns. | 33 | O14 |
| Prestonfield Golf Course | 33 | O15 |
| Prestonfield Pk. | 33 | O14 |
| Prestonfield Rd. | 33 | O14 |
| Prestonfield Sch. | 33 | O14 |
| Prestonfield Terr. | 33 | O14 |
| Priestfield Av. | 33 | O14 |
| Priestfield Cr. | 33 | O14 |
| Priestfield Gdns. | 33 | O14 |
| Priestfield Gro. | 33 | O15 |
| Priestfield Rd. | 33 | O15 |
| Priestfield Rd. N. | 33 | O15 |
| Primrose Cr., Dalk. | 50 | V9 |
| Primrose St. | 12 | O18 |
| Primrose Terr. | 30 | K15 |
| Primrose Terr., Dalk. | 50 | V9 |
| Primrose Bank Rd. | 11 | L19 |
| Prince Regent St. | 12 | N19 |
| Princes St. | 6 | L16 |
| Princes Street Gardens | 6 | M16 |
| Princess Alexandra Eye Pavilion | 6 | M15 |
| Princess Margaret Rose Hosp. | 41 | M11 |
| Promenade | 23 | R17 |
| Promenade | 24 | U16 |
| Promenade Terr. | 22 | R17 |
| Prospect Bank Cr. | 13 | O18 |
| Prospect Bank Gdns. | 13 | O18 |
| Prospect Bank Gro. | 13 | P18 |
| Prospect Bank Pl. | 13 | P18 |
| Prospect Bank Rd. | 13 | O18 |
| Prospect Bank Sch. | 13 | O18 |
| Prospect Bank Terr. | 13 | P18 |
| Protein Frac. Centre | 43 | P12 |
| Pryde Av. | 49 | R8 |
| Pryde Terr. | 48 | R8 |

| | | |
|---|---|---|
| Quality St. | 9 | G18 |
| Quality St. La. | 9 | G18 |
| Quarry Cl. | 20 | N15 |
| Quarry Cotts. | 35 | R14 |
| Quarry Howe* =Deanpark Gro. | | |
| Quarryfoot Gr.* =Quarryfoot Gdns. | | |
| Quarryfoot Gdns. | 49 | R8 |
| Quarryfoot Pl. | 49 | R8 |
| Quarryhole Pk. | 12 | O18 |
| Quayside St. | 12 | N19 |
| Queen Charlotte La.* =Queen Charlotte St. | | |
| Queen Charlotte St. | 12 | O19 |
| Queen Margaret Coll. | 17 | F16 |
| Queen St. | 6 | L17 |
| Queen St. Gdns. | 6 | M17 |
| Queen St. Gdns. E. | 6 | M17 |
| Queen St. Gdns. W. | 6 | M17 |
| Queen's Av. | 18 | H17 |
| Queen's Av. S. | 18 | J17 |
| Queen's Bay Cr. | 23 | S16 |
| Queen's Cr. | 32 | N14 |
| Queen's Dr. | 21 | O16 |
| Queen's Gdns. | 18 | J17 |
| Queen's Hall, The | 20 | N15 |
| Queen's Park Av. | 21 | O17 |
| Queen's Pk. Ct. | 21 | P16 |
| Queen's Rd. | 18 | J17 |
| Queen's Walk | 34 | Q14 |
| Queensberry House Hospital | 20 | N16 |
| Queensferry Rd. | 8 | E18 |
| Queensferry St. | 6 | J16 |
| Queensferry St. La. | 6 | L16 |
| Queensferry Terr. | 18 | K17 |
| Quilts, The | 12 | N19 |
| Quilts Wynd | 12 | N19 |
| Rae's Gdns. | 49 | R8 |
| Raeburn Pl. | 19 | L17 |
| Raeburn St. | 19 | L17 |
| Ramsay Annexe (Stevenson Coll.) | 22 | Q17 |
| Ramsay Gdn. | 6 | M16 |
| Ramsay La. | 6 | M16 |
| Ramsay Pl. | 22 | R17 |
| Randolph Cliff | 6 | L16 |
| Randolph Cr. | 6 | L16 |
| Randolph Hall | 6 | L16 |
| Randolph La. | 6 | L16 |
| Randolph Pl. | 6 | L16 |
| Rankeillor St. | 7 | N15 |
| Rankin Av. | 32 | N13 |
| Rankin Dr. | 32 | N13 |
| Rankin Rd. | 32 | N14 |
| Rannoch Gro. | 17 | F17 |
| Rannoch Pl. | 17 | F17 |
| Rannoch Rd. | 17 | F17 |
| Rannoch Terr. | 16 | F17 |
| Ransfield | 26 | A13 |
| Ransome Gdns. | 16 | F17 |
| Ratcliffe Terr. | 32 | N14 |
| Ratho Park Golf Course | 26 | B13 |
| Ratho Park Rd. | 26 | A13 |
| Ravelrig Pk. | 44 | B9 |
| Ravelrig Rd. | 44 | B10 |
| Ravelrig Hill | 44 | B9 |
| Ravelston Ct. | 18 | J16 |
| Ravelston Dykes | 18 | J16 |
| Ravelston Dykes La. | 18 | H16 |
| Ravelston Dykes Rd. | 18 | H17 |
| Ravelston Gdn. | 18 | J16 |
| Ravelston Golf Course | 18 | H17 |
| Ravelston Heights | 18 | J17 |
| Ravelston House Gro. | 18 | J17 |
| Ravelston House Ln. | 18 | J17 |
| Ravelston House Pk. | 18 | J17 |
| Ravelston House Rd. | 18 | J17 |
| Ravelston Pk. (st) | 18 | K16 |
| Ravelston Pk. | 18 | H17 |
| Ravelston Pl.* =Belford Rd. | | |
| Ravelston Rise | 18 | J16 |
| Ravelston Terr. | 19 | K17 |
| Ravenscroft Gdns. | 43 | Q11 |
| Ravenscroft Pl. | 43 | Q11 |
| Ravenscroft St. | 43 | Q11 |
| Ravenswood Av. | 33 | O13 |
| Redbraes Gro. | 12 | M18 |
| Redbraes Pk. | 12 | M18 |
| Redbraes Pl. | 12 | M18 |
| Redford | 40 | J11 |
| Redford Av. | 40 | J11 |
| Redford Bk. | 40 | J11 |
| Redford Barracks | 40 | J12 |
| Redford Cr. | 40 | J11 |
| Redford Dr. | 40 | H11 |
| Redford Gdns. | 40 | J11 |
| Redford Gro. | 40 | J12 |
| Redford Ln. | 40 | J11 |
| Redford Neuk | 40 | J11 |
| Redford Pl. | 40 | J12 |
| Redford Rd. | 40 | J11 |
| Redford Terr. | 40 | J11 |
| Redford Walk | 40 | J11 |
| Redgauntlet Terr. | 33 | P13 |
| Redhall Av. | 29 | H13 |
| Redhall Bank Rd. | 29 | H13 |
| Redhall Cr. | 29 | H13 |
| Redhall Dr. | 29 | H13 |
| Redhall Gdns. | 29 | H13 |
| Redhall Gro. | 29 | H13 |
| Redhall House Dr. | 30 | H13 |
| Redhall Pk. | 29 | H13 |
| Redhall Pl. | 29 | H13 |
| Redhall Rd. | 29 | H13 |
| Redhall Vw. | 30 | H13 |
| Redheughs Av. | 28 | E14 |
| Redheughs Muir | 28 | E14 |
| Redheughs Rigg | 28 | E15 |
| Reekies Ct.* =Nicholson St. | | |
| Regent Bridge* =Waterloo Pl. | | |
| Regent Gdns. | 7 | N17 |
| Regent Pl. | 21 | O17 |
| Regent Rd. | 7 | N16 |
| Regent Road Pk. | 7 | N17 |
| Regent St. | 23 | R16 |
| Regent St. La. | 23 | R16 |
| Regent Terr. | 7 | N17 |
| Regent Terr. Mews | 7 | N17 |
| Regis Ct. | 8 | E18 |
| Register Ho. | 7 | M17 |
| Register Pl. | 7 | M17 |
| Reid Terr. | 19 | L17 |
| Reid's Cl. | 7 | N16 |
| Reid's Ct.*=Canongate | | |
| Relugas Gdns. | 32 | N14 |
| Relugas Pl. | 32 | N14 |
| Relugas Rd. | 32 | N14 |
| Research Av. One | 37 | D12 |
| Research Av. Two | 37 | D12 |
| Research Park Rd. | 37 | D12 |
| Restalrig Av. | 21 | P17 |
| Restalrig Circus | 13 | P18 |
| Restalrig Cr. | 13 | P18 |
| Restalrig Dr. | 21 | P17 |
| Restalrig Gdns. | 21 | P17 |
| Restalrig Ho. | 21 | P17 |
| Restalrig Pk. | 13 | O18 |
| Restalrig Rd. | 13 | O18 |
| Restalrig Rd. S. | 21 | P17 |
| Restalrig Sq. | 13 | P18 |
| Restalrig Terr. | 12 | O18 |
| Riccarton Av. | 38 | D11 |
| Riccarton Cr. | 38 | E11 |
| Riccarton Dr. | 38 | D11 |
| Riccarton Gro. | 38 | E11 |
| Riccarton Mains | 38 | E12 |
| Riccarton Mains Rd. | 38 | E11 |
| Riccarton Sch. | 38 | D10 |
| Richmond La. | 7 | N16 |
| Richmond Pl. | 7 | N16 |
| Richmond Terr. | 19 | L16 |
| Riding Pk. | 8 | E18 |
| Rillbank Cr. | 20 | M15 |
| Rillbank Terr. | 20 | M15 |
| Ringwood Pl. | 42 | O12 |
| Rintoul Pl. | 19 | L17 |
| Riselaw Cr. | 41 | L12 |
| Riselaw Pl. | 41 | L12 |
| Riselaw Rd. | 41 | L12 |
| Riselaw Terr. | 41 | L12 |
| Ritchie Pl. | 31 | K15 |
| Riversdale Cr. | 18 | J15 |
| Riversdale Gro. | 18 | J16 |
| Riversdale Rd. | 18 | J16 |
| Riverside Gdns., Muss. | 24 | U15 |
| Roanshead Rd., Dalk. | 50 | V8 |
| Robb's Ln. | 30 | J14 |
| Robb's Loan Gro. | 30 | J14 |
| Robert Burn's Mews, Dalk. | 50 | V10 |
| Robert Burns Dr. | 33 | O13 |
| Robertson Av. | 30 | J15 |
| Robertson's Cl. | 7 | N16 |
| Robertson's Cl., Dalk.* =St. Andrew St. | | |
| Rocheid Pk. | 10 | K18 |
| Rocheid Path | 11 | L18 |
| Rochester Terr. | 31 | L14 |
| Rockville Terr. | 49 | R8 |
| Roddinglaw | 26 | C14 |
| Roddinglaw Rd. | 26 | C14 |
| Rodney St. | 20 | M17 |
| Roman Fort (Rems.) | 8 | F19 |
| Romero Pl. | 33 | N15 |
| Ronaldson's Wharf* =Sandport Pl. | | |
| Rose Pk. | 11 | L19 |
| Rose St. | 6 | L16 |
| Rose St. La., N. | 6 | L16 |
| Rose St. La., S. | 6 | L16 |
| Rosebank Cem. | 12 | N18 |
| Rosebank Cotts. | 6 | L16 |
| Rosebank Gdns. | 11 | L30 |
| Rosebank Gro. | 11 | L19 |
| Rosebank Rd. | 11 | L19 |
| Rosebery Cr. | 19 | K16 |
| Rosebery Cr. La. | 19 | K16 |
| Rosebery Ho. | 19 | K16 |
| Roseburn Av. | 18 | J16 |
| Roseburn Cliff | 18 | K16 |
| Roseburn Cr. | 18 | J16 |
| Roseburn Dr. | 18 | J16 |
| Roseburn Gdns. | 18 | J16 |
| Roseburn Pk. | 18 | J16 |
| Roseburn Pl. | 18 | J16 |
| Roseburn Sch. | 18 | J15 |
| Roseburn St. | 18 | J15 |
| Roseburn Terr. | 18 | J16 |
| Rosefield Av. | 22 | R16 |
| Rosefield Av. La. | 22 | R16 |
| Rosefield La. | 22 | R16 |
| Rosefield Pk. | 22 | R16 |
| Rosefield Pl. | 22 | R16 |
| Rosefield St. | 22 | R16 |
| Rosemount Bdgs. | 6 | L16 |
| Roseneath Pl. | 32 | M15 |
| Roseneath St. | 32 | M15 |
| Roseneath Terr. | 32 | M15 |
| Rosevale Pl. | 13 | O18 |
| Rosevale Terr. | 13 | O18 |
| Roseville Gdns. | 11 | M19 |
| Ross Gdns. | 32 | N14 |
| Ross Pl. | 32 | N14 |
| Ross Rd. | 33 | O13 |
| Rossie Pl. | 21 | O17 |
| Rosslyn Cr. | 12 | N18 |
| Rosslyn Terr. | 12 | N18 |
| Rothesay Mews | 19 | K16 |
| Rothesay Pl. | 19 | L16 |
| Rothesay Pl., Muss. | 25 | V15 |
| Rothesay Terr. | 19 | L16 |
| Roull Gro. | 29 | F15 |
| Roull Pl. | 29 | G15 |
| Roull Rd. | 29 | F15 |
| Rowallan Ct.* =Craigievar Wynd | | |
| Rowan Tree Av. | 45 | D10 |
| Rowan Tree Gro. | 45 | D10 |
| Rowan Tree Pl. | 45 | D10 |
| Roxburgh Pl. | 7 | N16 |
| Roxburgh St. | 7 | N16 |
| Roxburgh Terr.* =Drummond St. | | |
| Royal Bank | 7 | M17 |

| | | |
|---|---|---|
| Royal Blind Sch. | 32 | N14 |
| Royal Botanic Gdn. | 11 | L18 |
| Royal Burgess Golf Course | 8 | E29 |
| Royal Circus | 6 | L17 |
| Royal Commonwealth Pool | 32 | N15 |
| Royal Cr. | 20 | M17 |
| Royal (Dick) Veterinary Coll. | 32 | N15 |
| Royal Edinburgh Hosp. | 31 | L14 |
| Royal High Sch., The | 9 | F18 |
| Royal High Sch., The (Primary) | 21 | P16 |
| Royal Highland Showgrd. | 14 | A15 |
| Royal Hospital for Sick Children | 32 | M15 |
| Royal Infirmary | 7 | M15 |
| Royal Mile Sch. | 7 | N16 |
| Royal Museum of Scotland (Chambers St.) | 7 | M16 |
| Royal Museum of Scotland (Queen St.) | 7 | M17 |
| Royal Observatory | 32 | M13 |
| Royal Park Pl. | 21 | O17 |
| Royal Park Terr. | 21 | O17 |
| Royal Scottish Acad. | 6 | M16 |
| Royal Terr. | 7 | N17 |
| Royal Terr. Gdns. | 7 | N17 |
| Royal Terr. Mews | 7 | N17 |
| Royal Victoria Hosp. | 18 | K17 |
| Royston Mains Av. | 10 | J19 |
| Royston Mains Cr. | 10 | J19 |
| Royston Mains Gdns. | 10 | K19 |
| Royston Mains Gr. | 10 | K19 |
| Royston Ho. | 10 | J20 |
| Royston Mains Pl. | 10 | J19 |
| Royston Mains Rd. | 10 | K19 |
| Royston Mains St. | 10 | J19 |
| Royston Sch. | 10 | K19 |
| Royston Terr. | 11 | L18 |
| Rudolph Steiner Sch. | 31 | K14 |
| Russell Pl. | 11 | L19 |
| Russell Rd. | 18 | K16 |
| Rustic Cotts.* =Colinton Rd. | | |
| Rutherford Dr. | 33 | O13 |
| Rutland Ct. | 6 | L16 |
| Rutland Pl.*=West End | | |
| Rutland Sq. | 6 | L16 |
| Rutland St. | 6 | L16 |
| Ryehill Av. | 13 | O18 |
| Ryehill Gdns. | 13 | O18 |
| Ryehill Gro. | 13 | O18 |
| Ryehill Pl. | 13 | O18 |
| Ryehill Terr. | 13 | O18 |
| Saddletree Loan | 33 | P13 |
| Safeway Shopping Centre (Gyle) | 16 | F15 |
| Safeway Shopping Centre (Silverknowes) | 9 | G18 |
| Safeway Shopping Centre (Piershill) | 21 | P17 |
| Safeway Superstore (Hunter's Tryst) | 40 | K11 |
| St. Alban's Rd. | 32 | M14 |
| St. Andrew Pl. | 12 | O29 |
| St. Andrew Sq. | 7 | M17 |
| St. Andrew St., Dalk. | 50 | U10 |
| St. Andrew's Ho. | 7 | N17 |
| St. Anthony Ct.* =St. Anthony St. | | |
| St. Anthony La.* =St. Anthony St. | | |
| St. Anthony Pl. | 12 | N19 |
| St. Anthony St. | 12 | N19 |
| St. Augustine's Sch. | 28 | F14 |
| St. Augustine's Sch. Sports Grd. | 11 | L18 |
| St. Barnabas Ct. | 43 | Q12 |
| St. Bernard's Cr. | 6 | L17 |
| St. Bernard's Pl.* =Saunders St. | | |
| St. Bernard's Row | 19 | L17 |
| St. Bernard's Well | 6 | L17 |
| St. Catherine's Gdns. | 17 | H15 |
| St. Catherine's Pl. | 32 | N15 |
| St. Catherine's Sch. | 43 | O11 |
| St. Cecilia's Hall | 7 | N16 |
| St. Clair Av. | 12 | O18 |
| St. Clair Pl. | 12 | O18 |
| St. Clair Rd. | 12 | O18 |
| St. Clair St. | 12 | O18 |
| St. Clair Terr. | 31 | K13 |
| St. Colme St. | 6 | L16 |
| St. Colm's Coll. | 11 | L18 |
| St. Columba's Hospice | 11 | L19 |
| St. Crispin's Sch. | 32 | N14 |
| St. Cuthbert's Sch. | 30 | J14 |
| St. David's Pl.* =Morrison St. | | |
| St. David's Sch. | 10 | J18 |
| St. David's Sch., Dalk. | 50 | U9 |
| St. David's Sch. | 50 | V9 |
| St. David's Terr.* =Morrison St. | | |
| St. Denis and Cranley Sch. | 31 | K14 |
| St. Fillan's Terr. | 31 | L13 |
| St. Francis' Sch. | 34 | Q14 |
| St. George's Sch. | 18 | K16 |
| St. Giles' Cathedral | 7 | M16 |
| St. Giles Centre | 29 | G14 |
| St. Giles' St. | 7 | M16 |
| St. James Centre | 7 | M17 |
| St. James' Pl. | 7 | M17 |
| St. James' Pl.* =Cathedral La. | | |
| St. John St. | 7 | N16 |
| St. John Vianney Sch. | 33 | O13 |
| St. John's Av. | 17 | G15 |
| St. John's Cr. | 17 | G15 |
| St. John's Gdns. | 17 | G15 |
| St. John's Pl.* =Holyrood Rd. | | |
| St. John's Rd. | 16 | F15 |
| St. John's Sch. | 22 | R16 |
| St. John's Terr. | 17 | G15 |
| St. Joseph's Sch. | 29 | G14 |
| St. Katharine's Brae | 42 | O11 |
| St. Katharine's Cr. | 42 | O11 |
| St. Katharine's Ln. | 42 | O11 |
| St. Leonard's Bk. | 7 | N15 |
| St. Leonard's Crag | 7 | N15 |
| St. Leonard's Hill | 7 | N15 |
| St. Leonard's La. | 7 | N15 |
| St. Leonard's St. | 20 | N15 |
| St. Margaret's Pk. | 16 | F15 |
| St. Margaret's Rd. | 32 | L14 |
| St. Margaret's Sch. | 47 | P9 |
| St. Margaret's Sch. | 33 | O14 |
| St. Margaret's Sch. Senior Coll. | 33 | O14 |
| St. Mark's La. | 23 | R16 |
| St. Mark's Pk. | 12 | M18 |
| St. Mark's Pl. | 23 | R16 |
| St. Mark's Sch. | 40 | K12 |
| St. Mary's Cathedral (Episc.) | 6 | L16 |
| St. Mary's Cathedral (R.C.) | 7 | M17 |
| St. Mary's Music Sch. | 6 | L16 |
| St. Mary's Pl. | 23 | S16 |
| St. Mary's Pl. La. | 23 | S16 |
| St. Mary's Sch. | 7 | M17 |
| St. Mary's Sch., Leith | 13 | O19 |
| St. Mary's St. | 7 | N16 |
| St. Michael's Av., Muss. | 25 | V15 |
| St. Nicholas' Sch. | 30 | J15 |
| St. Ninian's Dr. | 16 | F16 |
| St. Ninian's Rd. | 17 | F16 |
| St. Ninian's Sch. | 21 | P17 |
| St. Ninian's Terr. | 31 | K13 |
| St. Patrick Sq. | 7 | N15 |
| St. Patrick St. | 7 | N15 |
| St. Patrick Sch.*=Cowgate | | |
| St. Patrick's Sch. | 7 | N16 |
| St. Peter's Bdgs.* =Gilmore Pl. | | |
| St. Peter's Pl. | 19 | L15 |
| St. Peter's Sch. | 31 | L14 |
| St. Peter's Sch. Annexe | 20 | M15 |
| St. Raphael's | 32 | M14 |
| St. Ronan's Terr. | 31 | L13 |
| St. Serf's Sch. | 18 | K16 |
| St. Stephen Pl.* =St. Stephen St. | | |
| St. Stephen St. | 19 | L17 |
| St. Teresa's Pl. | 31 | K14 |
| St. Thomas of Aquin's Sch. | 6 | M15 |
| St. Thomas Rd. | 32 | M14 |
| St. Vincent St. | 6 | L17 |
| Salamander Pl. | 13 | O19 |
| Salamander St. | 13 | O19 |
| Salisbury Pl. | 32 | N15 |
| Salisbury Rd. | 32 | N15 |
| Salmond Pl. | 21 | O17 |
| Salters Rd., Dalk. | 50 | V10 |
| Salter's Gr., Dalk. | 50 | V10 |
| Salter's Terr., Dalk. | 50 | V10 |
| Saltire Ct. | 6 | L16 |
| Saltire Society*=High St. | | |
| Salvesen Cr. | 9 | H19 |
| Salvesen Gdns. | 9 | H19 |
| Salvesen Gro. | 9 | H19 |
| Salvesen Terr. | 9 | H19 |
| Sandford Gdns. | 22 | R16 |
| Sandport | 12 | O19 |
| Sandport Pl. | 12 | N19 |
| Sandport St. | 12 | N19 |
| Sauchiebank | 19 | K15 |
| Saughton Av. | 30 | J15 |
| Saughton Cem. | 30 | H14 |
| Saughton Cr. | 17 | H15 |
| Saughton Gdns. | 17 | H15 |
| Saughton Gro. | 17 | H15 |
| Saughton Ln. | 17 | H15 |
| Saughton Mains Av. | 29 | G14 |
| Saughton Mains Bk. | 29 | H14 |
| Saughton Mains Cotts.* =Saughton Mains Gdns. | | |
| Saughton Mains Dr. | 29 | G14 |
| Saughton Mains Gdns. | 29 | G14 |
| Saughton Mains Gro. | 29 | H14 |
| Saughton Mains Ln. | 29 | G14 |
| Saughton Mains Pk. | 29 | G14 |
| Saughton Mains Pl. | 29 | G14 |
| Saughton Mains St. | 29 | G14 |
| Saughton Mains Terr. | 29 | G14 |
| Saughton Pk. (st.) | 17 | H15 |
| Saughton Pk. | 30 | H15 |
| Saughton Prison | 29 | H14 |
| Saughton Rd. | 29 | G14 |
| Saughton Rd. N. | 29 | G15 |
| Saughtonhall Av. | 18 | H15 |
| Saughtonhall Av. W. | 18 | H15 |
| Saughtonhall Circus | 18 | J15 |
| Saughtonhall Cr. | 18 | H15 |
| Saughtonhall Dr. | 18 | H15 |
| Saughtonhall Gdns. | 18 | J15 |
| Saughtonhall Gro. | 18 | J15 |
| Saughtonhall Pl. | 18 | H15 |
| Saughtonhall Terr. | 18 | J15 |
| Saunders St. | 19 | L17 |
| Savile Pl. | 32 | N14 |
| Savile Terr. | 32 | N14 |
| Saxe-Coburg Pl. | 19 | L17 |
| Saxe-Coburg St. | 19 | L17 |
| Saxe-Coburg Terr.* =Saxe-Coburg St. | | |
| School Brae | 8 | E19 |
| School Brae | 48 | R9 |
| School Gr. | 49 | R9 |
| Sciennes | 32 | N15 |
| Sciennes Gdns. | 32 | N15 |
| Sciennes Hill Pl.* =Sciennes | | |
| Sciennes House Dr.* =Sciennes | | |
| Sciennes House Pl. | 32 | N15 |
| Sciennes Pl. | 32 | N15 |
| Sciennes Rd. | 32 | M15 |
| Sciennes Sch. | 32 | M15 |
| Sciennes St. E.* =Causewayside | | |
| Scollon Av. | 49 | S8 |
| Scone Gdns. | 21 | P17 |

| | | |
|---|---|---|
| Scotch Whisky Heritage Centre | 6 | M16 |
| Scotland St. | 20 | M17 |
| Scotland St. La. E. | 20 | M17 |
| Scotland St. La. W. | 20 | M17 |
| Scott Monument | 7 | M16 |
| Scottish Agricultural College | 32 | N13 |
| Scottish Experience, The | 7 | N16 |
| Scottish Gall. | 6 | L16 |
| Scottish Marine Biological Association | 11 | M19 |
| Scottish National Gall. of Modern Art | 19 | K16 |
| Scottish National Portrait Gall. | 7 | M17 |
| Scottish Poetry Library | 7 | N16 |
| Scottish Travel Centre | 7 | M17 |
| Scottish Widows | 20 | N15 |
| Scottish Youth Hostel Association Office | 31 | L15 |
| Scottish Zoological Pk. | 17 | G16 |
| Seacot | 13 | P18 |
| Seafield Av. | 13 | P18 |
| Seafield Cem. | 13 | P18 |
| Seafield Crem. | 13 | P18 |
| Seafield Ind. Estate | 22 | Q17 |
| Seafield Pl. | 13 | P18 |
| Seafield Moor Rd. | 46 | M9 |
| Seafield Recreation Grd. | 13 | Q18 |
| Seafield Rd. | 13 | P18 |
| Seafield Rd. E. | 22 | Q17 |
| Seafield St. | 13 | P18 |
| Seafield Terr.* =Seafield Av. | | |
| Seafield Way | 13 | Q18 |
| Seaforth Dr. | 18 | J17 |
| Seaforth Terr. | 18 | J17 |
| Sealcarr St. | 10 | K20 |
| Seaport St.* =Bernard St. | | |
| Seaview Cr. | 23 | S16 |
| Seaview Terr. | 23 | S16 |
| Second Gait | 37 | D12 |
| Semple St. | 6 | L16 |
| Seton Pl. | 32 | N15 |
| Shadepark Cr., Dalk. | 50 | U10 |
| Shadepark Dr., Dalk. | 50 | U10 |
| Shadepark Gdns., Dalk. | 50 | U10 |
| Shaftesbury Pk. | 30 | K14 |
| Shandon Cr. | 30 | K14 |
| Shandon Pl. | 30 | K14 |
| Shandon Rd. | 30 | K14 |
| Shandon St. | 30 | K14 |
| Shandon Terr. | 30 | K14 |
| Shandwick Pl. | 6 | L16 |
| Shanter Way | 33 | O13 |
| Sharpdale Ln. | 33 | O14 |
| Shawfair | 33 | S13 |
| Shaw's Pl. | 12 | N18 |
| Shaw's Sq.* =Gayfield Sq. | | |
| Shaw's St. | 12 | N18 |
| Shaw's Terr. | 12 | N18 |
| Sheriff Brae | 12 | N19 |
| Sheriff Ct. | 7 | M16 |
| Sheriff Pk. | 12 | N19 |
| Shore | 12 | O19 |
| Shore Pl. | 12 | O19 |
| Shorthope St., Muss. | 25 | V15 |
| Shrub Mount | 22 | R17 |
| Shrub Pl. | 20 | N17 |
| Shrub Pl. La.* =Shrub Pl. | | |
| Sienna Gdns. | 32 | N15 |
| Sighthill Av. | 29 | G13 |
| Sighthill Bk. | 28 | F13 |
| Sighthill Ct. | 28 | F13 |
| Sighthill Cr. | 28 | F13 |
| Sighthill Dr. | 28 | F13 |
| Sighthill Gdns. | 29 | F13 |
| Sighthill Gr. | 28 | F13 |
| Sighthill Gro. | 29 | G13 |
| Sighthill Health Centre | 28 | F13 |
| Sighthill Ind. Estate | 28 | E14 |
| Sighthill Ln. | 28 | F13 |
| Sighthill Neuk | 28 | F13 |
| Sighthill Pk. (st.) | 29 | F13 |
| Sighthill Pk. | 28 | F14 |
| Sighthill Pl. | 28 | F13 |
| Sighthill Rise | 28 | F13 |
| Sighthill Rd. | 28 | F13 |
| Sighthill Sch. | 28 | F13 |
| Sighthill St. | 28 | F13 |
| Sighthill Terr. | 29 | F13 |
| Sighthill Vw. | 28 | F13 |
| Sighthill Wynd | 28 | F13 |
| Silverknowes Av. | 9 | G18 |
| Silverknowes Bk. | 9 | G18 |
| Silverknowes Brae | 9 | G18 |
| Silverknowes Ct. | 9 | G18 |
| Silverknowes Cr. | 9 | G18 |
| Silverknowes Dell | 9 | G18 |
| Silverknowes Dr. | 9 | G18 |
| Silverknowes Eastway | 9 | G18 |
| Silverknowes Gdns. | 9 | G19 |
| Silverknowes Golf Course | 9 | G19 |
| Silverknowes Gr. | 9 | H18 |
| Silverknowes Gro. | 9 | G19 |
| Silverknowes Hill | 9 | G18 |
| Silverknowes Ln. | 9 | G18 |
| Silverknowes Midway | 9 | H29 |
| Silverknowes Neuk | 9 | H18 |
| Silverknowes Pk. | 9 | G19 |
| Silverknowes Parkway | 9 | G19 |
| Silverknowes Pl. | 9 | G19 |
| Silverknowes Rd. | 9 | G19 |
| Silverknowes Rd. E. | 9 | G18 |
| Silverknowes Rd. S. | 9 | G18 |
| Silverknowes Sch. | 9 | H18 |
| Silverknowes Southway | 9 | H18 |
| Silverknowes Terr. | 9 | G18 |
| Silverknowes Vw. | 9 | H18 |
| Simon Sq. | 7 | N16 |
| Simpson Memorial Maternity Pavilion | 6 | M15 |
| Sir Harry Lauder Rd. | 22 | R16 |
| Slaeside | 45 | C9 |
| Slateford Rd. | 30 | J14 |
| Slateford Sta. | 30 | J14 |
| Sleigh Dr. | 21 | O17 |
| Sleigh Gdns. | 21 | P17 |
| Sloan St. | 12 | N18 |
| Smeaton Gro. | 25 | V14 |
| Smithfield St. | 30 | J15 |
| Smith's Pl. | 12 | N18 |
| Smithy Green Av. | 51 | R12 |
| Society* =Chambers St. | | |
| Solicitor's Bdgs.* =Cowgate | | |
| Somerset Pl. | 13 | O18 |
| Sour Howe | 40 | K11 |
| South Barnton Av. | 9 | G18 |
| South Beechwood | 17 | H15 |
| South Bridge | 7 | M16 |
| South Charlotte St. | 6 | L16 |
| South Clerk St. | 20 | N15 |
| South College St. | 7 | M16 |
| South East Circus Pl. | 6 | L17 |
| South Ettrick Rd. | 31 | K14 |
| South Fort St. | 12 | N19 |
| South Gayfield La.* =Gayfield Sq. | | |
| South Gillsland Rd. | 31 | K14 |
| South Gray St. | 32 | N14 |
| South Gray's Cl. | 7 | N16 |
| South Groathill Av. | 18 | J17 |
| South Gyle Access | 28 | F14 |
| South Gyle Bdwy. | 28 | E14 |
| South Gyle Cres. | 28 | E14 |
| South Gyle Gdns. | 28 | E15 |
| South Gyle Ln. | 28 | E15 |
| South Gyle Mains | 28 | E15 |
| South Gyle Pk. | 28 | E15 |
| South Gyle Rd. | 28 | F15 |
| South Gyle Sta. | 28 | E15 |
| South Gyle Wynd | 28 | F14 |
| South Lauder Rd. | 32 | N14 |
| South Laverockbank Av. | 11 | M19 |
| South Learmonth Av. | 19 | K17 |
| South Learmonth Gdns. | 19 | K17 |
| South Lorne Pl. | 12 | N18 |
| South Maybury | 16 | E15 |
| South Meadow Walk* =Meadow Pl. | | |
| South Mellis Pk. | 22 | Q16 |
| South Morningside Sch. | 31 | L13 |
| South Morton St. | 23 | S16 |
| South Oswald Rd. | 32 | M14 |
| South Oxford St. | 32 | N15 |
| South Pk. | 11 | M19 |
| South St. Andrew St. | 7 | M17 |
| South St. David St. | 7 | M16 |
| South St., Muss. | 24 | U15 |
| South St., Dalk. | 50 | U10 |
| South Sloan St. | 12 | N18 |
| South Trinity Rd. | 11 | L19 |
| Southfield Bk. | 22 | Q15 |
| Southfield Farm Gro. | 22 | Q16 |
| Southfield Gdns. E. | 22 | Q16 |
| Southfield Gdns. W. | 22 | Q16 |
| Southfield Hosp. | 43 | P12 |
| Southfield Ln. | 22 | Q15 |
| Southfield Pl. | 22 | R16 |
| Southfield Pl. N.* =Southfield Sq. | | |
| Southfield Pl. S.* =Southfield Sq. | | |
| Southfield Rd. E. | 22 | Q15 |
| Southfield Rd. W. | 22 | Q15 |
| Southfield Sq. | 22 | Q15 |
| Southfield Terr. | 22 | Q15 |
| Southfield Villas* =Stanley St. | | |
| Southhouse Av. | 42 | O11 |
| Southhouse Bdwy. | 42 | O10 |
| Southhouse Cr. | 43 | O10 |
| Southhouse Gdns. | 42 | O10 |
| Southhouse Gro. | 42 | O10 |
| Southhouse Medway | 43 | O11 |
| Southhouse Paths | 43 | O11 |
| Southhouse Rd. | 42 | O11 |
| Southhouse Sq. | 43 | O10 |
| Southhouse Terr. | 43 | P11 |
| Soutra Ct. | 43 | O11 |
| Spa Pl. | 22 | R17 |
| Spalding Cr., Dalk. | 50 | U10 |
| Spence St. | 33 | N15 |
| Spencer Pl. | 11 | L19 |
| Spey St. | 12 | N18 |
| Spey St. La. | 12 | N18 |
| Spey Terr. | 12 | N18 |
| Spiers Pl. | 12 | N19 |
| Spinney, The | 43 | P11 |
| Spittal St. | 6 | L16 |
| Spittalfield Cr.* =St. Leonard's St. | | |
| Spottiswoode Rd. | 32 | M15 |
| Spottiswoode St. | 32 | M15 |
| Spring Gdns. | 21 | O17 |
| Springfield Bdgs.* =Springfield St. | | |
| Springfield | 12 | N18 |
| Springfield St. | 12 | N18 |
| Springvalley Gdns. | 31 | L14 |
| Springvalley Terr. | 31 | L14 |
| Springwell Ho. Health Centre | 31 | K15 |
| Springwell Pl. | 19 | K15 |
| Springwood Pk. | 42 | O12 |
| Spylaw Av. | 39 | G12 |
| Spylaw Bank Rd. | 39 | G12 |
| Spylaw Ho. | 39 | H11 |
| Spylaw Pk. (street) | 39 | G12 |
| Spylaw Pk. | 39 | H11 |
| Spylaw Rd. | 31 | K14 |
| Spylaw St. | 39 | H11 |
| Square, The | 51 | R12 |
| Stable La. | 31 | L14 |
| Stafford St. | 6 | L16 |
| Stair Pk. | 18 | J16 |
| Stanedykehead | 42 | N11 |
| Stanhope Pl. | 19 | K16 |
| Stanhope Pl. W.* =Stanhope Pl. | | |

| | | |
|---|---|---|
| Stanhope St. | 19 | K16 |
| Stanley Pl. | 21 | O17 |
| Stanley Rd. | 11 | M19 |
| Stanley St. | 22 | R16 |
| Stanwell St. | 12 | N18 |
| Stapeley Av. | 22 | Q17 |
| Starbank Pk. | 11 | M19 |
| Starbank Rd. | 11 | M19 |
| Stark's Cotts. | 40 | K12 |
| Station Brae | 22 | R16 |
| Station Ln. | 45 | C10 |
| Station Rd. | 17 | G15 |
| Station Rd. | 48 | P8 |
| Station Rd., Dalk. | 50 | T9 |
| Station Rd., Muss. | 24 | U15 |
| Stead's Pl. | 12 | N18 |
| Steils, The | 31 | K12 |
| Steel's Pl. | 31 | L14 |
| Stenhouse Av. | 29 | H14 |
| Stenhouse Av. W. | 29 | H14 |
| Stenhouse Cotts. | 29 | H14 |
| Stenhouse Cr. | 29 | H14 |
| Stenhouse Cross | 29 | H14 |
| Stenhouse Dr. | 29 | G14 |
| Stenhouse Gdns. | 29 | H14 |
| Stenhouse Gdns. N. | 29 | H14 |
| Stenhouse Gro. | 29 | H14 |
| Stenhouse Mill Cr. | 29 | H14 |
| Stenhouse Mill La. | 29 | H14 |
| Stenhouse Mill Wynd | 29 | H14 |
| Stenhouse Pl. E. | 29 | H14 |
| Stenhouse Pl. W. | 29 | H14 |
| Stenhouse Rd. | 29 | H14 |
| Stenhouse Sch. | 29 | H14 |
| Stenhouse St. E. | 29 | H14 |
| Stenhouse St. W. | 29 | G14 |
| Stenhouse Terr. | 29 | H14 |
| Stennis Gdns. | 43 | P12 |
| Stevenlaw's Cl.* =High St. | | |
| Stevenson Av. | 30 | J15 |
| Stevenson Coll. of Further Education | 28 | F14 |
| Stevenson Dr. | 29 | H14 |
| Stevenson Gro. | 30 | J15 |
| Stevenson Rd. | 30 | J15 |
| Stevenson Terr. | 30 | J15 |
| Stewart Av. | 37 | D10 |
| Stewart Cr. | 37 | D10 |
| Stewart Gdns. | 37 | D10 |
| Stewart Pl. | 37 | D10 |
| Stewart Rd. | 37 | D10 |
| Stewartfield | 12 | M18 |
| Stewart Terr. | 30 | J15 |
| Stewart's Melville Coll. | 19 | K17 |
| Stewart's Melville Coll. Sports Grd. | 11 | K18 |
| Stirling Rd. | 11 | L19 |
| Stockbridge Health Centre | 6 | L17 |
| Stockbridge Sch. | 19 | L17 |
| Stoneybank Av., Muss. | 24 | U14 |
| Stoneybank Cr., Muss. | 24 | U14 |
| Stoneybank Ct., Muss. | 24 | U15 |
| Stoneybank Dr., Muss. | 24 | U15 |
| Stoneybank Gdns., Muss. | 24 | U15 |
| Stoneybank Gdns. N., Muss. | 24 | U15 |
| Stoneybank Gdns. S., Muss. | 24 | U14 |
| Stoneybank Gr., Muss. | 24 | U14 |
| Stoneybank Pl., Muss. | 24 | U14 |
| Stoneybank Rd., Muss. | 24 | U14 |
| Stoneybank Terr., Muss. | 24 | U14 |
| Stoneyhill Av., Muss. | 24 | U15 |
| Stoneyhill Cr., Muss. | 24 | U15 |
| Stoneyhill Ct. | 24 | U15 |
| Stoneyhill Dr., Muss. | 24 | U15 |
| Stoneyhill Farm Rd., Muss. | 24 | U15 |
| Stoneyhill Gr., Muss. | 24 | U15 |
| Stoneyhill Ho. | 24 | U15 |
| Stoneyhill Pl., Muss. | 24 | U15 |
| Stoneyhill Rise, Muss. | 24 | U15 |
| Stoneyhill Rd., Muss. | 24 | U15 |
| Stoneyhill Terr., Muss. | 24 | U15 |
| Stoneyhill Wynd, Muss. | 24 | U15 |
| Storrie's Alley*=Giles St. | | |
| Strachan Gdns. | 17 | H17 |
| Strachan Rd. | 18 | H17 |
| Straiton Pl. | 23 | R16 |
| Straiton | 47 | O9 |
| Straiton Caravan Park | 47 | O9 |
| Straiton Mains | 47 | O9 |
| Straiton Rd. | 47 | N8 |
| Strathalmond Ct. | 8 | D18 |
| Strathalmond Gr. | 8 | D29 |
| Strathalmond Pk. | 8 | D17 |
| Strathalmond Rd. | 15 | D17 |
| Strathearn Pl. | 31 | L14 |
| Strathearn Rd. | 32 | M14 |
| Strathfillan Rd. | 32 | M14 |
| Strawberry Bk. | 50 | T9 |
| Stuart Cres. | 16 | E16 |
| Stuart Gr. | 16 | E16 |
| Stuart Pk. | 16 | E16 |
| Stuart Sq. | 16 | E16 |
| Stuart Wynd | 16 | E16 |
| Student Centre | 7 | M16 |
| Succoth Av. | 18 | J16 |
| Succoth Ct. | 18 | J16 |
| Succoth Gdns. | 18 | J16 |
| Succoth Pk. | 18 | J16 |
| Succoth Pl. | 18 | J16 |
| Suffolk Rd. | 32 | N14 |
| Summer Bk. | 20 | M17 |
| Summer Pl. | 11 | M18 |
| Summer Trees Ct. | 33 | O13 |
| Summerfield Gdns. | 13 | O18 |
| Summerfield Pl. | 13 | O18 |
| Summerhall | 32 | N15 |
| Summerhall Pl.* =Causewayside | | |
| Summerhall Sq. | 32 | N15 |
| Summerside Pl. | 12 | M19 |
| Summerside St. | 12 | M19 |
| Sunbury Mews | 19 | K16 |
| Sunbury Pl. | 19 | K16 |
| Sunbury St. | 19 | K16 |
| Sunnybank Pl. | 21 | O17 |
| Sunnybank Terr. | 21 | O17 |
| Sunnyside | 21 | O17 |
| Surgeon Sq.* =Infirmary St. | | |
| Surgeons' Hall | 7 | N16 |
| Surrey Pl.*=Borthwick Pl. | | |
| Surrey Sq.* =Sutherland St. | | |
| Sutherland St. | 19 | K16 |
| Swan Spring Av. | 41 | L12 |
| Swanfield | 12 | N19 |
| Swanston Av. | 41 | L11 |
| Swanston Cr. | 41 | L11 |
| Swanston Cott. | 41 | K10 |
| Swanston Cotts. | 41 | L10 |
| Swanston Dr. | 41 | L10 |
| Swanston Gdns. | 41 | L11 |
| Swanston Golf Course | 41 | K10 |
| Swanston Gr. | 41 | L11 |
| Swanston Gro. | 41 | L10 |
| Swanston Ho. | 40 | K10 |
| Swanston Ln. | 41 | L11 |
| Swanston Muir | 40 | K11 |
| Swanston Pk. | 41 | L11 |
| Swanston Pl. | 41 | L11 |
| Swanston Rd. | 41 | L10 |
| Swanston Row | 41 | L11 |
| Swanston Terr. | 41 | L11 |
| Swanston Vw. | 41 | L11 |
| Swanston Way | 41 | L11 |
| Sycamore Gdns.* =Saughton Rd. N. | | |
| Sycamore Terr | 17 | G15 |
| Sydney Pk. | 22 | Q17 |
| Sydney Pl. | 22 | Q17 |
| Sydney Terr. | 22 | Q17 |
| Sylvan Pl. | 20 | M15 |
| Synagogue | 32 | N15 |
| Tait St., Dalk. | 50 | U10 |
| Talbot Rice Art Gall. | 7 | M16 |
| Talisman Pl. | 33 | O13 |
| Tanfield | 11 | M18 |
| Tanfield La. | 11 | M18 |
| Tantallon Pl. | 32 | N15 |
| Tarvit St. | 6 | L15 |
| Tay St. | 31 | K15 |
| Taylor Gdns. | 12 | N19 |
| Taylor Pl. | 21 | O17 |
| Taylor Pl., Dalk. | 50 | V9 |
| Telephone Ho. | 30 | J15 |
| Telfer Subway | 19 | K15 |
| Telferton | 22 | Q17 |
| Telford Coll. of Further Education | 10 | K18 |
| Telford Dr. | 10 | J18 |
| Telford Gdns. | 10 | J18 |
| Telford Pl. | 10 | J18 |
| Telford Rd. | 10 | J17 |
| Temple Park Cr. | 31 | K15 |
| Templeland Gro. | 16 | F16 |
| Templeland Rd. | 16 | F16 |
| Tennant St. | 12 | N18 |
| Teviot Pl. | 7 | M16 |
| Teviotdale Pl. | 19 | L17 |
| Theatre Workshop | 19 | L17 |
| Third Gait | 37 | D12 |
| Thirlestane La. | 32 | M14 |
| Thirlestane Rd. | 32 | M15 |
| Thistle Ct.*=Thistle St. | | |
| Thistle Foundation Homes | 34 | Q14 |
| Thistle Pl. | 19 | L15 |
| Thistle St. | 6 | M17 |
| Thistle St. La., N.E. | 6 | M17 |
| Thistle St. La., N.W. | 6 | M17 |
| Thistle St. La., S.E. | 6 | M17 |
| Thistle St. La., S.W. | 6 | M17 |
| Thomas Clouston Clinic | 30 | K20 |
| Thomson Cr. | 38 | E11 |
| Thomson Dr. | 38 | E11 |
| Thomson Gro. | 38 | E11 |
| Thomson Rd. | 38 | E11 |
| Thomson's Ct.* =Grassmarket | | |
| Thorburn Gro. | 40 | J11 |
| Thorburn Rd. | 40 | H11 |
| Thorntree Side | 12 | O18 |
| Thorntree St. | 12 | O18 |
| Thornville Terr. | 13 | O18 |
| Thornybank Ind. Est. | 50 | V10 |
| Thornybauk | 6 | L15 |
| Threipmuir Av. | 45 | C8 |
| Threipmuir Gdns. | 45 | C8 |
| Threipmuir Pl. | 45 | C8 |
| Ticket Centre and Tattoo Office | 7 | M16 |
| Timber Bush | 12 | O19 |
| Tinto Pl. | 12 | N18 |
| Tipperlinn Rd. | 31 | L14 |
| Tobago Pl.* =Morrison St. | | |
| Todhills | 51 | R11 |
| Tolbooth Wynd | 12 | N19 |
| Tollcross | 19 | L15 |
| Tollcross Sch. | 6 | L15 |
| Torduff Reservoir | 39 | G10 |
| Torduff Rd. | 39 | H10 |
| Torphichen Pl. | 6 | L16 |
| Torphichen St. | 6 | L16 |
| Torphin Hill Golf Course | 39 | G10 |
| Torphin Rd. | 39 | G11 |
| Torrance Pk. | 16 | F17 |
| Torsonce Rd., Dalk. | 50 | T9 |
| Toward Ct.* =Craigievar Wynd | | |
| Tower Farm | 42 | N12 |
| Tower Pl. | 12 | O19 |
| Tower St. | 12 | O19 |
| Tower St. La. | 12 | O19 |
| Towerbank Sch. | 23 | R17 |
| Town Hall, Leith | 12 | N19 |
| Town Hall, Portobello | 22 | R16 |
| Trafalgar La. | 12 | N19 |
| Trafalgar St. | 12 | N19 |
| Traprain Rd. | 48 | P8 |
| Traprain Terr. | 48 | P8 |

Traquair Park E. 17 G15
Traquair Park W. 17 G15
Traverse Theatre 6 L16
Trefoil Sch. 27 C13
Trench Knowe 41 L11
Tressilian Gdns. 33 O13
Trinity Acad. 11 M19
Trinity Acad., Telford Coll. Annexe 12 M19
Trinity Ct. 11 L19
Trinity Cr. 11 L19
Trinity Gro. 11 L19
Trinity Mains 11 L30
Trinity Mains* =East Trinity Rd.
Trinity Rd. 11 L19
Trinity Sch. (Primary) 12 M19
Tron Sq. 7 M16
Tryst Pk. 40 K11
Turlies, The 39 H12
Turnbull's Entry* =Potterrow
Turner Av. 44 B10
Turner Pk. 44 C10
Turnhouse Golf Course 15 C16
Turnhouse Farm Rd. 15 C17
Turnhouse Rd. 15 D16
Tyler's Acre Av. 29 G15
Tyler's Acre Gdns. 29 G15
Tyler's Acre Rd. 29 G15
Tynecastle Bdgs.* =McLeod St.
Tynecastle La. 18 K15
Tynecastle Pk. (Hearts F.C.) 18 K15
Tynecastle Pl.* =Gorgie Rd.
Tynecastle Sch. 18 K15
Tynecastle Sch. Annexe 30 J15
Tynecastle Terr.* =Gorgie Rd.

UCI Cinema 35 S14
Ulster Cr. 21 P16
Ulster Dr. 21 P16
Ulster Gdns. 21 P16
Ulster Gro. 21 P16
Ulster Terr. 21 P16
Union Ct*=Richmond Pl.
Union Pl. 7 N17
Union St. 7 N17
University Library 7 M15
University of Edinburgh 7 M16
Upper Bow 20 M16
Upper Broomieknowe 49 R8
Upper Coltbridge Terr. 18 K16
Upper Craigour 34 Q13
Upper Craigour Way 34 P13
Upper Cramond Ct. 8 E18
Upper Damside 19 L16
Upper Dean Terr. 19 L17
Upper Gilmore Pl. 19 L15
Upper Gilmore Terr. 19 L15
Upper Gray St. 32 N15
Upper Grove Pl. 6 L15
Usher Hall 6 L16
Usher Institute 32 M15

Valleyfield St. 19 L15
Vanburgh Pl. 12 O18
Vandeleur Av. 22 Q17
Vandeleur Gro. 22 Q17
Vandeleur Pl. 22 Q17
Veitch's Sq. 19 L17
Vennel 6 M16
Ventnor Pl. 33 O14
Ventnor Terr. 32 N14
Vernon Cotts.* =Pittville St. La.
Vexhim Pk. 35 R15
Victor Park Terr. 16 F16
Victoria Pk. 12 M19
Victoria Sch. 12 M20
Victoria St. 7 M16
Victoria Terr.* =Victoria St.
Victoria Terr., Muss. 25 W15
View Bk. 49 S8
Viewbank Av. 49 S9
Viewbank Cr. 49 S8
Viewbank Dr. 49 S8
Viewbank Rd. 49 R8
Viewbank Vw. 49 S8
Viewcraig Gdns. 20 N16
Viewcraig St. 20 N16
Viewfield 49 S8
Viewfield Rd. 39 G12
Viewforth 31 L15
Viewforth Gdns. 31 L15
Viewforth Sq. 31 L15
Viewforth Terr. 31 L15
Viewpark Gdns. 49 R8
Violet Bk.*=Spring Gdns.
Violet Terr. 31 K15
Vivian Terr. 9 G18

Waddell Pl. 12 N18
Wadingburn La. 48 Q9
Wadingburn Rd. 48 Q8
Wakefield Av. 22 Q17
Walker Cr. 49 S9
Walker St. 6 L16
Walker Terr. 19 L16
Walter Scott Av. 33 O13
Wanton Walls 35 T15
Wardie Av. 11 L19
Wardie Cr. 11 L19
Wardie Dell 11 L19
Wardie Gro. 11 K19
Wardie House La.* =Boswall Rd.
Wardie Pk. 11 L19
Wardie Rd. 11 L19
Wardie Sch. 11 L19
Wardie Sq. 11 L19
Wardie Steps 11 L19
Wardieburn Dr. 11 K19
Wardieburn Pl. E. 10 K30
Wardieburn Pl. N. 10 K19
Wardieburn Pl. S. 10 K19
Wardieburn Pl. W. 10 K19
Wardieburn Rd. 10 K19
Wardieburn St. E. 10 K19
Wardieburn St. W. 10 K19
Wardieburn Terr. 10 K19
Wardiefield 11 K19
Wardlaw Pl. 30 K15
Wardlaw St. 30 K15
Wardlaw Terr. 30 K15
Warrender Park Cr. 32 L15
Warrender Park Rd. 32 M15
Warrender Park Terr. 32 M15
Warriston 36 C11
Warriston Av. 11 M18
Warriston Cem. 11 M18
Warriston Cl.*=High St.
Warriston Cr. 11 M18
Warriston Crem. 11 M18
Warriston Dr. 11 L18
Warriston Gdns. 11 L18
Warriston Gro. 11 L18
Warriston Pl. 11 M18
Warriston Rd. 11 M19
Warriston Terr. 11 L18
Washington La. 19 K15
Washington St. 19 K15
Water St. 12 O19
Waterloo Pl. 7 M17
Waterside Ct.* =Coltbridge Av.
Water's Cl.*=Shore
Watertoun Rd. 32 N14
Watson Cr. 31 K15
Watson's Bdgs.* =Main St.
Watts Cl., Muss. 24 U15
Wauchope Av. 34 Q14
Wauchope Cr. 34 Q14
Wauchope Ho. 34 Q14
Wauchope Pl. 34 Q14
Wauchope Rd. 34 Q14
Wauchope Sq. 34 Q14
Wauchope Terr. 34 Q14
Waugh Path 49 S8
Waukmill Ln. 45 D10
Waverley Bridge 7 M16
Waverley Cr. 49 S8
Waverley Dr. 49 S8
Waverley Market 7 M16
Waverley Pk. (Abbeyhill) 21 O17
Waverley Pk. (Bonnyrigg) 49 S8
Waverley Park Terr. 21 O17
Waverley Rd. 49 S8
Waverley Rd., Dalk. 50 T9
Waverley Pl. 21 O17
Waverley Sta. 7 M16
Waverley Steps 7 M16
Waverley Terr. 49 S8
Weaver's Knowe Cr. 38 D11
Websters Land* =West Port
Wedderburn Ho., Muss. 25 V14
Wedderburn Terr., Muss. 25 V14
Wee Brae 49 R9
Weir Cr. 50 T9
Weir Ct. 29 F13
Well Ct. 19 L16
Wellington Pl. 12 O19
Wellington St. 7 N17
Wemyss Pl. 6 L17
Wemyss Pl. Mews* =Wemyss Pl.
West Adam St. 20 N16
West Annandale St. 20 M18
West Approach Rd. 6 L16
West Bow 6 M16
West Bowling Green St. 12 N19
West Brighton Cr. 22 R16
West Broompark 10 K20
West Bryson Rd. 31 K15
West Caiystane Rd. 41 L11
West Carnethy Av. 39 H11
West Castle Rd. 31 L15
West Catherine Pl. 18 K16
West Coates 18 K16
West College St. 7 M16
West Ct., Ravelston 18 J17
West Ct., Niddrie 34 Q14
West Craigs 16 D16
West Craigs Av. 16 D15
West Craigs Cr. 16 E15
West Craigs Gr. 16 E15
West Croft 26 A13
West Cromwell St.* =Cromwell Pl.
West Crosscauseway 20 N15
West Edge Farm 43 P10
West End 6 L16
West End Pl. 19 K15
West Ferryfield 11 K18
West Fountain Pl. 19 K15
West Gorgie Pk. 30 J14
West Grange Gdns.* =Grange Ln.
West Granton Cr. 10 H19
West Granton Dr. 10 J19
West Granton Gdns. 10 J19
West Granton Gr. 10 H19
West Granton Gro. 10 J19
West Granton Ln. 10 J19
West Granton Pl. 10 H19
West Granton Rd. 10 J19
West Granton Row 10 J19
West Granton Terr. 10 J19
West Granton Vw. 10 J19
West Harbour Rd. 10 K20
West Hermiston 27 D13
West Holmes Gdns., Muss. 24 U15
West Mains Rd. 32 N13
West Maitland St. 19 L16
West Mayfield 32 N14
West Mill La.* =Dean Path

| | | |
|---|---|---|
| West Mill Rd. | 39 | G11 |
| West Newington Pl. | 32 | N15 |
| West Nicolson St. | 7 | N16 |
| West Norton Pl. | 7 | N17 |
| West Park Pl. | 19 | K15 |
| West Pier | 10 | K20 |
| West Pilton Av. | 10 | J18 |
| West Pilton Bk. | 10 | H19 |
| West Pilton Cr. | 10 | H19 |
| West Pilton Crossway | 10 | J19 |
| West Pilton Dr. | 10 | J19 |
| West Pilton Gdns. | 10 | J19 |
| West Pilton Gr. | 10 | J19 |
| West Pilton Gro. | 10 | J19 |
| West Pilton Lea | 10 | J19 |
| West Pilton Ln. | 10 | J19 |
| West Pilton Pk. (street) | 10 | J19 |
| West Pilton Pk. | 10 | J18 |
| West Pilton Pl. | 10 | J19 |
| West Pilton Rise | 10 | J19 |
| West Pilton Rd. | 10 | J19 |
| West Pilton St. | 10 | J19 |
| West Pilton Terr. | 10 | J19 |
| West Pilton Vw. | 10 | J18 |
| West Port | 6 | M16 |
| West Port House | 6 | M16 |
| West Powburn | 32 | N14 |
| West Preston St. | 32 | N15 |
| West Princes St. Gdns. | 6 | M16 |
| West Register Ho. | 6 | L16 |
| West Register St. | 7 | M17 |
| West Relugas Rd. | 32 | M14 |
| West Richmond St. | 7 | N16 |
| West Savile Rd. | 32 | N14 |
| West Savile Terr. | 32 | N14 |
| West Shore Rd. | 10 | H20 |
| West Silvermills La. | 19 | L17 |
| West Straiton Cotts. | 47 | O9 |
| West Telferton | 22 | Q17 |
| West Tollcross | 6 | L15 |
| West Werberside | 10 | K18 |
| West Winnelstrae | 10 | K18 |
| West Woods | 10 | K18 |
| Westbank Ln. | 22 | R17 |
| Westbank Pl. | 22 | R17 |
| Westbank St. | 22 | R17 |
| Westburn Av. | 38 | F12 |
| Westburn Gdns. | 38 | F12 |
| Westburn Gro. | 38 | F12 |
| Westburn Middlefield | 38 | F12 |
| Westburn Park | 38 | F12 |
| Westburn Sch. | 28 | F13 |
| Wester Broom Av. | 28 | F15 |
| Wester Broom Dr. | 28 | F15 |
| Wester Broom Gdns. | 28 | F15 |
| Wester Broom Gro. | 28 | F15 |
| Wester Broom Pl. | 28 | F15 |
| Wester Broom Terr. | 28 | F15 |
| Wester Cl.* =Newhaven Main St | | |
| Wester Coates Av. | 18 | K16 |
| Wester Coates Gdns. | 19 | K16 |
| Wester Coates Pl. | 18 | K16 |
| Wester Coates Rd. | 18 | K16 |
| Wester Coates Terr. | 18 | K16 |
| Wester Craiglockhart Hill | 30 | J13 |
| Wester Drylaw Av. | 10 | H18 |
| Wester Drylaw Dr. | 10 | H18 |
| Wester Drylaw Pk. | 10 | J18 |
| Wester Drylaw Pl. | 10 | H18 |
| Wester Drylaw Row | 10 | J17 |
| Wester Hailes Centre | 38 | F12 |
| Wester Hailes Dr. | 39 | F12 |
| Wester Hailes Education Centre | 28 | F13 |
| Wester Hailes Health Centre | 29 | F13 |
| Wester Hailes Pk. | 39 | G12 |
| Wester Hailes Rd. | 28 | F13 |
| Wester Melville | 48 | Q9 |
| Wester Steil | 31 | K13 |
| Westerlea Sch. | 18 | J16 |
| Western Corner* =Saughtonhall Dr. | | |
| Western Gdns. | 18 | J16 |
| Western General Hosp. | 18 | K18 |
| Western Pl. | 18 | J16 |
| Western Terr. | 18 | J16 |
| Westfield | 49 | S9 |
| Westfield Av. | 30 | J15 |
| Westfield Ct. | 30 | J15 |
| Westfield Ct., Dalk. | 50 | T9 |
| Westfield Dr., Dalk. | 50 | T9 |
| Westfield Gro. | 50 | T9 |
| Westfield Pk. | 50 | T9 |
| Westfield Rd. | 30 | J15 |
| Westfield St. | 30 | J15 |
| Westgarth Av. | 39 | H11 |
| Westhall Gdns. | 31 | L15 |
| Westland Cotts.* =Ravenscroft Pl. | | |
| Westland Houses* =Ravenscroft Pl. | | |
| Westmill Ct.* =Westmill Rd. | | |
| Westmill Rd. | 49 | R8 |
| Westmill Wynd | 49 | R8 |
| Westmost Cl.* =Newhaven Main St. | | |
| Wheatfield Pl. | 30 | J15 |
| Wheatfield Rd. | 30 | J15 |
| Wheatfield St. | 30 | K15 |
| Wheatfield Terr. | 30 | J15 |
| Wheatsheaf La. | 50 | U10 |
| Whinhill Pk. | 29 | G14 |
| Whins Pl.*=Figgate St. | | |
| White Dales | 41 | M11 |
| White Hart St., Dalk.* =Buccleuch St. | | |
| White Ho. | 41 | K10 |
| White Pk. | 30 | K15 |
| White Pk. (Str.) | 30 | K15 |
| Whitehall Ct. | 18 | H17 |
| Whitehill Av., Muss. | 24 | U15 |
| Whitehill Dr., Dalk. | 50 | V9 |
| Whitehill Farm Rd., Muss. | 24 | U14 |
| Whitehill Gdns., Muss. | 24 | U14 |
| Whitehill Gr., Dalk. | 50 | V9 |
| Whitehill Mains | 35 | S14 |
| Whitehill Rd. | 35 | S14 |
| Whitehill St | 35 | S14 |
| Whitehorse Cl. | 7 | N16 |
| Whitehouse Ln. | 31 | L15 |
| Whitehouse Rd. | 8 | E18 |
| Whitehouse Terr. | 32 | M14 |
| Whitelaw | 38 | E12 |
| Whitelea Cr. | 44 | C8 |
| Whitelea Rd. | 44 | B8 |
| Whites Cl.* =St. Andrew St. | | |
| Whitingford | 12 | M19 |
| Whitson Cr. | 30 | H15 |
| Whitson Gro. | 30 | H15 |
| Whitson Pl. E. | 30 | H15 |
| Whitson Pl. W. | 30 | H15 |
| Whitson Rd. | 30 | H15 |
| Whitson Terr. | 30 | H15 |
| Whitson Walk | 30 | H15 |
| Whitson Way | 30 | H15 |
| Whyte Pl. | 21 | O17 |
| Wilfred Terr. | 21 | P17 |
| William Jameson Pl.* =Pipe St. | | |
| William Jamieson St.* =Pipe St. | | |
| William St. | 6 | L16 |
| William St. La., N.E. | 6 | L16 |
| William St. La., N.W. | 6 | L16 |
| William St. La., S.E. | 6 | L16 |
| William St. La., S.W. | 6 | L16 |
| Williamfield* =Rosefield Av. | | |
| Williamfield Sq.* =Rosefield Av. | | |
| Willowbank Row | 12 | M19 |
| Willowbrae Av. | 21 | P16 |
| Willowbrae Gdns. | 21 | P16 |
| Willowbrae Rd. | 21 | P16 |
| Willowpark Sch. | 30 | J15 |
| Wilson Av., Dalk. | 50 | V10 |
| Wilson's Pk. | 23 | R17 |
| Wilton Rd. | 32 | N13 |
| Windmill La* =Buccleuch Pl. | | |
| Windmill Pl.*=Chapel St. | | |
| Windsor Gdns., Muss. | 25 | W15 |
| Windsor Pk., Muss. | 25 | W15 |
| Windsor Park Dr., Muss. | 25 | W15 |
| Windsor Park Pl., Muss. | 25 | W15 |
| Windsor Park Terr., Muss. | 25 | W15 |
| Windsor Pl. | 23 | R16 |
| Windsor St. | 20 | N17 |
| Windsor St. La. | 20 | N17 |
| Windy Wynd, Muss. | 25 | V14 |
| Winton Dr. | 41 | M10 |
| Winton Gdns. | 41 | M10 |
| Winton Gro. | 41 | L11 |
| Winton Ln. | 41 | M10 |
| Winton Pk. | 41 | L10 |
| Winton Terr. | 41 | L10 |
| Wishart Av. | 49 | S8 |
| Wishart Pl. | 49 | T9 |
| Wishaw Terr. | 21 | O17 |
| Wisp Gr. | 34 | R14 |
| Wisp, The | 35 | R14 |
| Wolrige Rd. | 42 | O12 |
| Wolseley Cr. | 21 | P17 |
| Wolseley Gdns.* =Wolseley Cr. | | |
| Wolseley Pl.*= =Wolseley Cr. | | |
| Wolseley Terr. | 21 | P17 |
| Wood Pl. | 31 | L14 |
| Woodbine Terr. | 13 | O18 |
| Woodburn Av., Dalk. | 50 | V10 |
| Woodburn Bk., Dalk. | 50 | V10 |
| Woodburn Dr., Dalk. | 50 | U10 |
| Woodburn Gdns., Dalk. | 50 | V10 |
| Woodburn Gr., Dalk. | 50 | V9 |
| Woodburn Ho. | 31 | M14 |
| Woodburn Ln., Dalk. | 50 | V10 |
| Woodburn Medway, Dalk. | 50 | V10 |
| Woodburn Pk., Dalk. | 50 | V10 |
| Woodburn Pl., Dalk. | 50 | V9 |
| Woodburn Pl.* =Canaan La. | | |
| Woodburn Rd., Dalk. | 50 | U10 |
| Woodburn Sch., Dalk. | 50 | V10 |
| Woodburn St., Dalk. | 50 | V10 |
| Woodburn Terr. | 31 | L14 |
| Woodburn Terr., Dalk. | 50 | V9 |
| Woodburn Vw., Dalk. | 50 | V9 |
| Woodfield Av. | 39 | G11 |
| Woodfield Pk. | 39 | G11 |
| Woodhall Av. | 39 | F11 |
| Woodhall Bk. | 39 | G11 |
| Woodhall Dr. | 38 | F11 |
| Woodhall Gro. | 39 | G11 |
| Woodhall Mains | 39 | F11 |
| Woodhall Millbrae | 39 | G11 |
| Woodhall Rd. | 39 | G11 |
| Woodhall Terr. | 38 | F11 |
| Woodlands Gro. | 22 | Q15 |
| Woodside Gdns., Muss. | 25 | W15 |
| Woodside Terr. | 23 | S16 |
| Woodstock Pl. | 33 | O13 |
| Woodville Terr. | 13 | O18 |
| Woolmet Cr. | 51 | R12 |
| Wright's Houses | 20 | L15 |
| Wyvern Pk. | 32 | M14 |
| Yardheads | 12 | N19 |
| Yeaman La. | 19 | L15 |
| Yeaman Pl. | 19 | K15 |
| Yewlands Cr. | 42 | O12 |
| Yewlands Gdns. | 42 | O12 |
| Yoole Pl.*=Pipe St. | | |
| York Bdgs.*=Queen St. | | |
| York La. | 7 | M17 |
| York Pl. | 7 | M17 |
| York Rd. | 11 | M19 |
| Young St. | 6 | L16 |
| Young St. La., N. | 6 | L16 |
| Young St. La., S. | 6 | L16 |